Studies in Medieval and Renaissance Music

2

The Church Music
of Fifteenth-Century Spain

Spanish church music prior to the work of Francisco de Peñalosa at the end of the fifteenth century has been much neglected, partly because much of it is anonymous and scattered throughout a number of manuscripts. This book aims to redress the balance, identifying and examining nearly 70 pieces of surviving Latin sacred music written in Spain between 1400 and the early 1500s, and discussing them source by source; the author argues that they reveal a rapid and dramatic change, not only in style and sophistication, but in the level of self-consciousness they demonstrate, creating a new national music as Ferdinand and Isabella of Spain were creating a new nation. He moves on from this to set Peñalosa's work, written in a more mature, northern-oriented style which influenced Iberian composers for generations after his death, follows on from this pieces, in this context.

KENNETH KREITNER is Professor of musicology at the Scheidt School of Music at the University of Memphis.

Studies in Medieval and Renaissance Music

ISSN 1479-9294

General Editors
Tess Knighton and Andrew Wathey

This series aims to provide a forum for the best scholarship in early music; deliberately broad in scope, it welcomes proposals on any aspect of music, musical life, and composers during the period up to 1600, and particularly encourages work that places music in an historical and social context. Both new research and major re-assessments of central topics are encouraged.

Proposals or enquiries may be sent directly to the editors or the publisher at the UK addresses given below; all submissions will receive careful, informed consideration.

Dr Tess Knighton, Clare College, Cambridge CB2 1TL

Professor Andrew Wathey, Department of Music, Royal Holloway and Bedford New College, Egham Hill, Egham, Surrey TW20 0EX

Boydell & Brewer Ltd, PO Box 9, Woodbridge, Suffolk IP12 3DF

Already Published

The Church Music
of Fifteenth-Century Spain

Kenneth Kreitner

3120803 6789122
Mannes College of Music
Harry Scherman Library
150 W. 85th St.
New York, NY 10024
WITHDRAWN

THE BOYDELL PRESS

ML
3047
K74
2004
c. 1

© Kenneth Kreitner 2004

All Rights Reserved. Except as permitted under current legislation
no part of this work may be photocopied, stored in a retrieval system,
published, performed in public, adapted, broadcast,
transmitted, recorded or reproduced in any form or by any means,
without the prior permission of the copyright owner

First published 2004
The Boydell Press, Woodbridge

ISBN 1 84383 075 2

The Boydell Press is an imprint of Boydell & Brewer Ltd
PO Box 9, Woodbridge, Suffolk IP12 3DF, UK
and of Boydell & Brewer Inc.
668 Mt Hope Avenue, Rochester, NY 14620, USA
website: www.boydellandbrewer.com

A catalogue record for this title is available
from the British Library

Library of Congress Cataloging-in-Publication Data
Kreitner, Kenneth.
  The church music of fifteenth-century Spain / Kenneth Kreitner.
    p. cm. – (Studies in medieval and Renaissance music, ISSN 1479–9294 ; 2)
  Includes bibliographical references and index.
  ISBN 1–84383–075–2 (hardback : alk. paper)
  1. Church music – Spain – 15th century.   2. Church music – Catholic Church
  – 15th century. I. Title. II. Series.
  ML3047.K74 2004
  781.71'2'0094609031–dc22   2004000610

This publication is printed on acid-free paper

Typeset by Pru Harrison, Hacheston, Suffolk
Printed in Great Britain by
Antony Rowe Ltd, Chippenham, Wiltshire

Contents

Musical Examples

Abbreviations and Conventions

Bibliographic abbreviations

See bibliography for full citations.

Census-Catalogue	*Census-Catalogue of Manuscript Sources of Polyphonic Music, 1400–1550*, 5 vols.
DMEH	Casares Rodicio, ed., *Diccionario de la música Española e Hispanoamericana.*
MGG-P	Finscher, ed., *Die Musik in Geschichte und Gegenwart*, 2nd edn., Personenteil, 6 vols. finished at press time.
MGG-S	Finscher, ed., *Die Musik in Geschichte und Gegenwart*, 2nd edn., Sachteil, 9 vols.
MME	Monumentos de la Musica Española.
New Grove 1980	Sadie, ed., *The New Grove Dictionary of Music and Musicians*, 20 vols.
New Grove 2001	Sadie, ed., *The New Grove Dictionary of Music and Musicians*, 2nd edn., 29 vols.
RISM	*Répertoire Internationale des Sources Musicales.*

Clefs

- G Treble (G2)
- S Soprano (C1)
- M Mezzo-soprano (C2)
- A Alto (C3)
- T Tenor (C4)
- R Baritone (F3 or C5)
- B Bass (F4)
- K Contrabass (F5)

Sources

The musical manuscripts discussed here are called by a short name – sometimes a generally accepted nickname (e.g. the Cancionero de la Colombina, the Chigi codex), more often in the conventional city-plus-shelfmark form (e.g. Barcelona 454). For the most important of these sources, the full name and *Census-Catalogue* siglum are given in a note; others should be easily decoded by reference to the *Census-Catalogue* or other bibliographic aids.

Musical examples

Musical examples represent (except in a few cases as noted) my own editions, made from facsimiles or films of the original sources in consultation with the editions already extant. Note values are halved (also except as noted), and text underlay follows the indications of the manuscript as closely as practicable.

for Mona

Preface

I cannot remember becoming interested in the church music of fifteenth-century Spain. I mean I am reasonably sure, having, as I write this, just completed ten chapters on the subject, that I am interested in it now. And I seem to recall a time when I didn't much care one way or the other; but exactly what happened in between, I cannot quite say. Evidently there was some sort of threshold along the way that I crossed without noticing.

Instead, what I can see at this distance is three vague forces that pushed and pulled my curiosity into this direction over the years. The first, in the mid- and late 1980s, was the experience of writing a doctoral dissertation on civic music in fifteenth-century Barcelona and my frustration – common, I now know, to urban documentary studies, but at the time I assumed it was my problem alone – at being unable to pin a musical repertory onto the events I was describing. The second, beginning in the late stages of the dissertation and taking serious hold in the early 1990s, was my growing love for and fascination with the sacred music of Peñalosa, Escobar, and their contemporaries from the first decades of the sixteenth century. This was splendid music, splendid and idiosyncratic, the sort of thing that was obviously not just plagiarized from the north, but which at the same time could not have come out of nowhere. But as I tried to separate the northern and local elements in this music, it was a lot easier to find models for the former than the latter. And the third, throughout both of these scholarly phases and beyond, has been my day-today life as an academic musicologist, taking and then teaching courses in medieval and renaissance music, going to conferences on Busnoys, Binchois, Josquin, and so forth, attending fifteenth-century sessions at the AMS and IMS, reading the books and articles as they came out, and musing all the time – what did my Spain have to compare with this?

I knew part of the answer, of course. Cornago was Spain's Du Fay, Urrede its Ockeghem, the Cancionero de la Colombina its, say, Dijon chansonnier; and if all those comparisons seemed to favor the French, well, perhaps that was the nature of fifteenth-century music and we would have to be content with it. I had seen a little Spanish sacred music from this period, notably Cornago's mass, Urrede's *Pange lingua*, and the strange mixture of motets and mass movements, most of them small and anonymous, scattered through Colombina. But this music seemed to resist forming itself into a coherent and satisfying picture in my mind.

So I suppose it is fair to say that I already cared about Spanish church music in the fifteenth century and had spent some idle time wondering about it before 1992, when Emilio Ros-Fábregas finished his dissertation. Ros-Fábregas was ostensibly writing about one manuscript, but along the way he had also reëxamined the whole source situation from Spain in the late fifteenth and early sixteenth centuries and proposed new dates and stories for several important manuscripts. Perhaps none of his revisions was all that dramatic in itself, but seeing all the dates together like that was for

me, not an epiphany exactly, but a soft, gratifying sensation of fitness, like the
tumblers falling into place in a padlock. Suddenly it seemed possible to identify a fair
amount of church music in fifteenth-century Spain and, perhaps even more important, to make some chronological sense of it.

I began by making a handlist of the surviving repertory; this list, assembled from
manuscripts and composers that could be dated to Spain between 1400 and the early
1500s, was presented to the International Hispanic Music Study Group in Minneap-
olis in 1994 and has since been published in a memorial volume for Robert Snow. The
handlist at that point contained seventy-three compositions, of which only about two
thirds were available in modern edition. Next, then, I made working editions of the
unpublished pieces and began the task of sorting the repertory out liturgically, stylistically, and chronologically. The preliminary results of that phase were presented to the
American Musicological Society in New York in 1995.

This book represents a fleshing-out of some parts of that paper, a refinement of
others, a shamefaced retraction of a few things here and there. After all the additions,
deletions, and condensations, the handlist now stands at sixty-seven. There is some
fine music on the list, and I shall be proud if I can bring it to an appreciative audience.
And there is, to be honest, some music that makes you wonder a little about the people
who could have loved it. But love it they did, enough to make it up, sing it, and write it
down for reuse. And the act of imagining, with my Josquin-drenched ears, what it was
like to love this repertory and hunger for more, has been the best thing to come out of
this project. I believe this is not just a repertory but a story.

At the end of the fifteenth century, within a generation, Spanish sacred music and
its audience underwent a dramatic change. In 1490, the prevailing style for church
music in Spain was much simpler, more direct, more modest than the music we know
from the north. By the 1510s, the mainstream of Spanish church composers were fully
abreast of northern developments and writing in a fully mature contrapuntal style,
though a style that retained a peculiar – I would say self-conscious – local flavor of its
own. One composer, Juan de Anchieta, seems to be at the center of this story, and
behind him is not hard to see the desire of his patrons, Isabella and Ferdinand, to form
a national culture as they formed a nation.

I have had a lot of help. Most of the first draft was written during a faculty development leave awarded me by the University of Memphis in spring 1999; over the years
my department, now the Scheidt School of Music, has been generous with travel
grants and materials; and the College of Communication and Fine Arts has assisted
financially with publication.

I have been lucky also to have colleagues who can be counted on for practical help
and moral support; of the many, let me mention especially Janet Page, John David
Peterson, David Evans, James Richens, and Douglas Lemmon, who sadly did not live
to see the work finished. The department allowed me to teach two graduate research
seminars touching on my subject, one in 1994 on Spanish sacred music, and another
in 1998 on fifteenth-century Spain; a fair number of student projects from these seminars, plus a few theses and independent studies, are acknowledged gratefully in the
pages below, but everyone in these courses helped to focus my thoughts and make me
ask better questions of my material. I am thankful also to the Collegium Musicum for
indulging me (not that they were given a choice) in some experiments with this

repertory that have found their way into the narrative. And I have been humbled by the energy and good cheer of my factotums Deánna Stark, Dara Whaley, Lisa Higginbotham, Jessie Coyle, and in particular Craig Wiggins, who prepared my musical examples and happened to be on duty for the last, most drudgerous draft. Nathan Wilensky somehow got my computer to work, and Joyce Gordon, my Chief of Staff, did everything she could to make the book possible while I was trying to be an administrator.

Special thanks also go to my colleagues and friends at the University of Memphis Music Library: Ann Viles, Anna Neal, Carol Lowry, and Jenny Hinton. Other portions of the research were conducted at the Biblioteca de Catalunya in Barcelona and at the music library at the University of Illinois, where I got more than my share of help from Marlys Scarborough and Stacey Jocoy Houck.

Howard Mayer Brown may have started this whole thing when I was in graduate school by making me a bootleg microfilm of a manuscript that I still had probably better not mention, and in the years since, Brown's colleagues and successors have continued to be quick with the snail- and e-mail, offering advice, perspective, missing references, offprints, unpublished papers, proportional solutions, chapter commentaries, and comfort of mind often within hours of my requests. Among those interested in fifteenth-century music in general I am particularly grateful to Bonnie Blackburn, Jeffrey Dean, David Fallows, Barbara Haggh, Cristle Collins Judd, Herbert Kellman, Andrew Kirkman, Laura Macy, Honey Meconi, Robert Nosow, Susan Parisi, Alejandro Planchart, Joshua Rifkin, Elizabeth Randell Upton, and Rob Wegman; from the community of hispanic scholars, to Juan Carlos Asensio, Màrius Bernadó, Todd Borgerding, Pedro Calahorra, Juan José Carreras, Wolfgang Freis, Maricarmen Gómez, Jane Hardie, Bernadette Nelson, Michael Noone, Michael O'Connor, Greta Olson, Owen Rees, Emilio Ros-Fábregas, Roberta Schwartz, Graeme Skinner, Louise Stein, Robert Stevenson, Álvaro Torrente, Bruno Turner, and Grayson Wagstaff.

Tess Knighton has encouraged the project since before it started, set it on track when it derailed a couple of times, been a constant source of information and perspective, and at the end become the series editor for Boydell & Brewer. To her and everyone at B&B, especially Bruce Phillips, Caroline Palmer and Vanda Andrews, I am very grateful.

Finally, the dedicatee of this book has fed a lot of pets in my absence, endured some vacations in places known more for their bibliographic than their scenic splendors, taken on some horrendous home-repair projects while I sat in the back in my chair, and sung this music in such a way that I had to keep listening. To her above all I say thanks for sticking with it.

1

Eleven Days

At ten o'clock on Christmas eve 1478, Juan II of Aragón, aged eighty and in poor health since a hunting trip earlier in the month, sat down with his court at the bishop's palace in Barcelona and listened to his chapel singers perform some songs appropriate to the season – 'algunes cansons honestes', his chronicler Pere Miquel Carbonell later called them.[1] The king stayed up all night, heard three masses at home in the morning, went to church, and stood in the cold for some hours greeting the public. His health never recovered: within two weeks he took a serious turn for the worse, and on 19 January 1479, he died.

The death of Juan II is the sort of event that might well capture the imagination; for this, maybe more than any other, was the moment when Spain happened. Juan's eldest son, Carlos of Viana, had died in 1461, and his second son Ferdinand had married Isabella, princess and heir presumptive of Castile, in 1469; Isabella had succeeded to her throne in 1474. By the time of his father's death, then, Ferdinand had been King Regent in Castile for almost five years, and his succession to the Aragonese crown meant a powerful dynastic union, expected to become a real union in the next generation, of the two most powerful kingdoms on the peninsula. In 1492 Ferdinand would add Granada to their dominions, and in 1512 Navarra, essentially giving the Iberian peninsula the political boundaries it has today.

Thus the rise and fall of empires; the eyes of the music historian, however, go immediately to the scene Christmas eve when, to quote at more length,

> the matins of Christmas were said by the chaplains and singers in the great hall of the episcopal palace beginning around ten o'clock before midnight on that vigil, with some appropriate songs, and bringing the joy of the birth of the Son of God. And thus the king, in reverence to God and to his blessed mother, decided to remain devoutly in the hall all night until the day came.[2]

---

[1] Pedro Miquel Carbonell, *De exequiis sepultura et infirmitate Regis Joannis secundi*, in *Opúsculos inéditos del cronista catalan Pedro Miguel Carbonell*, ed. Manuel de Bofarull y de Sartório, Colección de documentos inéditos del Archivo General de la Corona de Aragón XXVII (Barcelona, 1864), pp. 137–320, quotation p. 155. For my earlier essay on this subject, see Kenneth Richard Kreitner, 'Music and Civic Ceremony in Late-Fifteenth-Century Barcelona' (Ph.D. diss., Duke University, 1990), pp. 334–87, which has been corrected and improved on in several respects by George Grayson Wagstaff, 'Music for the Dead: Polyphonic Settings of the *Officium* and *Missa pro defunctis* by Spanish and Latin American Composers before 1630' (Ph.D. diss., University of Texas, 1995), especially pp. 80–100.

[2] Carbonell, *De exequiis*, p. 155: '. . . se feu dir per los capellans e xandres en la sala maior del dit palau episcopal començant circa les X hores ans de la mija nit de la dita vigilia les matines de

The songs sung to Juan II in the bishop's house that night are not known for sure, but neither are they hard to imagine. The Cancionero de la Colombina, the most important source for Spanish music from this era, has some nine Castilian songs with Marian or Christmas texts, any of which would have been fine for the occasion. One of them, *Pues con sobra de alegría*, is even attributed to 'Enrrique', probably Enricus Foxer, also known as Enrique de Paris, who seems to have been in Juan's chapel at the end.[3] These are exactly the kind of surroundings we like to conjure up for the best fifteenth-century songs (and Enrique's are indeed among the best), and it is good to see music mentioned here in this scene of warmth right before the king's final decline.

Another part of the appeal of this image is that it nestles so comfortably against our musical expectations. The music of Juan del Encina and his companions in the Cancionero de Palacio has been very popular among modern performers and audiences of early music – as well it might, with its attractive tunes, catchy rhythms, limpid harmonies, and texts by turns courtly, pious, ironical, and smutty. This is the music most of us think of first when we think of Ferdinand and Isabella, and it seems only fitting that Ferdinand's father would spend Christmas listening to Encina's predecessors. But then one reads on in the chronicle, through the king's illness and death, the planning for the funeral, and the procession to the royal palace where his remains would lie in state from 20 January to 30 January – and then encounters another reference to polyphony:

> And moreover, for greater solemnity, for company for the royal body, and for the relief of the pains that the king's soul was enduring, all the chaplains, singers, and altarboys of his royal chapel stood there all day and night continuously while the royal body lay in the great hall where they had left it, singing in counterpoint in the way they were accustomed to sing in the king's chapel while he lived. And at night the chaplains and altarboys were accompanied by some monks from each order of the monasteries of Barcelona so that in order to get some rest and fulfill their vigils they could divide up among themselves and celebrate vespers, matins, and all other offices, with many devotions and innumerable prayers, asking all to our God for the good soul of their and our glorious king and lord.[4]

Nadal ab algunes cansons honestes e portants alegria de tal nativitat del fill de Deu. E axi lo Senyor Rey en reverentia de Deu e de la sua beneyta mare volgue en la dita sala star e devotament tota aquella nit fins que sobrevengue lo dia.'

[3] The standard edition of Colombina is Miguel Querol Gavaldá, ed., *Cancionero Musical de la Colombina*, MME XXXIII (Barcelona, 1971); the sacred songs include numbers 2, 3, 22, 64, 65, 72, 74, 75, and 78. On the biography of Enrique de Paris and his probable identification with the composer 'Enrrique', see Tessa Wendy Knighton, 'Music and Musicians at the Court of Fernando of Aragon, 1474–1516' (Ph.D. diss., Cambridge University, 1983), vol. I, p. 266 (later translated as Tess Knighton, *Música y músicos en la Corte de Fernando el Católico 1474–1516*, trans. Luis Gago [Zaragoza, 2001], p. 329), and Maricarmen Gómez Muntané, 'Enricus Foxer, alias Enrique de Paris († 1487/8)', *Nassarre* ix (1993), pp. 139–46.

[4] Carbonell, *De exequiis*, pp. 203–4: 'E encara per major solemnitat e companya del dit cors Real e relevatio de penes que passas la anima del dit Senyor Rey tots los capellans xandres e scholans de la sua capella Reyal stigueren aqui tots los dies e nits continuament tant com stech lo dit cors Real en la dita gran sala que may lo lexaren cantants a contrapunct e en aquella forma que acustumaven cantar en la capella del dit Senyor Rey quant vivia. E en les nits eren acompanyats los dits capellans e scholans de alguns frares de cascun orde dels monastirs de Barcelona per ço que ab algun repos passassen llurs vigilies es partissen aquelles entre ells car may cessaven de dir e celebrar vespres

This takes a little longer to assimilate. Surely Carbonell does not mean what he at first seems to mean: he is describing not eleven days of solid polyphony but rather a vigil, with various groups of local clergy sharing the duty of standing with the king's body and performing the daily office, possibly supplemented with extra prayers and so forth, mostly in monophonic chant according to the custom of the day.[5] And his word, *contrapunct*, is itself a little worrisome: at least in sixteenth-century Castilian, *contrapunto* would be a technical term used to distinguish improvised polyphony from written polyphony, *canto de órgano*, and it is hard to know at this distance exactly how precisely, if at all, Carbonell is making a distinction.[6] But his main message is clear: the royal chapel was there, its singers were the most conspicuous actors in this part of the drama, what was noteworthy about their presence was their polyphonic singing, and this singing, whether improvised or from a book, was a vital and vivid part of the whole sensory impression he took away from those days in the palace. Clearly Carbonell had the memory of music in his ears as he wrote his chronicle. But what did it sound like?

It's a curiously difficult question. If this scene had been set in 1579, it would be easy to come up with some suitably solemn music by Guerrero, or even the young Victoria, for our mind's ear. Or if it were, say, 1279, we might stitch something together between the Notre Dame manuscript Madrid 20486 and the Las Huelgas codex. Or if it were France or Italy, this would be the time of the middle-aged Ockeghem and the young Josquin. But Barcelona in 1479 is tough. The only manuscript that leaps to mind is the Cancionero de la Colombina, but as its name suggests, it is best known for its secular songs. Only two Spanish composers from around this time have achieved much of a profile today, and both are burdened with nettlesome asterisks: Juan de Urrede (fl. 1451–82) because he was a transplanted northerner and because he is more famous for his songs than for his sacred music, little of which has been available in modern edition, and Johannes Cornago (fl. 1420–75) because although his *Missa Ayo visto lo mappamundi* is well known today, it was almost certainly written in Italy. Neither Urrede nor Cornago, alas, seems a good bet for establishing a kind of baseline style for Spanish sacred polyphony in their time.

Yet Carbonell heard something during those eleven days in 1479, and his

matines e tots los altres officis ab moltes devotissimes e innumerables orations pregants tots a nostre Senyor Deu per la bona anima de llur e nostre glorios Rey e Senyor.'

5   See especially Wagstaff, 'Music for the Dead', pp. 92–4.

6   Most modern discussion of this issue has been derived from Juan Bermudo, *El libro llamado declaracion de instrumentos musicales* (Osuna, 1555; rept. Kassel, 1957), bk. 2 chs. 16–25, bk. 3 chs. 30–50, and bk. 5 chs. 16–17, 23–7. See also Wagstaff, 'Music for the Dead', pp. 85–91; Robert Stevenson, *Juan de Bermudo* (The Hague, 1960); Francisco José León Tello, *Estudios de história de la teoria musical* (Madrid, 1962), pp. 513–26; and an unpublished article by Todd Borgerding entitled '*Ay arte de contrapunto*: Improvised Vocal Polyphony and Ritual in Early Modern Spain', kindly sent to me by the author.

  Carbonell, in *De exequiis*, pp. 224–5, does once juxtapose the Catalan equivalents to both terms: describing a procession on 30 January he says that 'tots los xandres capellans e scholans de la capella del dit Senyor Rey los quals anaven tots vestits de gramalles e capirons de drap negre … axi anants e cantants a cant dorgue e contrapunct ab gran melodia e consonantia cantaven los psalms e officiaven com si fossen en la propria capella del Senyor Rey.' It is not clear whether he uses both terms because he means to describe two kinds of music, or merely in his habit of speaking in pairs of words.

description has hovered around me since I first read it fifteen years ago. I am now convinced that Spain maintained a substantial tradition of written church polyphony in the fifteenth century, but that it is not to be found quite where we habitually look for such things. It tends not to be the work of Great Men – a mentality that despite our best efforts is hard to shake off – but is largely anonymous and in many cases gives more a sense of collective than of personal creation. And it has been preserved rather haphazardly, not in large institutionally-created manuscripts of sacred polyphony but piecemeal, scattered through sources mostly devoted, like Colombina, to something else. Nor, as it has survived the accidents of the centuries, is it a very large repertory: only a handful of these manuscripts are currently known, and in my most liberal esti-mates I have never supposed that I was talking about more than a hundred extant compositions. But I think it is enough.

No one working in this field can proceed without acknowledging a deep debt to Higini Anglès, whose work on Spanish medieval and renaissance music began in the 1920s and was still underway at his death in 1969,[7] and to Robert Stevenson, whose *Spanish Music in the Age of Columbus* appeared in 1960 and has aged remarkably well: it remains the most accessible biographical source for Spanish composers before 1530 or so and the only full-length treatment of their musical style.[8] In the years since its publication, what we have gained above all is a somewhat refined sense of the chro-nology of things; this has been the result partly of Tess Knighton's efforts to illuminate the patterns of musical patronage by Ferdinand and Isabella;[9] partly of a number of important dissertations on the Spanish manuscripts of the period;[10] and partly of a new public interest, spurred by the Columbus quincentenary of 1992, in the music of the Spanish composers of Ferdinand and Isabella's courts.[11] The upshot of it all is that the *siglo de oro* of Spanish polyphony, which formerly seemed to begin with the first

[7] A number of Anglès's books and articles (most published, during the Franco period, under the Castilian version of his name) are cited in the bibliography; probably the most constantly influen-tial on me has been his series of editions and commentaries under the title *La música en la corte de los Reyes Católicos*, published as Monumentos de la Música Española, vols. I, V, X, and XIV (Barcelona, 1941–65). Volume XIV, the poetical commentary on the Cancionero de Palacio, was the work of Josep Romeu Figueras.

[8] Robert Stevenson, *Spanish Music in the Age of Columbus* (The Hague, 1960); most of Stevenson's composer biographies have been updated in at least a few particulars by Knighton in 'Music and Musicians', vol. I, pp. 246–302 (*Música y músicos*, pp. 321–49).

[9] See especially 'Music and Musicians'; *Música y músicos*; and Knighton's several articles in the bibliography below. I have also been much influenced by early drafts from her next book, *Music and Ceremony at the Court of Ferdinand and Isabella* (London, forthcoming), kindly sent to me in advance of publication.

[10] For some prominent examples: Robert Clement Lawes, Jr., 'The Seville Cancionero: Transcrip-tion and Commentary' (Ph.D. diss., North Texas State College, 1960); Norma Klein Baker, 'An Unnumbered Manuscript of Polyphony in the Archives of the Cathedral of Segovia: Its Prove-nance and History' (Ph.D. diss., University of Maryland, 1978); Jane Morlet Hardie, 'The Motets of Francisco de Peñalosa and their Manuscript Sources' (Ph.D. diss., University of Michigan, 1983); Owen Lewis Rees, 'Sixteenth- and Early Seventeenth-Century Polyphony from the Monastery of Santa Cruz, Coimbra, Portugal' (Ph.D. diss., Cambridge University, 1991); and Emilio Ros-Fábregas, 'The Manuscript Barcelona, Biblioteca de Catalunya, M. 454: Study and Edition in the Context of the Iberian and Continental Manuscript Traditions' (Ph.D. diss., City University of New York, 1992).

[11] See for example Kenneth Kreitner, 'Peñalosa on Record', *Early Music* xxii (1994), pp. 309–18.

publications of Cristóbal de Morales in the 1540s, now extends easily and more or less seamlessly back to the generation of Francisco de Peñalosa, Juan de Anchieta, and Pedro de Escobar – which then directs our gaze, or ought to, in turn toward their predecessors and influences.

Peñalosa, the most prolific of this group, the one most often copied into sources later in the sixteenth century, and the most famous today, joined the Aragonese royal chapel in May 1498;[12] no earlier document for him has been recovered, nor do his works appear in any of the known fifteenth-century sources. It seems reasonable, then, to suppose that most of his surviving compositions were written after the turn of the century, which in turn means that even if Peñalosa is the sort of composer who casts a long shadow, in this case the shadow has a fairly sharp edge: 1500 makes – in principle, difficult as it may be to enforce in practice – a convenient dividing line between the new musical Spain and the old. So my purpose here is simple and straightforward, a further refinement and extension of part of Stevenson's larger argument: I have tried to identify an early repertory of Spanish church polyphony and to pull it out from under Peñalosa's shadow for closer examination.

There are a myriad ways such an investigation could go, and I have no fantasy of exhausting them. I have begun by identifying sixty-seven pieces of Latin sacred music that I believe were written in fifteenth-century Spain; these appear in a handlist in the Appendix, and the reasons for including each are detailed in the chapters to come. And then I have looked at all the music I have found and tried to say what is worth saying about it – which inevitably means a mixture of what seems important as part of a historical narrative, and what seems interesting to me, what appeals to my own idiosyncrasies and musical tastes. I am not sure I can reliably unravel these impulses into separate strands; instead, perhaps this is a good time to pause for a moment and outline some of the vocabulary, and what I see to be the fundamental issues, behind this book.

Text

Sacred music, almost by definition, has a verbal text. I say *almost* because of course there was such a thing as organ music in the church service, and because some fifteenth-century Spanish churches used bands of wind instruments on occasion.[13] But since neither of these traditions contributes anything visible to the repertory until well into the sixteenth century, it is probably safe for present purposes to think of sacred music as music with sacred text, written for use in the Christian church service or in devotional or ceremonial situations outside church.

Another line must be drawn a bit more peremptorily. There exist from this time a number of pieces with sacred texts in Castilian: Enrique's *Pues con sobra de alegría*, mentioned earlier, is a particularly fine specimen.[14]

[12] Stevenson, *Spanish Music*, p. 146; Knighton, 'Music and Musicians', vol. I, p. 288 (*Música y músicos*, p. 340); Hardie, 'Motets of Peñalosa', p. 3.
[13] Kenneth Kreitner, 'Minstrels in Spanish Churches, 1400–1600', *Early Music* xx (1992), pp. 532–46.
[14] Castilian text from Querol, *Cancionero Musical de la Colombina*, pp. 35–6; on the tradition of vernacular Christmas songs in renaissance Spain, see especially Maricarmen Gómez, 'La polifonía

Pues con sobra de alegría	Now with excess of happiness
cantamos tu nasçimiento,	we sing your birth,
buen Jesús, por este día	good Jesus; through this day
guárdanos de perdimiento.	save us from loss.
Por intercesión de aquella	By the intercession of her
que te parió sin dolor,	who bore you without pain,
quedando madre y donzella,	remaining mother and maiden,
Tú, Dyos, ombre y señor,	You, God, man and lord,
haznos tú clara la vía	make clear the way
de nuestro conosçimiento;	of our knowledge;
por aqueste santo día	through this holy day,
guárdanos de perdimiento.	save us from loss.

Most of us would call this sacred music, which it certainly is under my my broad definition. This is why for my immediate purpose I prefer the term *church music*: these sacred vernacular songs have traditionally, and I believe rightly, been seen not as a kind of populist relative of the conventional masses and motets, but more as an offshoot of the secular musical and poetic traditions of the day. (Again, Enrique is a useful example: *Pues con sobra de alegría* alegría is actually a contrafactum, an alternate sacred text to his courtly song *Pues con sobra de tristura*.) Songs like this were written not for church, but for the sort of courtly-pious situation represented by, as we have seen, Christmas eve in the royal house of Aragón. Certain vernacular music did sometimes find its way into the church building, and I shall try to take account of it when appropriate. Otherwise, however, I shall be talking exclusively about music with text in Latin, suitable for use daily Catholic services.

These services were governed by an elaborate and highly structured liturgy, and most fifteenth-century church music, in Spain as elsewhere in Europe, was meant to fit into that liturgy. In the Franco-Flemish mainstream, however, it was also common for motets to be composed on newly-written, non-liturgical texts for use outside the regular services, or in processions, or sometimes to substitute for liturgical texts on special occasions. Many of the most famous compositions of the century fit this description; some, like Du Fay's *Nuper rosarum flores*, written for the dedication of the cathedral of Florence in 1436, refer to their occasion directly, and others, like Ockeghem's Marian motet *Intemerata Dei mater*, have more generic, broadly useful texts, but texts that clearly involve new poetry and not the heritage of centuries.[15] But neither of these northern trends seems to have caught on in fifteenth-century Spain; all but a few of our pieces take their texts directly from the mass and office.

Chant

In other words, most of this polyphony was meant to substitute for monophonic chant: it was not a distinct artistic entity so much as a fancier, more spectacular version of something habitual and familiar. Moreover, many, perhaps most of these

vocal española del Renacimiento hacio el Barroco: el caso de los villancicos de Navidad', *Nassarre* xvii (2001), pp. 77–114.

[15] For a thoughtful recent discussion, see especially Julie E. Cumming, *The Motet in the Age of Du Fay* (Cambridge, 1999).

polyphonic pieces are settings not just of the chant text, but of its music as well. And at this point the question gets complicated.

A fair number of our Spanish polyphonic compositions use tunes that can be found in the *Liber Usualis* and other chant collections published by the Vatican in the twentieth century. These pieces thus partook of the pan-European Gregorian tradition that survived, with Rome's encouragement (and suppression of the competition), into our own time. Others, however, are clearly tied to the local chant traditions of which Spain still had many in the fifteenth century. Variants in chant readings can be a useful clue to a polyphonic piece's date and place of origin; they have already proven their worth in certain mainstream repertories,[16] and they would seem to have especially intriguing possibilities in Spain, where the local differences can be dramatic. My original intent was to follow this path as strenuously as I could, but after a little while it became clear that if I did, I would come up with only premature conclusions. Our understanding of Spanish chant practices is still in, maybe not its infancy but its energetic toddlerhood; despite some very solid progress in recent years,[17] it is not yet possible to get the kind of control that we need to make the kind of judgements we would like to make. I have tried to identify my tunes in the Vatican sources when possible and to use the secondary literature on Spanish chant as effectively as I could. In a few cases I have looked through some local chant sources myself, but I have not made any systematic effort in this direction, and I warmly invite any reader to pick up where I have left off.

My more immediate interest has been in the treatment of the chant tunes, whatever their origin. The act of working a piece of monophonic chant into a polyphonic composition opens up an infinite range of possibilities, from the simplest parallel octaves to the rhythmic or harmonic extravagance of Ockeghem or, later, a Gesualdo, and the composer's fundamental job is to choose among those possibilities. Liturgical chant is normally – though not always, especially in Spain[18] – unmeasured, with set pitches but no set metrical rhythm; so the composer must decide whether to leave it unmeasured (an impossible choice for any but the simplest polyphony), give it a rigid regular rhythm, add a new more complex rhythm, or paraphrase it. And in the

---

16 For the promise that this sort of work offers, see for example Anne Walters Robertson, 'Which Vitry? The Witness of the Trinity Motet from the Roman de Fauvel', *Hearing the Motet: Essays on the Motet of the Middle Ages and Renaissance*, ed. Dolores Pesce (Oxford, 1997), pp. 52–81.

17 See, for example, Robert J. Snow, ed., *A New-World Collection of Polyphony for Holy Week and the Salve Service: Guatemala City, Cathedral Archive, Music MS 4*, Monuments of Renaissance Music IX (Chicago, 1996); Bruno Turner, 'Spanish Liturgical Hymns: A Matter of Time', *Early Music* xxiii (1995), pp. 473–82; Jane Morlet Hardie, 'Lamentations in Spanish Sources before 1568: Notes towards a Geography', *Revista de Musicología* xvi (1993), pp. 912–42; Màrius Bernadó, 'The Hymns of the *Intonarium Toletanum* (1515): Some Peculiarities', *Cantus Planus* i (1993), pp. 367–96; Manuel Pedro Ferreira, 'Braga, Toledo and Sahagún: The Testimony of a Sixteenth-Century Liturgical Manuscript', *Fuentes musicales en la península ibérica (ca.1250–ca.1550)*, ed. Maricarmen Gómez and Màrius Bernadó (Lleida, 2001), pp. 11–33; Wagstaff, 'Music for the Dead'; and other contributions by these authors in the bibliography. For a recent survey of the whole issue, see especially Maricarmen Gómez Muntané, *La música medieval en España* (Kassel, 2001), chapter 1.

18 See for example Turner, 'Spanish Liturgical Hymns', Bernadó, 'Hymns of the *Intonarium Toletanum*', and Jane Morlet Hardie, 'Proto-Mensural Notation in Pre-Pius V Spanish Liturgical Sources', *Studia Musicologica Academiae Scientiarum Hungaricae* xxxix (1998), pp. 195–200.

addition of the new polyphonic voices, the choices become more numerous: if the chant tune becomes a cantus firmus in one voice, the new voices can harmonize it in the same rhythm or accompany it in a faster rhythm. Or the chant can be woven into several of the voices at once, or the tune can be bypassed altogether and just the liturgical words set to completely different music. All of these decisions (and of course combinations of them) are the composer's to make, and they can be usefully seen by us as part of a continuum between the simplest pieces, most closely and obviously tied to the chant, and the most sophisticated and free.

Chronology

In using terms like *simplest* and *most sophisticated* I do not mean to imply a value judgement, or even a chronology exactly: chant harmonizations and free compositions, which I have placed at opposite ends of a spectrum, appear together in the same manuscripts and must have coexisted in performing life. But just as clearly, anyone writing polyphonic music in fifteenth-century Spain (or anytime, anywhere) did so within at least a vague sense of tradition and innovation. On the traditional side, different liturgical occasions bore different musical expectations; a psalm text suggested one kind of music, a Requiem another, a Marian antiphon another. Then as now, the job of the composer was to build on these expectations – obey them, distend them, or defy them. Some appreciation of the chronology of things, of what music composer X would have known when he wrote piece Y, of what was considered old-fashioned and avant-garde in any genre at any particular moment, is thus at the center of a critical understanding of any musical era.

Traditionally, at least for repertories before the age of music printing, this kind of chronology has had to be triangulated among datable compositions, manuscript studies, and composer biographies. It is a speculative business at best, and the more so for fifteenth-century Spain, where so much basic groundwork still needs to be laid. Datable pieces we have none in our repertory, at least not explicitly. There are a few vernacular songs in the cancioneros that refer to military victories and such, and I shall try to associate a handful of Latin sacred pieces to one occasion, the funeral of Prince Juan in 1497; but in the main, the straightforward liturgical character of most of the sacred music makes it all but impossible to assign a precise date to any one piece. For manuscript studies we are on somewhat firmer ground, especially since the work of Emilio Ros-Fábregas on Barcelona 454 and its concordant sources;[19] but still, no Spanish manuscript from this period has been dated to within less than a half-decade, some (like the largest, Tarazona 2/3) remain persistently baffling, and none of the major sources has been confidently placed before 1490.

Biographical information ought to be the most help of all, and at least in the case of Anchieta, whose whereabouts we generally know and whose biography can be divided into reasonably distinct phases, it does help to straighten things out. For most earlier composers, however, the data are just too few and flimsy to offer much of a handhold – not even for Cornago and Urrede, who merely disappear from the royal chapels in 1475 and 1482 and whose actual deaths are not recorded; if they in fact retired to their

19 Ros-Fábregas, 'Manuscript Barcelona'.

hometowns or went to a cathedral somewhere, they could easily have lived, sung, and written music for some decades more without attracting our attention.[20] And in any case, much of the sacred music in these sources is anonymous and much of the rest is ascribed with a single name (like 'Enrrique', or 'Madrid') fraught with maddening possibilities of misidentification.

In short, though I would love to organize this book along firm and clear chronological lines, there is no way at present to accomplish that; the best we can do is to proceed in an attitude of non-paralyzed caution. With a few exceptions for clarity, I shall be presenting the repertory one manuscript at a time, in what I believe to be their order of copying. At the end of each chapter I shall append a section on 'The Story So Far', in which we catch up on some chronological issues, and then I shall return to them in earnest in the last chapter. But one point is clear: it is time we started considering Spanish music between, say, 1470 and 1530 – elsewhere, from the late works of Du Fay through the early works of Arcadelt – as a sequence of repertories and not just one.

North and South

As much as we may come to love and admire this repertory, there will probably be no temptation to mistake it for the Crucible In Which Western Music Was Forged. The story of fifteenth-century music as we have all learned it took place mostly in north-western Europe (what is now northern France, Belgium, and the Netherlands) and among the many northern musicians working at the courts of Italy and elsewhere. Spain in the fifteenth century remained part of the periphery, caught between the middle ages and exciting innovations that were happening, for the most part, far away.[21]

Influence is a delicate thing to discuss fairly, especially at five hundred years' remove. The perhaps natural tendency to credit northern influence for all change in Spanish music over the course of the century – or, more insidiously, for any moments of contrapuntal complexity or sophistication, or anything we suddenly like – should of course be mistrusted. Yet there is no question that the osmotic pressure here was downward, that northern music had a lot more impact in Spain than Spanish music had abroad. True, Urrede's *Nunca fue pena mayor* had a fabulous international career at the end of the century, and a few other Spanish songs appear scattered as exotic novelties in the French chansonniers; but only one probable piece of sacred music from the Spanish repertory survives in a foreign source – the controversial *O bone Jesu*, which appeared under Compère's name in Petrucci's *Motetti de la Corona III* of 1519. The time would come when Spanish singers were particularly valued by the papal chapel and their way of singing sacred music world-famous, and when the phrase *more hispano* would have advertising value on the title page of a sacred print; but these are sixteenth-century phenomena. In fifteenth-century Spain, church music was something acted on from without.

The Pyrenees look like an impressive barrier on the map, but they are not hard to

---

20 For the cautionary tale of Juan Álvarez de Almorox, see below, p. 153, n. 43.
21 The most recent and comprehensive treatment of this subject is Reinhard Strohm, *The Rise of European Music, 1380–1500* (Cambridge, 1993).

cross or sail around. Castile and Aragón in the fifteenth century had strong dynastic and trading ties to the north and east alike, and throughout the period the peninsula was by no means isolated from the musical mainsteam. For the first three quarters of the century, Spanish courts did as so many Italian courts did, hiring French- or Flemish-trained singers and composers and bringing them down as ornaments to their own chapels. Figures like Urrede and, presumably, Enrique de Paris were among the last beneficiaries of this custom (which can be traced back in the royal court of Aragón at least to the mid-fourteenth century[22]).

Beginning in the 1470s, however, Ferdinand and Isabella seem consciously to have reversed this long habit and begun to hire their singers and composers locally.[23] They maintained a fascination with northern, especially Burgundian, ways of life and cere-mony and culture,[24] and the music of their composers beginning around 1500 shows northern influence in a number of explicit ways;[25] but the mechanism of influence had shifted decisively. After the succession of the Catholic Monarchs, Spanish musi-cians learned about the wider world by their own occasional trips abroad (e.g. Anchieta's time in the north, 1504–5, with the court of their daughter Juana), from northern musicians visiting Spain briefly (e.g. La Rue and Agricola, with Juana and her husband Philip the Fair in 1501–2 and 1506–8), and from musical repertories brought into Spain in written form from northern and Italian cities.[26]

It is clear, in short, that throughout the fifteenth century, Spanish composers had reasonably ready access to the music of northern Europe. The Segovia manuscript, with its rich mixture of local sacred and secular music with some of the most ambi-tious works of Obrecht, Isaac, Josquin, and so forth, is perhaps the most eloquent surviving sign that they and their patrons nurtured a kind of obsession with the musical mainstream, even as they may have stayed somewhat apart from it them-selves. Separating the foreign and local influences in a repertory is never done with easy security, but it is something to keep in mind throughout this study.

Eleven days and nights in the winter of 1479: after all that I can find to say about the church music of fifteenth-century Spain, and all that will remain unsaid for now, it is the royal chapel of Aragón, singing polyphony as they keep watch over their king's remains, convening for one last time before they must disperse, that has remained with me at day's end – partly, I suppose, because the visual image is so easy to conjure.

The room that Carbonell describes as the 'gran sala' in the Palau Reial Major must have been what is now called the Saló del Tinell, literally the banqueting hall; today it is one of the most famous rooms in Barcelona, revered by architectural historians as a

[22] María del Carmen Gómez Muntané, *La música en la casa real catalano-aragonesa durante los años 1336–1432* (Barcelona, 1977).
[23] On this, see for example Knighton, 'Music and musicians', especially vol. II, pp. 2–52 (*Música y músicos*, pp. 167–95).
[24] Tess Knighton, 'Northern Influence on Cultural Developments in the Iberian Peninsula during the Fifteenth Century', *Renaissance Studies* i (1987), pp. 221–37
[25] Kenneth Kreitner, 'Franco-Flemish Elements in Tarazona 2 and 3', *Revista de Musicología* xvi (1993), pp. 2567–86
[26] Stevenson, *Spanish Music*, pp. 134–5; Knighton, 'Music and Musicians', vol. I, pp. 251–2 (*Música y músicos*, pp. 323–4); Mary Kay Duggan, 'Queen Joanna and the Musicians', *Musica Disciplina* xxx (1976), pp. 73–95.

touchstone of the Catalan gothic and by tourists as the place where, according to legend anyway, Christopher Columbus was greeted by Ferdinand and Isabella after his return from the New World.[27] It is long and plain, with six huge stone arches spanning its width to give the effect of what Robert Hughes has called 'a very grand Quonset hut'.[28] Every time I have been there it has been utterly empty of furnishings, and, with only a single row of low windows along one wall, it has probably always been dark. It is the sort of room that must have heard laughter once, but that today enforces a sudden silence on the perkiest visitor. We stroll around talking in whispers that echo, most people, I imagine, speculating about where the king and queen might have sat and the explorer knelt. But my own mind is fixed more than a decade earlier, on Juan II and his singers – and above all their music, now lost but maybe not quite out of reach.

The sacred polyphony of fifteenth-century Spain has had little impact on the narrative of music history as it has lately been written. Gustave Reese's classic textbook of 1954, for one gauge, gave half a dozen pages (out of a thousand) to the subject, and his successors Howard Brown (1976), Allan Atlas (1998), and Leeman Perkins (1999) barely acknowledged it at all.[29] Perhaps, in perspective, that is as it should be, though I have to say it's a little discouraging to see the proportion go *down* over the decades. But it is much harder to maintain such an attitude on the floor of the Saló del Tinell. Other feet stood here too, and other voices bounced off these walls, and what they sang was as good as anything anyone in the room had ever heard. I believe it will be worth listening to.

27 Robert Hughes, *Barcelona* (New York, 1992), pp. 143–5; on the Columbus legend, see Agustí Duran i Sanpere, 'Cristofor Colom a Barcelona', in his book, *Barcelona i la seva història* (Barcelona, 1972–75), vol. II, pp. 623–5.

28 Hughes, *Barcelona*, p. 143; see also the photograph on p. 144.

29 Gustave Reese, *Music in the Renaissance* (New York, 1954), pp. 575–80; Howard Mayer Brown, *Music in the Renaissance* (Englewood Cliffs, 1976), pp. 237, devotes two paragraphs to the biographies of Cornago, Anchieta, Peñalosa, et al. and praises their sacred music generically (mentioning only one piece, the Cornago mass) before going on to the songs; Allan W. Atlas, *Renaissance Music: Music in Western Europe, 1400–1600* (New York, 1998), mentions Anchieta's *Missa de Beata Virgine* in a list of Marian masses on p. 310 and puts Anchieta and Peñalosa (with the wrong first name) in a list of *L'homme armé* masses on p. 149, but otherwise discusses only secular music from Spain at this time; and Leeman L. Perkins, in *Music in the Age of the Renaissance* (New York, 1999), gives an entire chapter (pp. 481–503) to 'Polyphony on the Iberian Peninsula' at this time, mentioning the existence of sacred music but taking all six of its musical examples from the song repertory.

2

The Catalan Ars subtilior

Is Spain part of Europe or not?

This unspoken question lies somewhere in the background of just about every-thing that has ever been written about Spanish cultural history. It has a simple answer: yes. Spain is attached to France, and that is all it needs. Yet at the same time there is something about the simple answer that doesn't satisfy, something compelling in W.H. Auden's description of 'that arid square, that fragment nipped off from hot/ Africa, soldered so crudely to inventive Europe.'[1] And while we today must be careful to remember how much of this impression comes from the political history of the twentieth century – Auden's poem was, significantly, written in 1937 – it is also true that Spain's sense of separateness goes back a long way and pervades its history and culture to the very center. If the church music of fifteenth-century Spain were just like the church music of everywhere else, you would be reading another book right now.

It is odd that medieval music, of all things, should be such an exception to what seems like an eternal verity. Yet there, apparently, we are. For each of the first three broad notational and stylistic bands into which we habitually divide the history of written polyphony, one of the most important and famous manuscripts has a strong Spanish connection: for unmeasured polyphony, we have the Codex Calixtinus; for the Notre Dame period, Madrid 20486; for the Franconian, the Las Huelgas codex. All of these sources are close to the center of music history as it has traditionally been written, and all, gratifyingly for the present purpose, are dominated by Latin sacred music.[2]

Nor, I should perhaps immediately add, are these famous sources anything like the whole story for Spanish medieval music. A great wealth of material, of a wide variety of periods and styles, has been uncovered by scholars taking a more local approach – one thinks immediately perhaps of Higini Anglès's astonishing early study of music in medieval Catalonia,[3] or José López-Calo's work in Galicia,[4] or more recently Kathleen

---

[1] W.H. Auden, 'Spain', in *Selected Poems*, ed. Edward Mendelson (New York, 1979), pp. 51–5, quotation p. 53; the poem is dated April 1937.

[2] I use the phrase 'strong Spanish connection' here circumspectly: all of these sources import substantial amounts of music from the north, and at least Calixtinus actually originated there. All of them, however, arrived in Spain early and presumably had a real role in Spanish polyphony during their active lives. On this issue see especially Maricarmen Gómez, 'Acerca las vías de difusión de la polifonía antigua en Castilla y León: del Códice Calixtino al Códice de las Huelgas', *El Códice Calixtino y la música de su tiempo*, ed. José López-Calo and Carlos Villanueva (La Coruña, 2001), pp. 163–80.

[3] Higini Anglès, *La música a Catalunya fins al segle XIII* (Barcelona, 1935).

[4] José López-Calo, *La música medieval en Galicia* (La Coruña, 1982).

Nelson's in Zamora[5] – who make it clear that sophisticated, and not necessarily isolated, traditions must lie just under the surface all over the peninsula, some of them presumably still awaiting discovery and recognition.

But for our purposes here it is the end of the middle ages, the late fourteenth century, the period often divided into the Ars nova and Ars subtilior, that promises the most immediate relevance. And this period does contain one piece with at least a certain name recognition: the so-called 'Barcelona mass', a series of mass ordinary movements copied together in a manuscript now at the Biblioteca de Catalunya.[6] We can come back to the Barcelona mass in a moment; more important, it is by no means an isolated example of a substantial piece of fourteenth-century music surviving in Spain. As Maricarmen Gómez has shown in two decades of publication, Spain – and specifically Catalonia – appears to have taken a very active role indeed in the musical culture of the late fourteenth century.[7]

5   Kathleen E. Nelson, *Medieval Liturgical Music of Zamora*, Musicological Studies LXVII (Ottawa, 1996); idem, '*Conlaudemus omnes pie* and *Deo nos agentes*: Polyphony in a Fourteenth-Century source of the Church of Zamora', *Fuentes musicales in la península ibérica (ca. 1250–ca. 1550)*, ed. Maricarmen Gómez and Màrius Bernadó (Lleida, 2001), pp. 109–19; and idem, 'Two Twelfth-Century Fragments in Zamora: Representatives of a Period in Transition', *Encomium Musicæ: Essays in Memory of Robert Snow*, ed. David Crawford and G. Grayson Wagstaff (Hillsdale, 2002), pp. 161–74.

6   The Barcelona mass has been published a number of times, perhaps most accessibly in Leo Schrade, ed., *The* Roman de Fauvel; *The Works of Philippe de Vitry; French Cycles of the Ordinarium Missæ*, Polyphonic Music of the Fourteenth Century I (Monaco, 1956; rept. 1974), hereafter abbreviated PMFC 1, and H. Stäblein-Harder, *Fourteenth-Century Mass Music in France*, Corpus Mensurabilis Musicæ XXIX (n.p., 1962), commentary in idem, *Fourteenth-Century Mass Music in France*, Musicological Studies and Documents VII (n.p., 1962); Stäblein-Harder's two publications, identically titled and dated, will hereafter be referred to as CMM 29 and MSD 7.

7   Gómez's name is spelled according to various conventions by various journals and publishers; her work on this repertory is contained principally in M.ª del Carmen Gómez Muntané, *La música en la casa real catalano-aragonesa durante los años 1336–1432* (Barcelona, 1977); María del Carmen Gómez, 'Neue Quellen mit mehrstimmiger geistlicher Musik des 14. Jahrhunderts in Spanien', *Acta Musicologica* l (1978), pp. 208–16; María del Carmen Gómez, 'Más códices con polifonía del siglo XIV en España', *Acta Musicologica* liii (1981), pp. 85–90; M.ª Carmen Gómez Muntané, 'El manuscrito M 971 de la Biblioteca de Catalunya (Misa de Barcelona)', *Butlletí de la Biblioteca de Catalunya* x (1982–84), pp. 159–290, reissued with a facsimile in 1989; M.ª Carmen Gómez, 'Musique et musiciens dans les chapelles de la maison royale d'Aragon (1336–1413)', *Musica Disciplina* xxxviii (1984), pp. 67–86; M. Carmen Gómez, 'Un nuevo manuscrito con polifonía antiqua en el Archivo Diocesano de Solsona', *Recerca Musicologica* v (1985), pp. 5–11; María del Carmen Gómez, 'Quelques remarques sur le répertoire sacré de l'Ars nova provenant de l'ancien royaume d'Aragon', *Acta Musicologica* lvii (1985), pp. 166–79; Giulio Cattin and Francesco Facchin, with Maria del Carmen Gómez, eds., *French Sacred Music*, Polyphonic Music of the Fourteenth Century XXIII (Monaco, 1989), hereafter abbreviated PMFC 23; and M.ª Carmen Gómez Muntané, *El Llibre Vermell de Montserrat: Cantos y danzas s. XIV* (Barcelona, 1990); Mª Carmen Gómez, 'Autour du répertoire du XIVe siècle du manuscrit M 1361 de la Bibliothèque Nationale de Madrid', *L'Ars Nova Italiana del Trecento* vi (1992), pp. 193–207; M.ª Carmen Gómez Muntané, *Polifonía de la Corona de Aragón: Siglos XIV y XV*, Polifonía Aragonesa VIII (Zaragoza, 1993); Maricarmen Gómez, 'Una fuente desatendida con repertorio sacro mensural de fines del medioevo: el contoral del convento de la Concepción de Palma de Mallorca [E-Pm]', *Nassarre* xiv (1998), pp. 333–72; M.ª Carme Gómez i Muntané, *La música medieval*, 3rd edn. (Barcelona, 1998), which is not a general survey as its title might indicate, but focuses on Catalan music only; and Maricarmen Gómez Muntané, *La música medieval en España* (Kassel,

Gómez has collated some twenty manuscripts, none of them large and a few very fragmentary indeed, that appear to have circulated within Spain in the years around 1400: Barcelona 144, Barcelona 853, Barcelona 853b, Barcelona 853c/d, Barcelona 971 (which contains the Barcelona mass and is, at twelve folios, the biggest), Barcelona 971b–Girona (two fragments that belong together but are now in separate libraries), Barcelona 971c, Barcelona 2, Burgos s.s., Girona 33/II, Madrid 1474/17, Madrid 1361, Montserrat 1 (otherwise known as the Llibre Vermell), Palma de Mallorca s/n, Solsona 109, Tarragona (1), Tarragona (2), Tarragona (3), Valladolid 29/7, and Vic V.60.[8] And in them she locates, by my count, a perhaps surprising total of sixty-one compositions. Nearly all are edited in volumes 1, 5, and 23 of the series Polyphonic Music of the Fourteenth Century, which for convenience shall be my standard reference.[9]

I advance the phrase 'Catalan Ars subtilior' with some caution. In several important senses, this music is not particularly Catalan: though all but a few of the manuscripts seem to have spent their active lives in or around Catalonia – mostly, it seems, in and around the francophilic (and, we should remember, itinerant) Aragonese royal court – they did not necessarily all originate below the Pyrenees and they contain a good deal of music that clearly was imported. And 'Ars subtilior' is also a potentially controversial term; I use it here not in the way it is sometimes used, to refer to a specific, often spectacular musical style, but more neutrally as a name for something that does not as yet have a tidy name: the music of the period between, say, Machaut and Dunstaple, and in particular that music produced and distributed within the Avignonese papal obedience. We can return to this point at the end of the chapter; for now, whatever they might be called, these sixty-odd sacred compositions appear to form a repertory reasonably unified in style and by geography, and the clearest available background to the sacred music of fifteenth-century Spain in general.

2001), especially pp. 219–80. These works understandably overlap a great deal, and in my citations I have not attempted to be exhaustive.

8   List from PMFC 23, p. 462, updated after Gómez, *Música medieval en España*, pp. 247 ff. For descriptions, see Gilbert Reaney, *Manuscripts of Polyphonic Music (c. 1320–1400)*, RISM B.IV.2 (Munich: Henle, 1969), 88–103, updated by Gómez in *Música en la casa real*, vol. 2, pp. 3–8 and the other articles etc. in the previous note. See also Bernat Cabero Pueyo, 'El fragmento con polifonía litúrgica del siglo XV, E-Ahl 1474/17: Estudio comparativo sobre el Kyrie *Summe clementissime*', *Anuario Musical* xlvii (1992), pp. 39–80.

9   The one exception is a Credo found in Palma s/n after the publication of PMFC and edited by Gómez in 'Una fuente desatendita', pp. 344–50. PMFC 1 contains the five movements of the Barcelona mass, unnumbered, on pp. 139–64, and an additional Agnus on pp. 136–7. Four motets are edited in Frank Ll. Harrison, with Elizabeth Rutson and A.G. Rigg, eds., *Motets of French Provenance*, Polyphonic Music of the Fourteenth Century V (Monaco, 1968), numbers 9, 10, 23, and 34. The remainder of the repertory is in PMFC 23, numbers 8, 14, 17, 18, 20, 22–26, 31, 36, 39–41, 51, 54, 56, 62, 63, 69, 86, 88, 95–104, 106, 107, 110–17, 121, 122, 126, 128, 129, A1, and A2. Many of the pieces in this repertory are edited elsewhere as well, notably Stäblein-Harder, CMM 29, and Gómez, *Música en la casa real*, vol. 2.

The Barcelona Mass

Of the sixty-one pieces I am putting into this repertory, twenty have concordances in sources outside Spain, most prominently the Apt manuscript (thirteen instances) and the Ivrea codex (eight): the Catalan Ars subtilior, like so many of its Spanish predecessors, was not a geographically isolated repertory but one with strong connections to traditions outside the peninsula. A very small handful of compositions have Spanish concordances only: they may indeed be local products, and we shall look at them in more depth shortly. The rest are unica, and about any one of them, barring some other evidence like a composer's name, it is difficult to pronounce.

It is a repertory dominated by sacred genres, like its predecessors, and especially by the ordinary of the mass: some forty-five mass movements, about a third of them troped;[10] three Latin motets; one motet mixing French and Latin; two smaller liturgical works in Latin; and in the Llibre Vermell ten songs and canons for the Virgin, eight in Latin, one in Catalan, and one in Occitan. There are at least six quartets; the rest appear to be mostly trios with a few duos, though the number of fragmentary pieces makes it hard to give solid statistics.[11]

The only part of this repertory to have entered much into the big narrative of music history is the 'Barcelona mass', which is often cited, along with the similar 'Toulouse mass' and a few others, as part of an intermediary stage in the story of the polyphonic mass ordinary, between Machaut's mass and the English cyclic masses of the early fifteenth century.[12] And the Barcelona mass makes a convenient starting-point. It consists, in Barcelona 971, of five movements:

- a Kyrie, MTT clefs, found only in Barcelona 971;
- a Gloria, MMT clefs, with the trope 'Splendor Patris', found also in the Apt manuscript and Barcelona 2;
- a Credo, SAA clefs, attributed to 'Sortis', who is probably the Catalan composer Steve de Sort, with concordances in Apt, the Ivrea codex, a manuscript in Rochester, and the Toulouse mass;
- a Sanctus, STA clefs, with the trope 'Sacrosanctus pater / Sanctus miro gaudio', for which 971 is the unique source; and
- a four-voice Agnus Dei, SMRR clefs, also an unicum in Barcelona 971.[13]

Hanna Stäblein-Harder, in her pioneering study of this repertory, introduced three basic categories to describe it: motet style, in which two active, texted voices are supported by a slow-moving textless tenor; discant style, in which one voice is active

---

[10] My count, from the PMFC volumes plus the Palma manuscript, includes 5 Kyries, 7 troped Kyries, 11 Glorias, 4 troped Glorias, 11 Credos, 2 Sanctus, 1 troped Sanctus, 3 Agnus Deis, and 1 troped Agnus. See also Gómez, *Música medieval en España*, pp. 254–7, for a table that makes a few calls differently.

[11] I include the three monophonic works in the Llibre Vermell among in my statistics because they are written in mensural notation and are clearly of a piece with the polyphony in the manuscript.

[12] See for example Richard Hoppin, *Medieval Music* (New York, 1978), pp. 389–91.

[13] Edited by Schrade in PMFC 1, pp. 139–64; Stäblein-Harder, in CMM 29, separates the movements, numbering them 19, 25, 47, 56, and 72. See also Gómez, 'Manuscrito M 971' and *Música medieval en España*, pp. 257–62.

and texted and the others are slow-moving and textless; and simultaneous style, in which all the voices are texted and generally move together.[14] This scheme, and especially her flexible and sensitive application of it, have stood up well over the years,[15] and the Barcelona mass happens to provide textbook examples of all three types and one specimen that crosses the boundaries: the Kyrie she calls simultaneous, the Gloria and Credo discant, the Sanctus motet (it is even bitextual), and the Agnus a mixture of all three.[16]

There is no reason, at this point in history, why a single mass could not contain all these divergent styles. But the circumstantial evidence – the pattern of concordances, the lone attribution in the middle, and the variations of cleffing – all points to the fundamental disunity of this mass. Maybe whoever copied it meant the five movements to be sung together (the actual voice ranges would not be altogether impossible, especially for a choir with more than one on a part), but there is almost no chance that they were written as a unit. Gómez has noticed some connections between the Kyrie and Agnus and raised the possibility that the Barcelona mass may be made from bits of two preexisting masses; but in the end she calls Barcelona 971 'a little musical anthology ordered by a collector',[17] and I am inclined to agree, adding only that the copyist probably put the five movements together more for tidiness to the eye than for practicality to the voice or unity to the ear. Indeed, if Stäblein-Harder's stylistic categories correspond to something that they were sensitive to back then, it is not hard to imagine the movements being chosen as a kind of encyclopedia of available musical styles.[18]

So the Barcelona mass is probably not a mass, at least in the way we use the term for later music; but is it from Barcelona? Again, probably not. The Credo is attributed to a composer of presumed Catalan birth, but it also appears in a number of Avignonese sources outside Spain, including the most central, Apt and Ivrea. Where it was actually written thus seems less important than the obvious fact that it was part of the repertory circulating internationally. The Gloria too is in Apt and thus a likely import; the Kyrie, Sanctus, and Agnus are all unica, and in their case, in the absence of any clear stylistic or liturgical connection, it is impossible to determine. In short, the Barcelona mass, with all its interesting features, seems for our present purpose merely to confirm what we might have guessed from the raw statistics: that somebody in Catalonia around 1400 took a special interest in polyphonic music for the ordinary of the mass, and that he was not content to drink the water from his own well.

---

[14] Stäblein-Harder, MSD 7, especially pp. 16–18; I have replaced her word *instrumental* with the more neutral *textless* in light of subsequent thinking about performance practice.

[15] For some refinements, see Hoppin, *Medieval Music*, pp. 378–84, and Reinhard Strohm, *The Rise of European Music, 1380–1500* (Cambridge, 1993), pp. 23–4.

[16] Stäblein-Harder, MSD 7, pp. 35, 39–41, 57–9, 67–8, and 78–9.

[17] Gómez, 'Quelques remarques', especially pp. 172–7, quotation p. 177: '. . . une petite anthologie musicale commandée par un collectionneur'.

[18] This is in fact Hoppin's view in *Medieval Music*, p. 391.

Sort, Tallender, and Perrinet

Of the sixty-one pieces in this repertory, only ten have attributions in the Spanish sources or elsewhere. All the attributions are short and at least potentially ambiguous; none, to my eye anyway, can be fastened securely to any vivid historical figure. Yet there are three attribution-personality pairs that seem to offer the possibility of an explicit, if hypothetical, Catalan connection for some pieces of music.

Steve de Sort, an Augustinian monk, was singer, organist, and possibly minstrel at the Aragonese court for some years: he was in the chapel of Juan I in 1394-1395 at least, then in that of María de Luna for some time, and then in that of María's husband Martín I from 1398 to 1406; he was alive but absent from court, possibly nearing death, in March 1407. He was probably a native Catalan; Sort is and was a small town in the Pyrenees west of Seu d'Urgell. He may have been an influential teacher within the court, and he is probably the composer of the Credo of the Barcelona mass, which is attributed to 'Sortis' in Apt and Barcelona 971, and mysteriously inscribed 'de regis' in Ivrea. A Gloria (Polyphonic Music of the Fourteenth Century, volume 23, number 8) attributed to 'Depansis' in Apt and anonymous in Ivrea, is attributed to 'Sortis' in Solsona 109, but this may be a mistake.[19]

There is a Credo (PMFC 23:54) attributed in Apt to 'Tailhandier', in the Barcelona-Girona fragments to 'p. Talhendenj' [=Talhenderii?], and in Munich 29775 to 'flors'; it is also anonymous in one non-Spanish and two Spanish sources. It is presumably the work of one of an illustrious family: Anthoni Tallender (1360–1443), also known as 'Mossen Borra', a famous jester-musician-diplomat who served the Aragonese courts in Barcelona and Naples; one of his three sons Anthoni II (profession unknown), Johan (canon of the cathedral of Barcelona), and Leonart (singer at the Aragonese court under Ferdinand I in 1414 and Alfonso the Magnanimous in 1417); or either of Anthoni II's sons Anthoni III (a lawyer) and Pere (who may have served in the chapel of María of Aragón in the 1430s and 1440s). Of these, the last has been the usual favorite because of the *p* in the one attribution and because of a surviving musical treatise with the title *Incipit lectura per Petrum Talhanderii ordinata tam super cantu mensurabili quam inmensurabili.* Yet if all of the above is correct, Pere could not have been born much before 1400 and thus would seem to be too young to have written this piece (or the chanson by 'Taillandier' in Chantilly 564); so the *p* in Barcelona-Girona may be wrong or there may be more musical Tallenders yet to be discovered.[20] Whoever wrote the Credo, though, it surely must have been someone in this Barcelona family.

---

[19] Biographical details from *New Grove* 1980, s.v. 'Sortes', by Gilbert Reaney; Gómez, *Música en la casa real*, vol. 1, pp. 92–8 et passim; idem, 'Manuscrito M 971', pp. 194–5 et passim, and idem, *Música medieval en España*, pp. 231–6, 249, 260, and 262. On the attribution in Solsona 109, see PMFC 23, p. 466. I shall adopt Gómez's Catalan names for all of these musicians. Karl Kügle, in the 'Sortes' article of *New Grove* 2001, suggests that 'Sortis' may not be a composer attribution at all.

[20] See Stäblein-Harder, MSD 7, pp. 62–3; *New Grove* 1980, s.v. 'Tailhandier, Pierre', by Ursula Günther; Gómez, *Música en la casa real*, vol. 1, pp. 102–3 and 107; Allan W. Atlas, *Music at the Aragonese Court of Naples* (Cambridge, 1985), pp. 109–10; *Gran enciclopèdia catalana*, 2nd edn., s.v. 'Tallander, Antoni', by Eulàlia Duran i Grau; Alejandro Planchart, 'Music in the Christian

And then there is the Credo (PMFC 23:51) attributed in Padua 684 to 'Perneth', in Strasbourg 222 to 'Prunet', and in Apt to 'Bonbarde', also anonymous in two Spanish sources and one non-Spanish. For only a few of the most recent opinions: Gómez favors Perrinet Prebostel, an organist, singer, and instrumentalist at Alfonso's court from at least 1425 to 1431;[21] Gilbert Reaney, in his *New Grove* entry, suggests Perrinet Rino, a shawm player who served Alfonso from 1416 to 1418, or Pierre Fontaine of Rouen and the Burgundian court, or Perrinet d'Acx, at the Navarrese court from 1374 to 1386;[22] and the editors of PMFC 23 say the composer was 'certainly the bombard-player "Patrequi de la bonbarda",' whose orgins are unspecified but who was paid by the Aragonese court in 1393.[23] In the end, there are just too many Peters in the world for me to be sure who this composer is: the index in Gómez's book[24] lists over fifty musicians or potential musicians connected with the Aragonese court with some variation on the name 'Pere' – not to mention all the Pierres, Pietros, and so forth outside Spain. For now, we cannot rely on this Credo, or the two works by 'Pelliso' that Gómez assigns to the same composer, as Catalan creations.[25]

In short, the biographical approach does not yield much music to identify securely with the Iberian peninsula. Such is the nature of the late middle ages, where attributions are rare and cryptic and biographical data are sketchy to nonexistent. But these two Credos by Sort and Tallender may be the most solid cases we have of mass music that was written in Spain at this time, and they are worth a closer look.

They are, in fact, rather alike. Both are in three voices, for a falsettist and two conventional male singers (basically MAA clefs for Sort, MRR for Tallender, though the actual clefs are variable). Both are in one meter throughout: Sort's setting is in what works out to 6/8 in modern transcription, Tallender's in 2/4.[26] Both divide the text to the creed into not the two to four large sections familiar from the renaissance, but little discrete bits of a sentence or less: Tallender's, for example, is broken into sixteen sections of mostly ten to fifteen bars long[27] for a choppy stop-and-start quality in performance. Both are good straightforward examples of what Stäblein-Harder

Courts of Spain', *Musical Repercussions of 1492*, ed. Carol E. Robertson (Washington, 1992), pp. 149–66, especially pp. 154 and 156; PMFC 23, pp. xiv and 486–8; *New Grove* 2001, s.v. 'Tailhandier, Pierre', by Maricarmen Gómez; and Gómez, *Música medieval en España*, pp. 249 and 260.

21 Gómez, *Música en la casa real*, vol. 1, pp. 110–11.

22 *New Grove* 1980 and 2001, s.v. 'Perrinet', by Gilbert Reaney; Reaney's dates for Rino are supplemented by Gómez in *Música en la casa real*, vol. 1, pp. 45 and 47. See also Stäblein-Harder, MSD 7, pp. 66–7.

23 PMFC 23, p. xiv; the 1393 reference is from Gómez, *Música en la casa real*, vol. 1, p. 169 n. 132; see also Strohm, *Rise of European Music*, pp. 26–35 for a detailed discussion of this piece.

24 Gómez, *Música en la casa real*, vol. 1, pp. 230–1

25 Ibid., vol. 1, p. 111; see also pp. 263–4 on Francisco de Campania, whose identity is similiarly in doubt.

26 Both of the main published editions of the Tallender Credo, in PMFC 23, p. 54, and Stäblein-Harder's in CMM 29, no. 51, combine bars of 2/4 into what amounts to 4/4 or sometimes 6/4; plain 2/4 seems clearer for the present comparison, and I have adopted it for Ex. 2.1. My editions for this chapter quarter the original note values (so that a semibreve becomes a quarter note) in accordance with the usual convention, rather than halving them (semibreve becomes a half note) as in the rest of the book.

27 In my barline-scheme; see the previous note. Tallender's sections range between 7 and 23 bars, and Sort's are a bit longer, from 9 (the opening) to 31 (the Amen).

calls the discant style, with the lower voices textless and moving mostly in half and quarter notes and the superius texted and moving substantially faster. Example 2.1 shows the opening of Tallender's setting as it appears in Barcelona-Girona.[28]

Ex. 2.1 Tallender, Credo, bb. 1–16

Some Anonymi

Again: the Credos of Sort and Tallender may have been written on Catalan soil by composers of Catalan birth, but they were in every sense part of an international tradition; Sort's has in fact been called, startlingly but with, on reflection, some justice, 'the most popular liturgical composition of the fourteenth century'.[29] This is in itself worthy of a pause to knit the brow: it will be more than a hundred years before another piece of undisputed Spanish sacred polyphony is found in a source outside the Iberian peninsula.

Identifying a more purely local tradition at the end of the fourteenth century, a body of music that originated on the peninsula and never spread elsewhere, is a more difficult matter. The number of unica among the sixty-one pieces clearly points to some kind of local repertory, but it is very hard to say, in default of other information, whether any particular piece belongs to it or not. Two anonymous compositions seem, however, to offer at least the beginnings of what we are looking for.

The more ambitious of these is *Kyrie: Rex inmense maiestatis–Dulcis potens* (PMFC 23: 23), which seems to have been widely distributed within Spain – it appears today

[28] Edited after PMFC 23, p. 54, with variants as detailed on p. 487. In bars 5–6 (their 3) I have followed the instructions explicitly; in 10–11 (their 6) I have made an editorial emendation. The three Catalan sources all have different contratenors: Barcelona-Girona concords with Apt, and Barcelona 853b and 2 have their own, similar to each other but still distinct; see p. 487.

[29] María del Carmen Gómez, 'Sobre el papel de España en la música europea del siglo XIV y primer tercio del siglo XV', *España en la música de occidente*, ed. Emilio Casares Rodicio, Ismael Fernández de la Cuesta, and José López-Calo (Madrid, 1987), vol. 1, pp. 45–7, quotation p. 45: '. . . la composición litúrgica más popular del siglo XIV, a juzgar por el número de copias que se han conservado (nueve en total)'.

whole in Barcelona 971 and fragmentarily in Barcelona 971b (an originally separate source), Barcelona 853c/d, and the Castilian Madrid 1474/17 – but does not survive in any foreign manuscript. It is a troped mass movement in the form of an isorhythmic motet: each of the three parts of the Kyrie is preceded by a long poetic introduction, or rather two, for the cantus I and cantus II have different texts. As was common with Kyrie tropes, the new portions transform the structure from Kyrie-Christe-Kyrie to Father-Son-Holy Spirit: for example, the texts to the first section:[30]

Cantus I	Cantus II
Rex inmense maiestatis	Dulcis, potens, pater pie
Et summe potencie,	Meritis sancte Marie
Vive fons virginitatis,	Super astra sedens dux,
Magne providencie,	Gencium dele peccata
Spes cuncte felicitatis	Kyrie eleison.
Lavans unda venie,	
Alme iudex equitatis,	
Dispensator sobrie,	
In die calamitatis,	
Lumen refulgencie	
Tu nobis convocatis	
Pande pulchra facie,	
Kyrie eleison.	

All three sections work the same way, with the Kyrie text preceded in the cantus I by twelve lines of verse and in the cantus II by four.

This precisely ordered verbal structure then supplies the basic architecture for the musical setting, which is a fine example of Stäblein-Harder's 'motet style'.[31] The three big sections become three isorhythmic periods in the slow-moving tenor, which is in alto clef and in 971 is given no text of its own (only an incipit from the cantus I text to identify it). The wordier cantus I, in soprano clef, moves considerably faster, working mostly in quarter and eighth notes, and the cantus II, also in soprano clef but with a much shorter text, establishes a rhythmic middle ground. (In the first 22 bars, for example, the cantus I sings fifteen words, the cantus II five.) Example 2.2 gives the first twelve and the last twenty-one bars of the first period, which will show that the three voices, despite their contrast in rhythmic style, are carefully constructed to go together, with frequent points of obviously deliberate coincidence (bb. 7–8, 12, 51–52). Especially impressive is the end of each period, where the trope ceases and the original text appears at last: all three times, the cantus parts mimic each other's rhythm, dovetailing their acclamations for a kind of call-and-response effect that ties the preceding together nicely and emphasizes the underlying structure. It is, on the whole, one of the most effective pieces of planning and craftsmanship in the whole repertory.

Ave regina cælorum (PMFC 23:86) is found in the Barcelona-Girona fragments and in Barcelona 853b; it is the only other piece (apart from one monophonic song in the Llibre Vermell) with Spanish concordances only. It is in SST clefs, i.e. for two high voices (falsettists or boys?) and one tenor or baritone; its meter is not specified but

30 Texts from PMFC 23, pp. 472–3.
31 Stäblein-Harder actually puts it first in her edition and commentary; see her commentary in MSD 7, pp. 22–3.

Ex. 2.2 *Kyrie: Rex inmense*, bb. 1–12, 46–66

must be ○. It takes its text from the familiar Marian antiphon, but uses neither of the tunes in the *Liber Usualis*.[32] And as Example 2.3 shows, it presents a notable stylistic contrast to the Kyrie trope: here the voices all move together, phrase by short phrase, in what Stäblein-Harder calls the simultaneous style. To the eye it suggests perhaps Dunstaple or something from the Old Hall manuscript, though the ear accustomed to the rich elegance of the English music may be struck by the rawer, emptier sound of this continental piece.

There remain, of course, a great many anonymous works among the pages of Barcelona 971 and its companions, but the rest have French concordances or no concordances anywhere. It seems reasonable to suppose that among the latter (and conceivably the former) are at least a few specimens of what we are looking for –

[32] *Liber Usualis*, pp. 274–5 and 278.

Ex. 2.3 *Ave Regina cælorum*, bb. 1–9

Spanish creations that never migrated north – but until more sources turn up, or perhaps more likely, until we get a better grip on local liturgical and chant traditions, it will be hard to make much of a case for any of them in particular. One manuscript does, however, seem to offer an especially privileged view of a local Catalan tradition: the famous Llibre Vermell.

The Llibre Vermell

The Llibre Vermell was copied between 1396 and 1400 for pilgrims to the Benedictine monastery of Montserrat, on a weird and impressive mountain northwest of Barcelona. Among its 137 folios, otherwise devoted to nonmusical texts (official documents, accounts of miracles, homiletic materials, a calendar, etc.), are seven (21v–27) of music; these form a gathering but are not otherwise distinguished in paper or hands from their surroundings.[33] They preserve ten pieces of music whose purpose is made clear by an inscription on folio 22:

> Because sometimes the pilgrims holding night vigil in the church of Santa Maria of Montserrat wish to sing and dance, and also by day in the plaza, and only decent and devout songs are allowed there, the songs above and below are written. And these must be used decently and sparingly, not disturbing those who continue in their prayers and devout contemplations . . .[34]

---

[33] Bibliographic information from Gómez, *Llibre Vermell*, pp. 16–18. This small facsimile, edition, and commentary will be my standard source; the pieces are also edited in PMFC 23, numbers 95–103. See also Francesc Xavier Altés i Aguilo, ed., *Llibre Vermell de Montserrat: Edició facsímil parcial del manuscrit núm. 1 de la Biblioteca de L'Abadia de Montserrat*, Llibres del Mil·lenari II (Barcelona, 1989) for a luxuriously printed full-size full-color facsimile with a mostly literary commentary, and Gómez, *Música medieval en España*, pp. 265–72.

[34] Transcribed in Gómez, *Llibre Vermell*, p. 19: 'Quia interdum peregrini quando vigilant in ecclesia

This sort of thing should never be taken quite at face value, of course, but in the present case it does seem to fit: the ten pieces show a remarkable variety of forms and styles, but on the whole they do have a popular flavor that strikes the attention right away and contrasts with the selfconsciousness of the service music we have been examining. It is indeed the kind of music that one might provide for people to entertain themselves in a respectable manner without disturbing the prayers of their fellow pilgrims.

The ten pieces appear to be ordered by subject. The first two make specific reference to Montserrat and the statue of the Virgin which the pilgrims were coming to see; the first, for example, begins, 'O Virgo splendens hic in monte celso . . .' Items 3 through 9 have more generic Marian texts, and the last, helpfully illustrated with a picture of a skeleton in a box, exhorts us to abjure sin because death is coming. Two of the pieces are in Catalan: LlV 5 is a monophonic tribute to the seven joys of the Virgin, and LlV 9 is a two-voice bitextual virelai. There are also three Latin monophonic songs (LlV 6, 7, and 10). This leaves five items of Latin polyphony for our story here.

Three are actually simple canons, of two types. The first, *O Virgo splendens* (LlV 1) is written in meterless black chant notation, so that each period must have not the same number of beats but the same number of notes, performed presumably in an even rhythm. It is preceded with the tagline 'Antiphona dulcis armonia dulcissime Virginis Marie de Monteserrato', and the harmony is indeed sweet:[35]

Ex. 2.4 *O Virgo splendens*, bb. 1–3

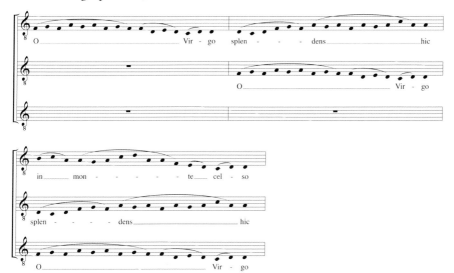

The other two canons, *Laudemus Virginem* and *Splendens ceptigera* (LlV 3 and 4), are both written (as is the rest of the music in the manuscript) in black mensural notation,

Beate Marie de Monte Serrato volunt cantare et trepudiare, et etiam in platea de die, et ibi non debeant nisi honestas ac devotas cantilenas cantare, idcirco superius et inferius alique sunt scripte. Et de hoc uti debent honeste et parce, ne perturbent perseverantes in orationibus et devotis contemplationibus in quibus omnes vigilantes insistere debent pariter et devote vaccare.'
[35] See also Gómez's commentary on this piece in ibid., pp. 23–9, where she shows some of its interrelationships with other items in the manuscript.

and both have the rubric 'Caça de duobus vel tribus.' They have simple rhythms and short canonic periods, twelve bars of 2/4 in the case of *Splendens*, and only six for *Laudemus*:

Ex. 2.5 *Laudemus Virginem*, bb. 1–10

This is about as simple a round as you could teach to a three-year-old, yet there is something strangely compelling about it – or perhaps compulsive is a better word; once started, especially with other people, it is a hard piece to stop singing. The image of it offering some comfort to a group of pilgrims laboring up the mountain is – to me anyway – irresistible.

Stella splendens (LlV 2) and *Mariam matrem* (LlV 8) both use variants of the virelai form, AbbaA, which was popular in the vernacular songs of France and Italy at this time and which had a Spanish precedent in the Cantigas de Santa María a century and a half earlier, but which was everywhere rare in Latin sacred music. These two pieces may thus be contrafacta of secular works, or polyphonic versions of a kind of popular sacred music that had been around for a long time without surviving on paper. *Stella splendens* is a more or less pure specimen of the form, though the A section is made up of two similar phrases with different cadences; it is in two voices, TT or RR clefs,[36] and shows solid, vigorous two-part polyphony:

Ex. 2.6 *Stella splendens*, bb. 1–10

Mariam matrem has essentially the same form as *Stella*, though it looks different on the page because the repetition of the B section is written out; but it too has an A section made of two similar phrases (its structure, in other words, could be expressed as AA' bb aa' AA'). Its texture, however, is much more complex and sophisticated: it is in three voices, STT clefs (this is the only high clef among the polyphonic works of the manuscript), and its top line, while perhaps not offering much competition to the spectacular productions we usually associate with the Ars subtilior, has some of the syncopation and suppleness that we have come to expect from the late fourteenth century. It is quite a lovely piece, as the opening and the first B section will show:

---

[36] Normal clef designations don't quite work for this piece because it is written on a four-line staff; both voices have an F clef on the second line from the bottom, and their ranges are identical.

Ex. 2.7 *Mariam matrem*, bb. 1–8, 15–21

The Story So Far

I have included this chapter mostly as a matter of perspective. True, the music of what I am calling the Catalan Ars subtilior was sung into the early fifteenth century, and some of it was no doubt actually written after 1400; yet somehow it does not register as a tradition *of* the fifteenth century. So I have not put any of this music into my handlist of fifteenth-century sacred music, preferring to explore it as a foundation for, and a contrast to, what will come next.

Even as a foundation, however, this repertory has proven strangely wobbly: in trying to describe it I have found myself rocking continually back and forth between two stereotypes. On the one side there is the notion of Spain, and particularly the Aragonese royal court, as an outpost of the Ars subtilior – the music of the Avignonese papacy, the music that Reinhard Strohm has made so bold as to call the 'central tradition' of European polyphony during the Great Schism.[37] Such, I suppose, is the established view: if you have been reading my footnotes carefully you may have noticed that Stäblein-Harder's edition of the mass music and all three relevant volumes of PMFC have the words 'French' or 'in France' prominently in their titles, and none mentions Spain at all. This has long struck me as an injustice, or at least an unfortunate but influential oversimplification; hence, rocking to the other side now, my own perhaps overzealous efforts to reverse the trend and establish some sort of Spanish voice amid this international repertory. But I have found no such distinctive voice. Among the fifty-one pieces of Latin sacred polyphony in the main group of Spanish manuscripts (leaving the Llibre Vermell aside for now) I have identified two pieces by composers who seem to have stronger Catalan connections than French, two pieces of exclusively Spanish transmission (which, given the vagaries of manuscript survival,

---

[37] Strohm, *Rise of European Music*, pp. 1–61.

may not mean much), and a host of dim but as yet unprovable possibilities. Nor is there any obvious way in which the style or form of this putatively native music is different from those of its northerly neighbors.

This, then, is the first thing to say about the Catalan Ars subtilior: that the stereotypes I brought to it – or, to put perhaps a more positive face on things, the archetypes we all tend to bring to the study of Spanish repertories – are just wrong here. The court of Aragón at the end of the fourteenth century was not a colony of a tradition clearly centered elsewhere; but neither was it really a culture of its own, receiving some influences from the mainstream but also developing separately on its own. Catalonia, so far as the surviving polyphony tells the story, was simply a full participant, exporting as well as importing, in a tradition that extended not to national or linguistic boundaries but to the boundaries of the Avignonese papal obedience.

The second thing to say about the Catalan Ars subtilior, or maybe it should have been the first, is that there is a lot of it. Fifty-one pieces of Latin, or mostly Latin, sacred music – for I am still keeping the Llibre Vermell out of the discussion for now – is a sizable repertory, comparing very favorably with the sixty-seven that I shall put in my handlist for the whole fifteenth century. Perhaps even more dramatic and puzzling, there are forty-five mass ordinary movements here; there, eight.

And the third observation about this music is that it is not the Ars subtilior we were taught in college, with its fantastic rhythmic intricacies, its mixed meters, its long syncopations, its notational calculus. This style was confined to songs, and only a relatively few songs at that – songs that may well have been sung in Barcelona and wherever the court was staying (the Ars subtilior composers Trebor and Gracián Reyneau both spent time in its chapel, and Solage has left three pieces dedicated to Juan I and Violante[38]), but which have not been preserved there. But no, the sacred music, in France, Italy, and Spain alike, was a much plainer, more sedate affair. This is what we should expect, of course, and it would be wrong to look for mass movements with all the hair-raising excitement of a Matteo da Perugia song. Yet there is no way around the observation that this repertory, despite its abundance and centrality, has so far had relatively little appeal for modern listeners, falling for most of us somehow behind the rhythmic energy of Ciconia, but also behind the suppleness and ingenuity of Machaut and Landini before it and the glorious sonority of Dunstaple and Du Fay after.

The Llibre Vermell has had greater success in today's marketplace, but as part of the story here it is more puzzling. For it was copied at about the same time as the other sources, and not that many miles away, and in the same notation, but musically it has little in common with the rest of the Catalan Ars subtilior. The music of the Llibre Vermell was compiled for a specific and specialized purpose – the pious entertainment of pilgrims to an isolated shrine. It is a response to a very different pressure: where Barcelona 971 and so forth were presumably part of the royal and other courtly milieus of Barcelona, and thus their music a part of the Aragonese monarchy's effort to position itself in an international cultural community, the Llibre Vermell was aimed at the spiritual needs of lay people. Its simple Latin rounds, its strophic monophonies, its sacred songs in Catalan, and its Latin virelai-oids all register as freaks somehow, as sacred versions of popular secular music, as shadows of a kind of

---

[38] For a recent summary, see Gómez, *Musica medieval en España*, pp. 239–46.

music that normally didn't get written down. It is good, and rare, to be able to see that kind of music, even imperfectly.

The Catalan Ars subtilior is, in short, a surprisingly large repertory, with a rich range of styles, with solid connections to the European mainstream and with, in the Llibre Vermell, visible roots in native soil. At least the northeast corner of Spain, at the end of the fourteenth century, was part of Europe *and* maintained traditions of its own. It is difficult to reconcile this plenitude and diversity with the – from our point of view anyway – blank spot that came right afterward and with the music that emerged from there.

3

Barcelona 251 and Paris 967

For all the strength of the Catalan Ars subtilior, it has no clear successor among the music that has survived. In Barcelona the Aragonese court and the cathedral continued to support polyphonic choirs,[1] and an inventory of the Barcelona cathedral's possessions taken in 1421 recorded four books that seem to have contained music beyond chant:

> Item: another book called a Prosarium, all with red covers; it begins on the second folio with *Magna de terris* and ends *Amen*, in song.
>
> Item: another book, of medium size, of tooled red leather, of various songs in Latin and vernacular; it begins on the second folio with *In se* and ends on the last with *Ballem*.
>
> Item: another small book, covered with tooled red leather, of old counterpoint; it has written on the first folio *Viderunt* and ends on the last *Samsonis*.
>
> Item: another book, covered in green, of various songs in notation, and prose in Latin; it begins on the first and also the second folio with *Iube Dompne* and ends on the last with *Regem glorie*.[2]

But all of these sources, and everything that these choirs sang, and all the polyphonic music that may have been sung elsewhere on the peninsula for the first half of the fifteenth century have vanished without any clear trace; there is now about a fifty-year gap in the repertory.

A number of things happened in the early 1400s that must have had some impact on the church music of Spain. In 1417 the Council of Constance brought an end to the

---

[1] On the court, see M.ª del Carmen Gómez Muntané, *La música en la casa real catalano-aragonesa durante los años 1336–1432* (Barcelona, 1977), especially pp. 82–112; on the cathedral, see Josep Maria Gregori i Cifré, 'La música del renaixement a la catedral de Barcelona, 1450–1580' (Doctoral thesis, Universitat Autònoma de Barcelona, 1986), especially pp. 1–72, and Kenneth Richard Kreitner, 'Music and Civic Ceremony in Late-Fifteenth-Century Barcelona' (Ph.D. diss., Duke University, 1990), especially pp. 216–33.

[2] Higini Anglès, *La música a Catalunya fins al segle XIII* (Barcelona, 1935), pp. 129–130: 'Item alium librum *Prosarium* vocatum per totum cum cohopertis de rubeo; incipit in secundo folio *magna de terris* et finit *amen* in cantu.

Item alium librum mediocrem de corio rublo lavorato, *de diversis cantilenis in latino et vulgari*; incipit in secundo folio *in se* et finit in ultimo *ballem*.

Item alium librum parvum, cohopertum de corio rubeo laborato, *de contrapuncto antiquo*; habet in primo folio scriptum *viderunt* et finit ultimo *samsonis*.

Item alium librum, cohopertum viridi, *de diversis cantilenis in nota, et prosa in latino* incipit in primo et etiam in secundo foliis *iube dompne* et finit in ultimo *regem glorie*.' (Emphasis as given by Anglès.)

Great Schism by denouncing the line of popes in Avignon, and the musical styles popular under the Avignonese obedience declined in popularity in the years afterward.[3] After the succession of Alfonso the Magnanimous to the throne in 1416, the Aragonese monarchy that had been the patrons of this music turned its attention instead more toward diplomacy and conquest, with a corresponding drop in the economic fortunes and cultural resources of Catalonia, the rise of a fashion for things Italianate, and, beginning in the 1440s, the actual removal of the court and its singers to Naples.[4] And at some point during this period, the black notation of the Ars subtilior sources was overtaken by the white notation of the later renaissance, with the possible result that a great many earlier manuscripts began to seem obsolescent and discardable: note that one of the books listed above was already, in 1421, described as containing 'contrapuncto antiquo'.

At the moment there is not much to submit as evidence of what was being sung in the cathedrals, parish churches, and court chapels of Spain after the decline of the Ars-subtilior tradition in Catalonia. One intriguing bit of homorhythmic two-voice polyphony, in black notation, on the text *Gaude virgo mater Christi* was recently spotted by Robert Nosow in an altarpiece by Gonçal Peris (†1451), probably painted in Valencia but now in the Nelson-Atkins Museum of Art in Kansas City. Its fragmentary nature and unusual transmission oblige me to omit this composition from the handlist, but as Nosow points out, its presence at least shows that polyphonic notation was something familiar enough to have visual symbolic use for a painter in the early to mid-fifteenth century.[5]

The next conventional polyphonic source from anywhere in Spain was copied in Catalonia in probably the early 1450s, and it gives little sign of any strong continuity, much less of progress, in written polyphony over the first half of the century. The three polyphonic compositions in Barcelona 251 may or may not be fair representatives of their era, but they make the only logical place to resume our narrative. Along with them we can then consider three pieces from Paris 967, a manuscript which is as yet undated and may be later, but which seems to belong to the same world. Both are basically chant manuscripts with a few polyphonic interpolations, and the music of both is far from what we might expect from the time of Du Fay.[6]

---

3   The story is perhaps best told by Reinhard Strohm in *The Rise of European Music, 1380–1500* (Cambridge, 1993); but see also his essay 'The Close of the Middle Ages', in *Antiquity and the Middle Ages*, ed. James McKinnon (Englewood Cliffs, 1990), pp. 269–312, especially 271–6.

4   See Allan W. Atlas, *Music at the Aragonese Court of Naples* (Cambridge, 1985).

5   Robert Nosow, 'Early Fifteenth-Century Spanish Polyphony from an Altarpiece in Kansas City', paper read at the IMS Congress, Leuven, August 2002. I am grateful to Dr. Nosow for sharing this paper and his edition in advance of publication.

6   In an earlier version of my handlist, published as Kenneth Kreitner, 'The Church Music of Fifteenth-Century Spain: A Handlist', in *Fncomium Musicæ: Essays in Memory of Robert J. Snow*, ed. David Crawford and G. Grayson Wagstaff (Hillsdale, 2002), pp. 191–207, I added six more pieces to this group, from Seville 82-4-33 and 82-4-33 *bis* (now renumbered 56-5-24 and 56-5-24 *bis*), also a chant manuscript with a few polyphonic interpolations, and also traditionally dated from the fifteenth century (see *Census-Catalogue*, vol. III, pp. 143–4); but Todd Borgerding has since persuaded me that the polyphony is a later addition to the manuscript, so I have had to leave them out. I am grateful to Dr. Borgerding for his correspondence and for sending me an early draft of a paper entitled '*Ay arte de contrapunto*: Improvised Vocal Polyphony and Ritual in Early Modern Spain'.

Barcelona 251

Barcelona 251, sometimes called the Cantorale Sancti Ieronimi, is a manuscript of 144 folios, now at the Biblioteca de Catalunya but known to have originated at the monastery of Sant Jeroni de Murtra outside Barcelona, probably in the early to mid-1450s. It contains a variety of chants and liturgical prose appropriate to the life of a Jeronimite monastery, and toward the end three anonymous pieces, just five openings altogether, of polyphony in white notation.[7]

The first two, **Ad honorem . . . Ave regina cælorum** (handlist 9) and **Ad honorem . . . Salve regina** (handlist 10) are a matched pair, with very similar musical styles and nearly identical text. They were apparently meant not as self-sufficient motets but as stereotyped and more or less interchangeable introductions to the Marian antiphons. The first is followed by a polyphonic setting of the words 'Ave regina cælorum' and then, fainter and monophonic but evidently in the same hand, 'Alma', the second by polyphonic treatments of the words 'Salve regina' and 'Regina cæli'. The superius lines of *Alma redemptoris mater* and *Salve regina* at least are recognizable from their modern Gregorian counterparts.[8] No hint of the rest of each antiphon is given, nor space left for them; most likely the missing portions (and all of *Alma redemptoris*) were to be sung monophonically or in an improvised two-voice polyphony.

Both are in three voices of similar range, somewhere between baritone and tenor clef, though the clefs (and the number of lines in the staves) vary. All three lines are written in a white or blanked-out version of standard chant notation yielding a very simple note-against-note counterpoint, with only a few instances where a note in one part must be lengthened to accommodate two in another. It is a rhythmic approach more familiar from the twelfth century than the fifteenth, as Example 3.1 will show.

Barcelona 251's other polyphonic contribution is a **Credo** (handlist 5) in white mensural notation, in two voices, mostly in RR clefs.[9] The tenor (on the recto side of each opening) is based on Gregorian Credo IV throughout,[10] and its treatment is structurally unusual. The piece is divided into seventeen little segments of a sentence or so apiece, alternating between polyphonic portions in the mensuration ₵, transcribed as 6/8, with the chant paraphrased, and monophonic passages where the chant is given literally but carefully rhythmicized in C (2/4) – yet the monophonic portions are given only as incipits, implying that such rhythmic versions of the chant could be continued without written prompting. The polyphonic parts of the Credo are harmonically bland and rhythmically unadventurous: ornamented homophony for

[7] Its official name is Barcelona, Biblioteca de Catalunya, MS M 251 (*Census-Catalogue* siglum BarcBC 251). The best and only recent description of this manuscript is in Màrius Bernadó i Tarragona, 'El repertori himnòdic del *Cantorale Sancti Ieronimi* (Barcelona: Biblioteca de Catalunya, M 251)' (Licenciado thesis, Universitat Autònoma de Barcelona, 1992), especially pp. 5–15; Bernadó's estimate of the date is based (pp. 5–7) on paper and paleographic evidence.
[8] By the superius line I mean the upper line on each verso; for modern Gregorian tunes, see *Liber Usualis*, pp. 273 and 276.
[9] For a full edition of and commentary on this piece, see M.ª Carmen Gómez, 'A propósito de un Credo polifónico del "Cantorale S. Jeronimi" (E-Bd 251)', *Revista de Musicología* iv (1981), pp. 309–15.
[10] *Liber Usualis*, pp. 71–3.

Ex. 3.1 *Ad honorem . . . Ave Regina cælorum*

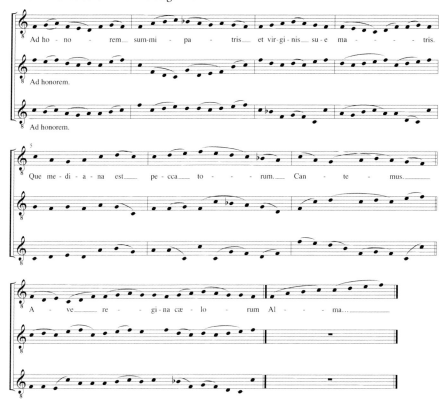

the most part, with a few moments of interest caused by syncopation or divisi and no rests till the 'Et iterum' section. Apart from the curious alternatim scheme, in short, the piece's style would not be at all out of place among the mass movements of Catalan manuscripts from fifty years earlier; whether was an old piece found and recopied, or a new piece in a style that hadn't changed much, is hard to say in such isolation. Example 3.2 shows the opening (with note values quartered).

It is hard to know exactly what to make of all three polyphonic pieces in Barcelona 251. They were copied in the 1450s and presumably performed for decades beyond; yet they give off a strong whiff of the middle ages. This was noticed as long ago as 1935, when Higini Anglès referred to the *Ad honorem* settings as a sign of a severe conservatism in Catalan music of the fifteenth century.[11] More recently, Márius Bernadò has noted the disposition of materials on some pages as evidence that the manuscript may actually have been copied from an earlier source[12] – which might explain some things but would not really change the force of Anglès's observation. Some musicians in

---

[11] Anglès, *Música a Catalunya*, p. 263: 'La producció, com la pràctica, de la polifonia primitiva a Catalunya, fou sempre concebuda en sentit molt conservador: ho prova el fet del manuscrit M. 250 [its number at that time] de la Biblioteca de Catalunya. . . . [M]algrat el tractar-se d'un *cantorale* copiat al segle XV, presenta dues composicions a tres veus escrites, també, seguint l'estil de la polifonia del segle XIII.'

[12] Bernadó, 'Repertori himnòdic', p. 5.

Ex. 3.2 Credo, bb. 1–20

Spain at midcentury, the only ones whose repertory we happen to know about, had a need for antique-style music and no other. We can return to this point after a look at another, equally puzzling little repertory.

Paris 967

Paris 967 is a short and luxurious manuscript: thirty-three parchment folios, with colored initials and marginal illustrations. Its first twenty-two openings are devoted to monophonic music for Holy Week (a somewhat unorthodox selection); the next seven to three polyphonic pieces, also for Holy Week; and the remainder to chant in honor of St. John the Evangelist.[13] Like Barcelona 251, then, it was intended principally as a liturgical chant collection: probably it was stored for most of the year and brought out only during its specialized seasons.

The origins of Paris 967 remain very mysterious, though some Castilian marginalia show that it was at least used in Spain. Amadée Gastoué, Günther Massenkeil, and Madeleine Bernard have all written about the manuscript very briefly; they are reluctant – as I am – to venture a precise date or provenance, though they see it as written in the late fifteenth or early sixteenth century, possibly for a nunnery.[14] Of all the sources I shall discuss in this book, this is the one with the scantiest secondary

---

[13] Paris, Bibliothèque Nationale, Département de Musique, Fonds du Conservatoire, MS Rés. F. 967 (*Census-Catalogue* ParisBNC 967).

[14] A. Gastoué, 'Manuscrits et fragments de musique liturgique, à la bibliothèque du Conservatoire, à Paris', *Revue de Musicologie* xiii (1932), pp. 1–9; Günther Massenkeil, 'Zur Lamentationskomposition des 15. Jahrhunderts', *Archiv für Musikwissenschaft* xviii (1961), pp. 103–14; idem, ed., *Mehrstimmige Lamentationen aus der ersten Hälfte des 16. Jahrhunderts*, Musikalische Denkmäler VI (Mainz, 1965), especially pp. 9*, 140–1, and 163; Madeleine Bernard, *Répertoire de manuscrits médiévaux contenant des notations muisicales, v. III: Bibliothèques Parisiennes Arsenal, Nationale (musique), Universitaire, École des beaux-arts et fonds privés* (Paris, 1974), p. 114. See also *Census-Catalogue*, vol. III, p. 17.

literature, and the number of unanswered questions must enforce a certain caution about placing it prematurely into a geographical or chronological framework. For now, however, it may be enough to say that its three polyphonic compositions seem to have led their musical lives in the Castilian-speaking area, that like those of Barcelona 251 they are of an unusual and apparently antique style,[15] and that they may fit better into this chapter than any other.[16] We may look at them in the order in which they appear.

Dona jube benedicere (handlist 33) is the first of the three; it was published and discussed in some detail by Massenkeil in a 1961 study of early polyphonic Lamentations.[17] It is in three voices, ARR clefs, labelled *tiple*, *tenor*, and *contrabasa*, and at 270 bars in my edition it is the longest piece in Paris 967 – indeed the longest single movement we shall see in this whole book.

It is a setting of Hebrews 9: 11–12 and 15, a text which also appears in the monophonic section of the manuscript (though on a different tune).[18] I cannot identify the tenor as a Lamentation tone, though with its narrow range and repeated note patterns (for example, A-G-F-G-F, identifiable at least eight times) it seems at least to be trying to evoke something of the sort. Its rhythms are slow and plodding, all in longs, breves, and semibreves, and the other voices harmonize it with relentless homophony broken only slightly at some cadences or, more rarely, in the middle of a phrase. Example 3.3 shows the first two sections.

Aleph. Quomodo obtexit (handlist 12) was also published by Massenkeil, in 1965 as part of a collection of renaissance Lamentation settings.[19] It is another work of imposing length (in my edition, 248 bars), in two voices, AR clefs. Its text is from Lamentations 2: 1–3, which also appears back in the monophonic portion of the manuscript;[20] the polyphonic setting, unlike *Dona jube*, uses a close paraphrase of the monophonic tenor. The upper voice harmonizes it mostly in homophony, fancier overall than *Dona jube* (with occasional minims!) and fancier still over the Hebrew letters and on 'Jerusalem'.

---

[15] Massenkeil, in 'Zur Lamentationskomposition', p.109, speculates that the polyphonic music may be from the early fifteenth century, but copied into the manuscript a good deal later.

[16] My thoughts on Paris 967 are much indebted to a correspondence with Jane Hardie, who has recently undertaken her own study of this manuscript as part of a long-term examination of Spanish Holy-week music. See especially Jane Morlet Hardie, 'Kyries tenebrarum in Sixteenth-Century Spain', *Nassarre* iv (1988), pp. 161–94; idem, 'Lamentations in Spanish Sources before 1568: Notes towards a Geography', *Revista de Musicología* xvi (1993), pp. 912–42; idem, 'Lamentations Chant in Spanish Sources: A Preliminary Report', in *Chant and its Peripheries: Essays in Honour of Terence Bailey*, ed. Bryan Gillingham and Paul Merkley, Musicological Studies LXXII (Ottawa, 1998), pp. 70–89; 'Proto-Mensural Notation in Pre-Pius V Spanish Liturgical Sources', *Studia Musicologica Academiae Scientiarum Hungaricae* xxxix (1998), pp. 195–200; idem, 'Circles of Relationship: Chant and Polyphony in the Lamentations of Francisco de Peñalosa', *Alamire Foundation Yearbook* iv (2000, published 2002), pp. 465–74; and idem, 'Lamentations Chants in Iberian Sources before 1568', in *Fuentes musicales en la Península Ibérica (ca. 1250–ca. 1550)*, ed. Maricarmen Gómez and Màrius Bernadó (Lleida, 2001), pp. 271–87. See also Robert J. Snow, ed., *A New-World Collection of Polyphony for Holy Week and the Salve Service: Guatemala City, Cathedral Archive, Music MS 4*, Monuments of Renaissance Music IX (Chicago, 1996), pp. 49–62.

[17] Massenkeil, 'Zur Lamentationskomposition', pp. 112–14.

[18] Folios 13–16.

[19] Massenkeil, ed., *Mehrstimmige Lamentationen*, pp. 140–1, commentary pp. 9* and 163.

[20] Folios 8v–10v.

Ex. 3.3 *Dona jube benedicere*, bb. 1–31

It has one notational curiosity: in a number of passages, small notes have been added, evidently later, on one or both staves. These have sometimes been interpreted as divisi passages, but the number of pointless dissonances and parallels suggests rather that the little notes represent an alternative reading that must involve both voices (see bb. 23–24, for instance). Both versions work fine, and there is little for the modern ear to prefer in either; possibly at some point there was some alteration made to the chant which had to be accommodated, or possibly the singers showed an aesthetic preference that is hard to discern at this distance. Either way, it is quite a simple elaboration of the chant: the tune is lightly paraphrased and put into a mensural rhythm, and the new voice generally sticks close to the old.

The third polyphonic composition in Paris 967 is **Kyrie . . . Qui passurus** (handlist 41). This is a setting of the 'Kyries tenebrarum', a troped or farsed Kyrie sung at the end of Lauds during Holy Week in a number of national traditions, with considerable local variation. As Jane Hardie has explained, in fifteenth- and sixteenth-century Spain the situation grew especially rich and complex.[21]

It is difficult to characterize the Kyries tenebrarum succinctly without oversimplifying, but essentially they consist of a series of short segments: repetitions of the

---

[21] See especially Hardie, 'Kyries tenebrarum' and 'Lamentations Chants in Iberian Sources'; for an earlier but still valuable discussion, see also idem, 'The Motets of Francisco de Peñalosa and their Manuscript Sources' (Ph.D. diss., University of Michigan, 1983), pp. 188–92.

Ex. 3.4 *Aleph. Quomodo obtexit*, bb. 1–26

acclamations 'Kyrie eleison' and 'Christe eleison' alternate with longer verses, many of them beginning with the word 'Qui', and the whole piece usually ends with 'Christus Dominus factus est. . .', derived from the Gradual for Maundy Thursday.[22] The substance and order of the segments changes significantly from source to source, and Hardie has collated some of these to draw a kind of liturgical geography for the region; for an accessible specimen, here is the text to a monophonic set, copied in a Catalan manuscript around 1400 and published by Anglès:[23]

> Kyrie eleyson.
> Kyrie eleyson.
> Qui passurus advenisti propter nos.
> Kyrie eleyson.
> Christe eleyson.
> Kyrie eleyson.
> Qui prophetice prompsisti: ero mors tua, o mors.
> Christe eleyson.
> Kyrie eleyson.
> Kyrie eleyson.
> Qui expansis in cruce manibus traxisti omnia ad te secula.
> Kyrie eleyson.
> Christus Dominus factus est obediens usque ad mortem.
> Mortem autem crucis.

A number of Spanish sources add rubrics assigning the various segments to different soloists and subchoirs, making the performance, in Hardie's words, 'a dramatic addition to the service in keeping with the ethos of the reenactment of Christ's Passion';[24] it is clear, then, that what we see in Paris 967 is a kind of analogue to the polyphonic Passion – a set of polyphonic modules that can be dropped into a

---

[22] *Liber Usualis*, pp. 655–6.
[23] Anglès, *Música a Catalunya*, p. 240, scholarly apparatus omitted.
[24] Hardie, 'Kyries tenebrarum', p. 163.

basically monophonic performance. How exactly this was supposed to work is not altogether clear; we have only the modules and not the frame, and our texts are found in too many of Hardie's sources to fit readily into any of her geographical patterns.[25] The entire piece is reproduced in Example 3.5, and the six polyphonic sections may be considered in order.

- *Kyrie eleison* (bb. 1–9). This corresponds to line 1 of the text as published by Anglès, and in each voice in the manuscript the music is followed by the words 'Christe eleison' and 'Kyrie eleison', suggesting that the same music is used for at least some of the repetitions of the basic acclamation.[26] The tenor is written in black chant notation, unmetered and read as though each note is a breve and the last a long; it bears the cantus firmus, nearly identical to the chant as given by Anglès. The other three voices are in white mensural notation, though all their notes are in fact breves and longs for a very stark set of block chords harmonizing the chant. The clefs are ATRB.
- *Qui passurus*... (bb. 10–27). For the four verses in the middle the altus drops out, leaving a three-voice texture, ARB clefs. The text here is from Anglès's line 3, and the tenor (still in black notation) is again similar to his chant. The outer voices are again in white notation, the bassus being a bit more active than the tenor and the superius still more so.
- *Qui expansis*... (bb. 28–61). This verse is longer and its superius even fancier than the previous; it takes its text from Anglès's line 11, but exhibits two important divergences from our model. First, this and the next verse are apparently reversed in order (though Hardie shows that this order is in fact the usual one and Anglès's the oddity[27]). And second, the cantus firmus is not the same tune as accompanies this text in Anglès but is closer to that given for 'Christus Dominus'.
- *Qui prophetice*... (bb. 62–79) and *Latro ipse*... (bb. 80–113). The text to 967's third verse is taken from Anglès's line 7, and the fourth from a line not in Anglès but well represented in other Spanish sources.[28] The music, all three voices, is identical to that for the previous two verses.
- *Mortem autem crucis* (bb. 114–19). The final acclamation is written in the same hand but is very distinct in appearance and sound: it is written in red ink, all voices are in white mensural notation, it is homophonic but without obvious reference to the chant as Anglès has it, and perhaps most important, it is in much higher SMAR clefs. Possibly it is set aside for performance by a separate choir using the same book.

It all adds up, at 119 bars, to another good-sized piece of music if – yet again – not a particularly memorable one from a contrapuntal point of view. But the polyphonic Kyries tenebrarum became a tradition that continued in Spain for a long time: in the chapters to come, we shall see examples, some of them quite conservative, in the Segovia manuscript and Barcelona 454, and other specimens are preserved even later in Tarazona 5, Toledo 21 and 22, and New York 392/278.[29]

---

[25] Ibid., especially pp. 167–71.

[26] A facsimile of folio 28v, showing these rubrics, can be found in Bernard, *Répertoire de Manuscrits*, plate LI. The superius has all three, Kyrie, Christe, and Kyrie; the other voices only the two.

[27] Hardie, 'Kyries tenebrarum', pp. 167–70.

[28] Ibid., pp. 167, 174–5.

[29] Ibid., p. 162 n. 3.

Ex. 3.5 *Kyrie ... Qui passurus*

Ex. 3.5 (cont.) *Kyrie . . . Qui passurus*

Ex. 3.5 (cont.) *Kyrie . . . Qui passurus*

Ex. 3.5 (cont.) *Kyrie . . . Qui passurus*

The Story So Far

It would be dangerous to try to build an elaborate and finely nuanced story out of the polyphony in Barcelona 251 and Paris 967. The six pieces are too few to support such a structure, too diverse to make up a coherent stylistic layer in themselves, and still – especially the ones in 967 – too chronologically ambiguous to form a secure bridge between what came before and after. Things may improve as we get to know these sources and their liturgical surroundings better or, maybe we can hope, as more Spanish sources from this mysterious period are recovered. But for now, for better or worse, these six pieces are the evidence there is, and they can be accounted for in two ways.

The first is that, for all their possible divergences, the two sources have a couple of important and unusual features in common. Both are, as we have seen, essentially chant manuscripts with small clumps of polyphony in the middle: the three pieces in Barcelona 251 may represent all the written polyphony that the monastery of Sant Jeroni needed for a year of liturgical singing, and those of Paris 967, all the written polyphony that its institution (unknown, but possibly a convent) needed for Holy Week. But the structure of these manuscripts gives, correctly I think, a vivid impression of the situation in which they were used: this kind of polyphony was but a small part of what went on in a church year, small enough that the institutions did not feel a need to prepare separate volumes of polyphony. Moreover, the polyphony in both is in low clefs: apart from the very last section of *Kyrie . . . Qui passurus*, there is no clef higher than alto, no note higher than F above middle C. Nor, as we have seen, is there any music that makes more than the most rudimentary technical demands. Is it possible, then, that what we are seeing in these two manuscripts is the difference between the polyphonic practices of Spanish monastic houses, which would presumably have had no boys or trained falsettists,[30] and the court and cathedral milieux behind our other sources?

My other thought does not necessarily contradict the first. In recent years we have come better to understand just how much improvised polyphony there could be, especially on a major feast day, in a late-medieval church.[31] Such unwritten practices are, practically by definition, shadowy, but no doubt they included a range of polyphonic techniques, from simple parallel organum, to note-against-note singing in oblique and contrary motion, to more florid organum with fancy improvised parts against a slow-moving tenor, to the tradition of *cantus planus binatim* in which note-against-note polyphony was improvised according to generally understood rules of counterpoint.[32] It is not currently clear, I should perhaps add, how deeply and broadly such practices had penetrated into late-medieval Spain, or what forms they took there.[33] But if we suppose – as surely we must – that improvised polyphony of some sort was more or less commonplace in Spanish religious institutions of the early fifteenth century, then the polyphonies of Barcelona 251 and Paris 967 start to make more sense.

The two *Ad honorem* settings and the outer portions of *Kyrie . . . Qui passurus* might be called three- and four-voice versions of *cantus planus binatim*; *Dona jube* and the Credo take the basic two-voice texture and add a mensural rhythm; and *Aleph. Quomodo obtexit* and the inner portions of the *Kyrie . . . Qui passurus* combine trio texture and rhythmic variety, yet still remaining, at the center, recognizable as a simple homophonic harmonization of the chant. All six pieces, in other words, are just one or two technical steps removed from simple improvised note-against-note counterpoint; and those one or two steps may have been just enough that the pieces could not be improvised but needed to be written down. We may be in the position here, then, of seeing the tip of a pyramid sticking above the sand, and not knowing how far down and out it goes.

No, the polyphonic compositions of Barcelona 251 and Paris 967 are not the obvious logical successors to the Catalan Ars subtilior. Most likely, when the spirit of the Ars subtilior subsided in Spain (assuming that it had ever been more than a local and rarefied curiosity), what replaced it was a tradition in which liturgical chant was mingled with improvised, not complex written, polyphony, and that in these six pieces we can start to envision the edges of such a tradition. The Credo, with its fourteenth-century rhythms, may be a survival from or echo of its Catalan past, but the others are better seen as coming out of a very different world – a world that may be a better representative, even though we can't see it very well, of what was really being sung in the churches, monasteries, and convents of Spain.

---

[30] The convent question complicates this thought, of course, but not seriously: nuns singing the music of Paris 967 could just have transposed it up.

[31] For a recent and sensitive example, see Frank A. D'Accone, *The Civic Muse: Music and Musicians in Siena during the Middle Ages and the Renaissance* (Chicago, 1997), pp. 63–97, 139–41, et passim.

[32] The best discussion of this issue is still F. Alberto Gallo, ' "Cantus planus binatim": Polifonia primitiva in fonti tardive', *Quadrivium* vii (1966), pp. 79–89.

[33] For a discussion of improvised polyphony in sixteenth-century Spain, see Borgerding, '*Ay arte de contrapunto*'.

4

The Cancionero de la Colombina and Paris 4379

Just as the Cancionero de Palacio has dominated our collective view of Spanish secular music in Josquin's time, so, it is probably safe to say, has the Cancionero de la Colombina done for Ockeghem's. And the recent discovery that a less famous source, a section of Paris 4379, is related to it only increases Colombina's allure.

Yet there is something misleading about the word *cancionero* in its modern name. Colombina is a songbook, in that most of its contents are Castilian songs; but it is not quite a chansonnier in the familiar French tradition of the day. Among its ninety-three surviving compositions are twelve pieces of Latin sacred polyphony; one must be a northern import from midcentury, but the others appear to be local. Paris 4379 adds five more sacred works to the list and offers a convenient opportunity to discuss two related pieces from the Chigi codex. Most of these are anonymous and unique to their manuscripts, which may help to explain their low profile today; but taken together, they are quite a substantial and varied repertory. They represent, for our purposes here, the earliest significant signs of a coherent body of polyphonic church music from fifteenth-century Spain.

Colombina

The origins and early history of the Cancionero de la Colombina (sometimes called the Seville cancionero) are not known. According to an unconfirmable bit of lore, the manuscript entered the great Colombina library when Ferdinand Columbus bought it in Seville in 1534,[1] but if so, it was clearly already something of an antique by that time. Colombina as a whole was probably finished in the early to mid-1490s (it contains one song about Ferdinand's final victory in Granada in 1492), but paleographic examination reveals a somewhat more complicated story.

In its present state, Colombina seems to represent a single long-term copying job interrupted by some years in the middle. Of its two broad chronological layers, it is the

---

[1] The manuscript's full name is Seville, Catedral Metropolitana, Biblioteca Capitular y Colombina, MS 7-1-28 (*Census-Catalogue* siglum SevC 7-1-28). The only clue to its acquisition is a somewhat mysterious passage from Simón de la Rosa y López, *Los seises de la catedral de Sevilla: Ensayo de investigación histórica* (Seville, 1904), p. 70 n. 1: 'El códice parece comprado en Sevilla por D. Hernando Colón en 1534.' No one since has been able to confirm this – see for example Robert Stevenson, *Spanish Music in the Age of Columbus* (The Hague, 1960), p. 196 n. 304 – but as chief of the Biblioteca de la Colombina, Rosa y López may have had access to materials now unknown.

later that contains the song from 1492; the earlier is hard to date, but most likely was copied between the late seventies and mid-eighties. Both halves have a striking number of pieces by one Juan de Triana, an otherwise minor composer who was presumably nearby, or at least familiar, during the whole period and who may even be the main scribe.[2]

Colombina has had no fewer than three modern editions: the first was by Robert Lawes in a dissertation completed in 1960;[3] this was followed in 1968 by Gertraut Haberkamp's edition[4] and in 1971 by Miguel Querol's volume in MME.[5] The Querol edition, though not always the most authoritative, is the most familiar and accessible, and I shall use its numbering system (with the initial Q) for simplicity.[6]

The Magnificat

We can begin with the **Magnificat** (nos. 83–5 in Querol's edition), which over the years has been something of a puzzle but which emerges as probably the oldest sacred piece in the manuscript. It covers three full openings, all in one hand, and a different hand from those of the pieces on either side; it is textless except for a couple of words; and on the last page it has large portions crossed out. Querol edited it as three separate pieces, but Lawes and Haberkamp both identified it as an incomplete Magnificat and edited it as such, with various hypothetical solutions to the problem of the deleted bits.[7]

A definitive answer has, however, been at hand since at least 1966, when Winfried Kirsch noticed not only that this was a Magnificat, but that it corresponded to an anonymous Magnificat on folios 73v–77 of Trent 88.[8] This composition, which is unpublished in modern edition but available in facsimile,[9] is unusual in having not

2   I make this case in more detail in Kenneth Kreitner, 'The Dates (?) of the Cancionero de la Colombina', *Fuentes musicales en la península ibérica (ca. 1250–ca. 1500)*, ed. Maricarmen Gómez and Màrius Bernadó (Lleida, 2001), 121–40.
3   Robert Clement Lawes, Jr., 'The Seville Cancionero: Transcription and Commentary' (Ph.D. diss., North Texas State College, 1960).
4   Gertraut Haberkamp, *Die weltliche Vokalmusik in Spanien um 1500* (Tutzing, 1968).
5   Miguel Querol Gavaldá, *Cancionero musical de la Colombina (siglo XV)*, MME XXXIII (Barcelona, 1971).
6   Users of Querol's edition should know, however, that it quarters the note values and puts barlines, in duple time, every two breves; as a result, it looks rather different from most editions of music of this period (including mine). Examples in this chapter will halve the note values and put barlines every breve.
7   Lawes, 'Seville Cancionero', pp. 141, 229, 330–1, 352, 365–6, 369–70; Haberkamp, *Weltliche Vokalmusik*, pp. 82–3, 250–4; Querol, *Cancionero Musical,* pp. 29, 86–8. See also Stevenson, *Spanish Music*, p. 207, as the first to notice that these might all be verses of the same Magnificat.
8   Winfried Kirsch, *Die Quellen der mehrstimmigen Magnificat- und Te Deum-Vertonungen bis zur Mitte des 16. Jahrhunderts* (Tutzing, 1966), p. 208, item number 115. So far as I can tell, even though this is the standard reference volume for Magnificats of the period, no one writing about Colombina has noticed this reference – including me: see for example Kenneth Kreitner, 'The Church Music of Fifteenth-Century Spain: A Handlist', *Encomium Musicæ: Essays in Memory of Robert Snow*, ed. David Crawford and Grayson Wagstaff (Hillsdale, 2002), pp. 191–207.
9   See *Codex Tridentinus 88* (Rome, 1970), pp. 148–55 (ms. folios 73v–77). Rebecca Lynn Gerber, in 'The Manuscript Trent, Castello del Buonconsiglio, 88: A Study of Fifteenth-Century Manuscript

the even or odd verses, but all twelve set in polyphony: verse 1 is in three voices, verse 2 in two, verse 3 in four, verse 4 in three, verse 5 in two but marked to add a voice in fauxbourdon, verse 6 in four, verse 7 in three, verse 8 in two, verse 9 in four, verse 10 in three, verse 11 in two, and verse 12 in four. The duos are in ¢ meter, the fifth verse in Φ, and the others all in O. Its clefs are, with occasional exceptions, MTTT.

A comparison of the two manuscripts shows what went wrong in Colombina: the Colombina scribe copied the first four verses successfully, leaving out the words except for a very few incipits. The fifth verse he also got right, including the text incipit, though he did not mark the fauxbourdon. As for the sixth verse, he copied the altus and bassus on folio 100r but for some reason didn't notice that there was no room on 99v for the superius and tenor, and in the process of scratching out these orphaned voices he accidentally eliminated verse 5's altus, which was caught between them.[10] The rest of the Magnificat was probably never there: folio 100 is the last of a gathering, but 100v has no trace of any Magnificat verse. Its clefs are basically MTTR.

Trent 88 was copied in Trent in the early 1460s,[11] which means that this piece is almost certainly northern and that it was written toward the middle of the century, much earlier than its copying into the late layer of Colombina. How it got to Spain is a good question, though the presence of Cornago's mass in Trent 88 may show a Neapolitan-Aragonese connection as yet imperfectly understood. In any case, it must be omitted from the handlist but not from our attention; its presence in Colombina is at the very least a sign of the the the continuing fascination that complex, even if antiquated, northern music had for some Spanish musicians in the 1490s. As an excerpt from verse three (Example 4.1) will show, it is an active piece but still maintains, in the frequent repetition of the pitch A in the superius and the fabordón-like monotony of the third and fourth bars, its relationship to the tradition of the monophonic Magnificat tone.

Juan de Triana

The Magnificat was, despite its early date, copied into the later portion of the Cancionero de la Colombina. The earlier part contains only three pieces of Latin sacred music. They are copied together on four openings near the end of the manuscript, far from the rest of their layer but easily recognized as having the same handwriting, luxurious page layout, and ornamental initials, and their placement on the first verso of a gathering shows that they were originally intended as the beginning of a separate section of church music to be attached later.[12] All three are attributed to Triana.

Juan de Triana's pre-eminence in the contents of the Cancionero de la Colombina seems to be exceeded only by his obscurity everywhere else. Of his twenty works in

Transmission and Repertory' (Ph.D. diss., University of California, Santa Barbara, 1984), p. 235, describes the piece but does not edit it.
[10] Querol number 83 corresponds to verses 1 and 2 of Trent; Q 84 to verse 3; Q 85 (which he calls *[Magnificat]* because it has the text 'Quia') to verse 4.
[11] Gerber, 'Manuscript Trent', p. 5 et passim; also *Census-Catalogue*, vol. III, pp. 224–5.
[12] Kreitner, 'Dates (?) of the Cancionero de la Colombina', 126.

Ex. 4.1 Magnificat, verse 3, bb. 1–8

Quia respexit...

Colombina, only three of the Castilian songs appear in Palacio (all anonymously), and to date only three documents about him have been found. They show him to have been a prebendary in the cathedral of Seville, probably though not necessarily in residence, from at least 1477 to 1480, and to have become a singer and the master of the choirboys at the cathedral of Toledo in 1483.[13] His name suggests that he or his forebears were from Triana, then a small town outside Seville.

Triana's three motets include two settings of the **Benedicamus Domino** (handlist 22–23, Q 80–81) and one of the hymn **Juste judex** (handlist 38, Q 82).[14] All three are much alike: all are in three voices, fully texted in all parts; all have two upper voices of equal range and one lower (SST, SSR, and SST clefs respectively); and all are written in an active contrapuntal style with occasional moments of imitation and frequent voice crossings between the sopranos. The second *Benedicamus Domino* (Example 4.2) will give the general flavor.

13 Stevenson, *Spanish Music*, pp. 195–6. The first document (Seville 1478) is transcribed in Lawes, 'Seville Cancionero', pp. 112–13, and the second (Seville 1480) in Rosa y López, *Seises*, pp. 347–8; only the third (Toledo 1483), partially transcribed by Stevenson on the same pages, describes Triana as a musician, but the name is probably unusual enough to connect the documents to one another and the attributions in Colombina, which give only his last name. See also François Reynaud, *La polyphonie tolédane et son milieu: Des premiers témoignages aux environs de 1600* (Brepols, 1996), pp. 101 and 142.

14 This text is no longer a hymn in the Vatican editions, but Bruno Stäblein, in *Monumenta monodica medii aevi I: Hymnen (I): Die mittelalterlichen Hymnenmelodien des Abendlandes* (Kassel, 1956), p. 498, identifies it in a Laon manuscript of the twelfth century, and anonymous polyphonic settings can also be found in Segovia s.s. (handlist 39; see below, p. 87) and in the Catalan Ars subtilior manuscript Madrid 1361; see for example Mª Carmen Gómez, 'Autour du répertoire du XIVe siècle du manuscrit M 1361 de la Bibliothèque Nationale de Madrid', *L'Ars nova italiana del Trecento* vi (1992), pp. 193–207. No two of these versions seem to share a tune.

Ex. 4.2 Triana, *Benedicamus Domino [ii]*, bb. 1–14

Robert Stevenson has described these as 'song-motets' – an awkward term perhaps, for it has had various meanings in various contexts,[15] but also an insightful description in some ways: these pieces do seem far removed from the other Latin music in Colombina, as we shall see, and closer to the manuscript's vernacular songs, and they would indeed seem (as Stevenson says) more at home in the private oratory than the cathedral.

Yet there is something odd going on here too. As songlike as these motets appear at first glance, they are set apart from the real Spanish songs of the day in some important ways. Of the twenty-four intact or reconstructable songs in this layer of Colombina, only one is texted in all voices, and none has two upper voices in the same clef.[16] In fact, in all of Colombina, there is just one song with two voices in soprano clef.[17] Moreover, Triana's motets seem to have an alliance to the chant tradition: the superius of the second *Benedicamus Domino* (Example 4.2 above) paraphrases the Benedicamus Domino from Gregorian Mass IV[18] – a popular tune, as we shall see, for Benedicamus settings and other mass movements in late fifteenth-century Spain. The

15 Stevenson, *Spanish Music*, p. 196. For a few other usages of the term, see Helen Hewitt, ed., *Petrucci: Harmonice Musices Odhecaton A* (Cambridge, 1942), pp. 69–72; Gustave Reese, *Music in the Renaissance* (New York, 1954), p. 94; Edward E. Lowinsky, ed., *The Medici Codex of 1518* (Chicago, 1968), vol. I, pp. 79 and 141; *The New Harvard Dictionary of Music*, s.v. 'Motet' (especially p. 511), and Julie E. Cumming, *The Motet in the Age of Du Fay* (Cambridge, 1999), pp. 177–9 and 201–4.

16 In Kreitner, 'Dates (?) of the Cancionero de la Colombina', I defined the rest of the layer as comprising Q 1–28; of these, 1, 3, 5, and 13 are defective and 6, 7, and 12 must be restored from concordances. The only fully texted song is Q 28, Triana's *Non puedes quexar*.

17 This is Q 93, *Pues que no tengo*, SSR clefs. Two other pieces have two soprano clefs: Q 39, *Omnipotentem senper adorant*, an SS Latin duo, and Q 76, an incomplete, crossed-out, and textless trio, SSR clefs apparently, that may have been intended as another motet.

18 *Liber Usualis*, p. 28.

other two I have not found, but the relative slowness and melodic contours of the top line of *Juste judex* (Example 4.3) may also betray a role as a cantus firmus.

Ex. 4.3 Triana, *Juste judex*, bb. 1–14

The unusual scoring of Triana's motets suggests a performing situation distinct from those of the other songs and the other church music in Colombina, and it is tempting to attach it to one of the few biographical facts we have for Triana. Triana was, as we have seen, named master of the *seises* or choirboys at Toledo cathedral in 1483; he may have continued in this position till 1490, when Pedro de Lagarto (a composer also, incidentally, represented in the later layer of Colombina) took over.[19] This was an old and distinguished ensemble, numbering six boys in Triana's time; and while we know more about its musical activities in the sixteenth century than in the fifteenth,[20] it is probable that, like most choirboys on the Continent at that point, they generally performed separate from the adult cathedral choirs, with their own repertories in which they would divide the upper parts and their master(s) would take the lower.[21] It is easy to imagine Triana writing these little motets either for pedagogical purposes or for use in a church or chapel service with his own group of boys.

---

[19] Reynaud, *Polyphonie tolédane*, pp. 101–2.
[20] Ibid., pp. 141–62, especially pp. 155–7.
[21] For three well-known examples: David Fallows, 'Specific Information on the Ensembles for Composed Polyphony, 1400–1474', *Studies in the Performance of Late Mediaeval Music*, ed. Stanley Boorman (Cambridge, 1983), pp. 109–59, especially pp. 110–17 and 120–6; Reinhard Strohm, *Music in Late Medieval Bruges* (Oxford, 1985), pp. 13–15, 22–3, 38–40, 44–6, et passim; and Craig Wright, *Music and Ceremony at Notre Dame of Paris, 500–1500* (Cambridge, 1989), pp. 185–90.

A mass and a motet

The later layer of Colombina, copied probably between the mid-1480s and the mid-1490s (but definitely not finished till after 1492), was a collaborative effort. It has one clear main scribe, who may be the same as the early layer's scribe, now making more efficient use of time and paper; but three other hands can be identified here and there too. This layer mixes courtly songs, rustic songs, church music, and even a couple of French chansons with no discernable overall plan.[22] We have already seen the fragmentary Magnificat that was also found in Trent 88, but this section also contains a fair selection of Latin works that seem to have originated in Spain. We can begin with the most substantial: a group of mass ordinary movements and a motet.

On folios 67v–69 are three pieces of music. They are all in the same hand, and not the same hand as the openings before or after. The first (Q45, MTTB clefs) has no text; the second (Q46, MATB) is crowded at the bottom of the pages and has 'Agnus' at the beginning and 'dona nobis pacem' at the end; the third (Q47, also MATB), spread over the other opening, has just the incipits 'Sanctus', 'Pleni', and 'Benedictus'. So the last two are easy: the remaining texts of the Agnus Dei and Sanctus are easily underlaid, and their top lines prove to paraphrase the Agnus and Sanctus of Gregorian mass XVIII, for ferias, or weekdays, of Advent and Lent.[23] Clearly these two pieces belong together, their position being reversed presumably for considerations of space – which then focuses attention on their predecessor and the possibility that it appears with them by design.[24]

The answer is yes: all three movements concord with an anonymous KSA mass in Toledo 21, copied in 1549. There it is called a **Missa de feria**, and so I shall call it here (handlist 1). The same mass appears, sometimes with slight changes and/or movements replaced or omitted, in Escorial 4 and 5, New York 278, Montserrat 750, Toledo s.s., and Toledo 24, and the underlying chants (Kyrie included) can be found in a Toledan print of 1562.[25] These three modest little pieces, then, are a modest little mass, Glorialess for penitential seasons. It is the closest thing to a conventional mass ordinary in the entire handlist, and it continued to be sung for a remarkably long time: some of the Escorial sources were copied at least a hundred years after Colombina.[26] Indeed, this fifteenth-century mass seems to be the earliest in a tradition that spread long and wide within the Spanish dominions; the manuscript Guatemala City 4, for

[22] Kreitner, 'Dates (?)of the Cancionero de la Colombina'.

[23] *Liber Usualis*, pp. 62–3; the Sanctus has been transposed down a tone in Colombina.

[24] Querol, in *Cancionero Musical*, p. 28, suggests that Q45 might be a Kyrie, but he offers no proof and adds no title nor text in his edition. The Kyrie in mass XVIII of the *Liber Usualis* is unrelated to Q45.

[25] For spotting this concordance and sharing all other information in this paragraph so far, I am grateful to Graeme Skinner; see also Soterraña Aguirre Rincón, *Ginés de Boluda (ca. 1545–des. 1604): Biografía y obra musical* (Valladolid, 1995), pp. 62–4, 117–22; José Sierra Pérez, *Fr. Martín de Villanueva: obras completas* (Escorial, 1997), pp. 37, 304–10; and Michael Noone, *Music and Musicians in the Escorial Liturgy under the Hapsburgs, 1563–1700* (Rochester, 1998), pp. 208–19, 223–6. The chants are found in Juan Rincon, *Processionarij Toletani prima pars* (Toledo, 1562), folios 136v (Kyrie), 141 (Sanctus), and 147v (Agnus). On the date of Toledo 21, see *Census-Catalogue*, vol. III, pp. 208–9; this piece is found on folios 3v–5.

[26] See especially Noone, *Music and Musicians*.

example, copied in Guatemala shortly after 1600, contains three *Missæ de feria*, all KSA and all based on the same chant tunes.[27]

The Kyrie is in two sections, of which (the Toledo sources make clear) the first represents the first eight repetitions (probably in alternation with chant) of a ninefold scheme, and the second the ninth. It is a little more contrapuntally ambitious than the Sanctus and Agnus, whose texture is represented by Example 4.4. The Pleni begins, as the Benedictus and Agnus do as well, with a written-out intonation, long enough to register as a bit of alternatim, and when the other voices enter, it swells to simple, direct, text-efficient polyphony, unpretentious but not uninteresting (notice, for instance, the altus of the Hosanna).[28]

Ex. 4.4 Sanctus, bb. 19–36

At 131 bars, **Salve sancta parens** (handlist 61, Q 63) is the longest piece in the Cancionero de la Colombina. Its superius paraphrases the Gregorian introit for Marian feasts, and it keeps the introit's structure and text except that the Alleluia is omitted (it falls over a page break and may have been done monophonically) and the psalm text 'Eructavit cor meum' is replaced by 'Virgo Dei Genitrix', from the gradual to the same feasts.[29] This would seem, then, to have been meant not as a polyphonic mass proper, but as a more generic Marian motet sewn together from existing liturgical items (an instructive comparison, perhaps, is Dunstaple's famous *Veni sancte/*

[27] Robert J. Snow, ed., *A New-World Collection of Polyphony for Holy Week and the Salve Service: Guatemala City, Cathedral Archive, Music MS 4*, Monuments of Renaissance Music IX (Chicago, 1996), especially pp. 29–33, pp. 89–91, and numbers 1, 4, and 8 in his edition.

[28] My example (and several others to come) follows the modern editions in ignoring an occasional peculiarity of the manuscript: a number of stems added to breves making them look like longs.

[29] *Liber Usualis*, pp. 1262–5.

Veni creator, which combines the text to the sequence for Pentecost with the music to the hymn for the same day).

Like the *Missa de feria*, *Salve sancta parens* is to be performed quasi-alternatim. Not everything is copied into the manuscript, but it is easily reconstructed:

Monophonic	Polyphonic
Salve. . .	. . . sancta parens,
	enixa puerpera Regem,
	qui cælum terramque regit
	in sæcula sæculorum.
[Alleluia. (?)]	
Virgo Dei [Genitrix,	
quem totus non capit orbis,]	
	in tua se clausit viscera
	factus homo.
Gloria [Patri et Filio,	
et Spiritui Sancto,]	
	sicut erat in principio,
	et nunc et semper,
	et in sæcula sæculorum.
	Amen.

This is a full-fledged entry into the repertory of the fifteenth-century motet – not a masterpiece of contrapuntal complexity perhaps, but a very satisfying composition, with a nice sense of drama and pacing. Above all one is struck by the subtle variety of rhythm within a basically homophonic approach: as the opening (Example 4.5) shows, at any moment there is usually at least one lower voice matching the rhythm of the superius, but all four voices seldom move together, and the lightly staggered entrances and exits and even little moments of imitation lend motion and energy without blurring the declamation or becoming fussy.

I have grouped the mass and the motet together because they are (apart from the Magnificat) the weightiest sacred pieces in Colombina; but they have much else in common. They are both anonymous. In a manuscript largely of trios, they are both in four voices, falsettist-tenor-tenor-bass. They paraphrase Gregorian chant in the top voice, and they employ alternatim between chant and polyphony – and the alternation is always between monophonic and full four-voice texture, with no duos. They are written in a basically homophonic style, with occasional prominent fabordón-like passages of declamation on a single chord, but with a rhythmic flexibility in the inner voices that ultimately elevates them above the usual run of fabordón. And they show a considerable sensitivity to the rhythm and phrase structure of the text, with phrases tending to be declamatory at the beginning and melismatic at the end.

I would suggest, then, that if the three Triana pieces in the early layer of Colombina represent a kind of archetype for the music of the choirboys in a Spanish cathedral, then the *Missa de feria* and *Salve sancta parens* may provide at least a provisional archetype for the mainstream of church music as performed by the adult choir in late-fifteenth-century Spain.

In this connection, it may be worth bringing up the Song of the Sibyl, whose two settings in Colombina are both in Castilian and thus out of our strict purview here. But the Song of the Sibyl was, in many cathedrals, church music: it was customarily sung on Christmas eve in the vernacular as a liturgical drama, with one choirboy

Ex. 4.5 *Salve sancta parens*, bb. 1–6

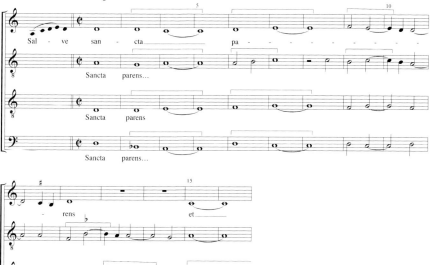

dressed in Sibylline garb and singing the apocryphal ancient prophecies in alternatim with the cathedral choir, who would repeat the first verse.[30] And in fact, the anonymous setting (Q 73, MTTB clefs, cantus firmus in the superius) fits the archetype very comfortably and was probably sung by the same people.[31]

Six smaller pieces

The half-dozen Latin pieces remaining in Colombina are all on a smaller scale – some, indeed, so small that one wonders why they were written down at all. Taken together, they refine but do not seriously challenge the image that we have from the Triana pieces and the larger compositions.

In exitu Israel (handlist 37, Q 68) is a fabordón or, in the more familiar Italian term, falsobordone – a polyphonic psalm formula, here given the opening of Psalm 113, but designed to be adaptable to a variety of line lengths. It thus has two very homophonic expandable passages, but ends each phrase with something a little more contrapuntal. Such a texture, and the piece's clefs (MATR) fit the archetype

---

30 There is a considerable literature on this custom, but for a recent summary see Maricarmen Gómez Muntané, *La música medieval en España* (Kassel, 2001), pp. 70–82. For primary sources see for example Richard B. Donovan, *The Liturgical Drama in Medieval Spain* (Toronto, 1958), pp. 39–50, 93–4, 120–5, 146–54, 160–7, et passim, and Higini Anglès, *La música a Catalunya fins al segle XIII* (Barcelona, 1935), pp. 288–302.

31 The other setting (Q 91) is by Triana; it is compatible with the archetype in its generally homophonic style, but its clefs are SMTB, and the cantus firmus is in the mezzo-clef line. Possibly, then, this is meant for a variant of the choirboy ensemble, with two adult men instead of just one.

established by the mass and *Salve sancta parens*, though the fabordón is of necessity even more homophonic and recitational than either.

   In exitu is the first of several fabordones we shall encounter in the fifteenth-century Spanish sources, and there is little to add to the extensive literature on this subject except to point out that in Murray Bradshaw's chronological inventory of falsobordoni worldwide, five of the first six manuscripts, with eleven of the first fifteen pieces, are from Spain, Portugal, or Aragonese Naples.[32] Whether this means the genre was invented or extensively developed on the Iberian peninsula, or if the Spanish were merely pioneers in writing it down and keeping it, is hard to know; for the present, it is enough merely to say that the fabordón was much cultivated in Spain in the late fifteenth century.

   Dic nobis Maria (handlist 28, Q 79) fits the archetype's voice distribution (SAAB, but with fairly restricted ranges) and generally homophonic texture (though the superius is a bit more florid than usual). The text is from the middle of *Victimæ paschali laudes,*the sequence for Easter,[33] and the tune of the chant is put into the tenor. This text and tune appear, however, as a separate bit of music in a great many late-medieval Easter plays from Spain and elsewhere, usually sung by a chorus representing angels or apostles,[34] and it is tempting to understand this little piece as an isolated choral moment from an otherwise unknown and otherwise largely monophonic liturgical drama for Easter.

   Qui fecit celum et terram (handlist 59, Q 77) isn't even a complete sentence: '. . . who made heaven and earth, amen.' Clearly it is intended as a response to something else, and indeed this text is found in a number of spots in the liturgy, perhaps most conspicuously as the last line of the Preces.[35] It is in only three voices, STR clefs, but otherwise, with its recitational beginning and more contrapuntal Amen, it fits the archetype reasonably well.

   O gloriosa Domina (handlist 55, Q 55) is a three-voice (STR) setting of a Marian hymn text and tune popular in fifteenth-century Spain though absent from the modern Gregorian liturgy.[36] The tune is paraphrased in the top voice, in triple meter reflecting the metrical chant of the original, and the lower voices exhibit the kind of lightly concealed homophony that has by now become familiar; what makes this piece unusual in Colombina, as Example 4.6 will show, is its stiff phrase-by-phrase structure, with every line of the hymn text separated by strong simultaneous rests in the music. It is reminiscent perhaps of an anonymous *Pange lingua* in the Neapolitan

---

[32] Murray C. Bradshaw, *The Falsobordone: A Study in Renaissance and Baroque Music,* Musicological Studies and Documents XXXIV (n.p., 1978), pp. 159–60. Bradshaw gave some manuscripts different dates from mine, and as a result he listed a few pieces that I do not; but this amounts to hairsplitting about what came before or after 1500, rather than a dispute about the role of Spain in the early history of polyphonic psalm formulæ.

[33] *Liber Usualis*, p. 780.

[34] For examples, see Donovan, *Liturgical Drama*, pp. 55 (Santiago de Compostela 1497), 85 (Vich 11th–12th c.), 86 (Vich 1413), 91 (Vich 14th c., in Catalan), 99–100 (Girona 1360), 101, 108 (Girona 13th–14th c.?), 109 (Girona 1360), 110 (Girona 15th c.), 131–2 (Palma 14th–15th c., in Catalan), and 141 (Gandía 1550); and Gómez, *Música medieval en España*, pp. 61–9.

[35] *Liber Usualis*, p. 232; see also p. 262[12], the short lesson for Sunday after Compline.

[36] It is in Barcelona 251, ff. 65v–66; for further information and concordances, see Màrius Bernadó i Tarragona, 'El repertori himnòdic del *Cantorale Sancti Ieronimi* (Barcelona: Biblioteca de Catalunya, M 251)' (Licenciado thesis, Universitat Autònoma de Barcelona, 1992), pp. 184–7.

manuscript Perugia 431;[37] but whether this a coincidence or a sign of foreign influence on Spanish music – or for that matter of Aragonese influence on the Neapolitan hymn – is hard to say at this distance. In any case, it is an attractive, vigorous little bagatelle.

Ex. 4.6 *O gloriosa domina*

Finally, Colombina has two short duos: **Laudate eum** (handlist 44, Q 29) sets Psalm 148, verse 2 in ST clefs, and **Omnipotentem semper adorant** (handlist 56, Q 39) sets a text from a procession hymn in SS clefs.[38] The manuscript gives no clue to what they are for, and neither has much precedent among Spanish sacred music of this time. They are among the least homophonic of the Latin pieces in Colombina, closer to bicinia elsewhere on the continent than to our Spanish archetypes; possibly they were extracted from longer pieces and recorded, as so many other duos were, as composition and/or singing exercises.[39]

---

[37] Edited in Allan W. Atlas, *Music at the Aragonese Court of Naples* (Cambridge, 1985), pp. 209–10; see also p. 137.

[38] Stäblein, *Hymnen (I)*, pp. 488–9, with different music.

[39] See for example Dietrich Kämper, 'Das Lehr- und Instrumentalduo um 1500 in Italien', *Die Musikforschung* xviii (1965), pp. 242–53, and Bruce Bellingham and Edward G. Evans, Jr., *Sixteenth-Century Bicinia: A Complete Edition of Munich, Bayerische Staatsbibliothek, Mus. Ms. 260*, Recent Researches in Renaissance Music XVI–XVII (Madison, 1974).

Paris 4379

Paris 4379 was assembled and bound by the Bibliothèque Nationale in 1885, from four separate clumps of musical pages – at least three of them, it now seems probable, pillaged from the Biblioteca de la Colombina in the years preceding.[40] Its fame today rests mostly on the first part, which can be fitted into the present gaps of the Colombina manuscript 5-1-43 to form one of the important French chansonniers of the late fifteenth century.[41]

For present purposes it is the fourth part, folios 69–92, that holds the most interest. Paris 4379/D, as we can call it, contains fourteen intact compositions and one fragment: it begins with nine French chansons (most with text incipits only), including works elsewhere attributed to Du Fay, Busnoys, and Basiron, and ends with an untexted single line. In the middle are five Latin sacred pieces: a *Domine non secundum* and a Gloria attributed to Madrid; an anonymous *Benedicamus Domino*; a *Nunc dimittis* attributed to Urrede; and a Magnificat which is anonymous here, but attributed to Urrede in Coimbra 12.

These would in themselves be a significant addition to the repertory of fifteenth-century Spanish church music; but in 1992 David Fallows raised the stakes further by pointing out that the page size, staff rulings, and hand(s) of 4379/D match those of the Cancionero de la Colombina.[42] Fallows's observations are the reason for grouping the two manuscripts together in one chapter here. Yet it seems unlikely that they were ever actually fastened together in real life: the pages of the Paris manuscript do not match up to gaps in the Seville source (in other words, we cannot posit the same sort of relationship as for 4379/A and 5-1-43), nor do they partake of either of the old foliations in the cancionero. And it might also be added that the contents of 4379/D (two-thirds French, one-third Latin) contrast sharply with those of the cancionero (four-fifths Castilian), and that not all of the former's scribal hands are easy to identify in the latter.[43] In short, the relationship between Paris 4379/D and the Cancionero de la Colombina is not a simple one: most likely the Paris folios are the work of the same atalier but a separate project. But clearly they come out of the same world and the same general time-span.

40 Paris, Bibliothèque Nationale, Département des Manuscrits, Nouvelles Acquisitions Françaises, MS 4379 (*Census-Catalogue* ParisBNN 4379). For its story and a bibliography, see *Census-Catalogue*, vol. III, pp. 29–31; the most significant addition to the bibliography since is David Fallows, 'I fogli parigini del *Cancionero Musical* e del manoscritto teorico della Biblioteca Colombina', *Rivista Italiana di Musicologia* xxvii (1992), pp. 25–40.

41 See especially Dragan Plamenac, 'A Reconstruction of the French Chansonnier in the Biblioteca Colombina, Seville', *The Musical Quarterly* xxxvii (1951), pp. 501–42; xxxviii (1952), pp. 85–117 and 245–77; Dragan Plamenac, ed., *Facsimile Reproduction of the Manuscripts Sevilla 5-1-43 & Paris N.A. Fr. 4379 (Pt. 1)*, Publications of Mediaeval Musical Manuscripts VIII (Brooklyn, 1962), and other items in the bibliography in the *Census-Catalogue* entry.

42 Fallows, 'Fogli parigini', especially pp. 26–9.

43 Using Fallows's inventory (ibid., 39–40) and my own identification of the hands in Colombina ('Dates (?) of the Cancionero'), I would (in many cases tentatively) assign numbers 2 and 3 to the early main hand; 5 and 14 to a transitional main hand; 1, 4, 6, 7, 8, 9, 13, and 15 to the late main; and 12 to the *O gloriosa* hand. Numbers 10 and 11 have the same scribe, but one whom I do not identify in Colombina.

On to the music. Juan de Urrede's international career and the wide distribution of his works earn him a separate treatment, and I shall reserve his two pieces for the next chapter. This leaves the works of Madrid and one anonymous composition.

The **Benedicamus Domino** setting (handlist 24, Fallows inventory[44] no. 12) is a modest little work, only 22 bars long, short enough to be included here in its entirety (Example 4.7). It is in three voices, SAT clefs, in a general style already familiar from the anonymi in the Cancionero de la Colombina: a chant paraphrase in the superius – the same tune, from Mass IV, that Triana used for his second *Benedicamus* (Example 4.2 above) – and a plain, mostly but not rigidly homophonic texture for the lower voices harmonizing. It is another specimen of what I consider to be the mainstream.

Ex. 4.7   *Benedicamus Domino*

---

44   Fallows, 'Fogli parigini', pp. 39–40.

Madrid

Two sacred pieces in 4379/D, one (or two) in the Chigi Codex, and four songs in the earliest layer of the Cancionero de Palacio[45] are attributed to a certain 'Madrid'. Traditionally the composer was thought to be Juan Fernández de Madrid, who sang in the Aragonese royal chapel from 1479 to at least 1482, but Tess Knighton has also made a strong claim for Juan Ruiz de Madrid, who joined the same chapel in 1493 and died in 1500 or 1501.[46] Nor are these necessarily all; Madrid in the fifteenth century was nothing near the metropolis it is today, but it was certainly no hamlet too small to produce musicians either.[47] We can return to his identity – or identities – after a look at the sacred music.

Domine non secundum peccata nostra (handlist 31, F 10), an unicum in Paris 4379/D, has sometimes been identified as two separate pieces, and indeed some peculiarities in the manuscript raise at least a momentary doubt.[48] Any question is dispelled, however, by the music: this is clearly a continuous setting of the tract for Ash Wednesday, omitting the verse 'Adjuva nos', which may have been done monophonically. Its superius is based on the Gregorian plainsong throughout, and the liturgical continuity of the text is confirmed by compatibility of clef and mode.[49] The

---

45 Higinio Anglés and Josep Romeu Figueras, eds., *La música en la corte de los Reyes Católicos: Cancionero Musical de Palacio (siglos XV–XVI)*, MME V, X, XIV (Barcelona, 1947–65), numbers 5, 13, 31, and 66. (Volumes of this edition will hereafter be named by their MME volume numbers.)
    The ascription of *Pues que Dios te fizo tal* (Palacio 5) has since been called into question by Rebecca L. Gerber in *Johannes Cornago: Complete Works*, Recent Researches in the Music of the Middle Ages and Renaissance XV (Madison, 1984), p. xiii, but the faint name on the recto page of the opening is clear on my film.

46 Stevenson, *Spanish Music*, pp. 177–9, *New Grove* 1980, s.v. 'Madrid, Juan Fernández de', by Isabel Pope, and *New Grove* 2001, s.v. 'Madrid, Juan Fernández de', by Tess Knighton, all favor Fernández. But Knighton, in 'Music and Musicians at the Court of Fernando of Aragón, 1474–1516' (Ph.D. diss., Cambridge University, 1983), vol. I, pp. 276–7, points out that Ruiz received a number of benifices, prebends, etc. from the crown and was evidently an important figure at court.

47 F. Rubio Piqueras, in *Música y músicos toledanos: contribución a su estudio* (Toledo, 1923), p. 52, mentions a certain Gonzalo Rodríguez de Madrid as chapelmaster at the Toledo cathedral in 1477. If Colombina and thereby 4379/D do prove to have strong Toledo connections, his name might be an intriguing one here; but his absence from Reynaud, *Polyphonie tolédane* does not attest to great or long importance in the musical community of the cathedral.

48 Anglés, in MME 10: 23, identified it as two pieces, *Domine non secundum* by Madrid and an anonymous *Domine ne memineris*; Stevenson, in *Spanish Music*, p. 177, continued to divide it in two, but suggested that Madrid may have been the composer of both. There are some odd inconsistencies of voice names (bottom voice called 'Contra' on the first opening, 'Contrat[en]or 2' on the second, 'Bassus' on the third), key signatures (flats on tenor and contra on the first, nowhere on the second, and contra and bassus on the third), and initials (ornamental initials, overlaid on existing voice designations, on the third opening, but neither of the other two, i.e. on neither of the openings where Anglés defined beginnings of pieces).

49 For the chant, see *Liber Usualis*, pp. 527–8. The superius is consistently in M clef, the altus in T, the tenor in R, and the bass in R for the first opening, B for the other two. And note especially bb. 23–4 of the edition, where Anglés would divide the composition: the three voices singing in his first piece come in for the second on exactly the same pitches, the newly singing altus entering two bars later.

Ex. 4.8 Madrid, *Domine non secundum*, bb. 81–108

first two lines of the tract are scored for a trio, superius-tenor-bassus; the third for all four voices; the fourth for superius and altus only; and the fifth for all four again.

Example 4.8 shows the ending of this piece. Its connection with the Spanish mainstream is evident in its use of the chant paraphrase in the top voice, in the occasional bursts of homophony, and, if the verse really was done monophonically, in the alternatim effect. But a closer look, or better yet a listen, puts us instantly into a very different world. This is partly the result of its dark, growly sound (its clefs are MTRB rather than the archetypal MATB), appropriate to the penitential text, and of the subtle contrast between the lighter triple meter of the duos and trios and the solid dignity of the four-voice sections. But perhaps most potent of all is its vigorous non-imitative counterpoint, very different from the homophony-plus-little-passing-ornaments that we saw in the lower lines of the *Benedicamus Domino* and the anonymi of Colombina. The top, chant-bearing line is still in the driver's seat – notice how, especially in the four-voice sections, its rhythm is carefully underlined by the bassus – but it is also a more or less equal partner in the whole contrapuntal scheme. It is the most sophisticated chant setting we have yet seen.

Madrid's **Gloria**, also an unicum in 4379/D (handlist 3, F 11), is in three voices, SMT clefs, the first two sections for all three voices and the third for superius and tenor. Unfortunately it survives both incomplete and corrupt: it sets only about half the Gloria text (up to '. . . Agnus Dei, Filius Patris'), it ends with an indecisive duo, and the last section can be reconstructed only partially. All of which is too bad, for in its completed state it must have been quite an impressive composition.

Robert Stevenson has edited the first section of this piece and singled the intact portions out for praise, observing that the opening quotes the introit for the feast of the Assumption, which may place this movement among the great Gaudeamus masses (or, I would add, at least making it a Marian mass, which would be almost as interesting), and he takes special pleasure in Madrid's harmonic innovations – the smooth modulation from D dorian to A-flat major in the first part, the profusion of first-inversion chords, and so forth.[50] Another bold stroke is Madrid's vertical juxtaposition, in the middle of the final duo, of ₵ mensuration in the tenor and ₵3 in the superius to indicate a contrast between what we would call 6/8 and 3/4 organization of the bar. This, alas, is the part that doesn't work; but presumably it worked once, and it is unique among this early Spanish repertory.

This ends Madrid's contributions to 4379/D. But at the very back of the Chigi codex are settings of the *Asperges me* and the *Vidi aquam,* both of them added in Spain by the manuscript's second scribe, in the mid- to late 1510s.[51] The first is attributed, faintly but legibly, to Madrid (on the page but not in the index); the second is unascribed but belongs so firmly with it that they must be considered together. This is as good a place as any.

The **Asperges me** (handlist 17) is in four voices, in the high clefs GAAT. It uses the text, and a variant of the standard Gregorian tune, from the antiphon and psalm for the blessing of the altar before mass.[52] Yet it is different from the chant settings we have seen so far, and from the previous works of Madrid: the monophonic intonations that open the antiphon, psalm, and doxology are all in the tenor, and the chant paraphrase is carried not as a cantus firmus in the top voice as we have seen so far, but in a complex fabric of imitative counterpoint. Right away, then, it seems to have a much more modern sound, as its opening passage (Example 4.9) shows.

The **Vidi aquam** (handlist 65) is a clear companion to its predecessor in the manuscript. The two belong together liturgically (the Vidi substitutes for the Asperges

---

[50] Stevenson, *Spanish Music,* pp. 177–9. For the Gaudeamus chant, *Liber Usualis,* pp. 1601–2.

[51] Vatican City, Biblioteca Apostolica Vaticana, MS Chigi C VIII 234 (*Census-Catalogue* VatC 234). For data, see in particular Herbert Kellman, 'The Origins of the Chigi Codex: The Date, Provenance, and Original Ownership of Rome, Biblioteca Vaticana, Chigiana, C.VIII.234', *Journal of the American Musicological Society* xi (1958), pp. 6–19, especially 8–9; and Herbert Kellman, ed., *Vatican City, Biblioteca Apostolica Vaticana, MS Chigi C VIII 234,* Renaissance Music in Facsimile XXII (New York,1987), especially p. ix.

[52] *Liber Usualis,* p. 11; the *Liber* begins the piece GA CBA BC D, where Chigi has GA CDB CDC D for the intonation.

Ex. 4.9 Madrid, *Asperges me*, bb. 1–17

during Paschal time), and it too uses the Gregorian tune[53] first for a monophonic intonation and then in a similar style of imitative counterpoint. Their placement together in Chigi is thus no accident, though *Vidi aquam* is missing its psalm and, with its SATT clefs, has a lower range. (Possibly the ranges were adjusted in performance and appear as they do in order to preserve the written pitch level of the chant.) I find little difficulty in accepting Herbert Kellman's suggestion that the attribution was meant for the pair,[54] or in thinking of this as another work of Madrid. At any rate, *Vidi aquam* is also a fine piece of music, with the same kind of vigorous counterpoint and

---

53 *Liber Usualis*, p. 12; in this case the intonation quotes the Gregorian tune exactly.
54 Kellman, *Vatican City*, p. ix; this corrects his earlier suggestion, in 'The Origins', p. 8, that the inscription might refer to the place of copying; Kellman in 1958 presumably did not know of Madrid the composer. Stevenson, incidentally, follows a flyleaf note in the manuscript to assert that the additions were made c.1490 (see *Spanish Music*, p. 179); but this date is decisively contradicted by Kellman.

variety of texture. If it is not by the same person who wrote *Asperges me*, it's a sound imitation of a very sound model. All of which raises once again the question: who is this Madrid?

I am satisfied that he is one person – that these four sacred pieces and the four songs are the work of the same composer, and a composer of considerable skill. Madrid's contrapuntal craftsmanship shows access to some rather sophisticated polyphony, and his use of the proportion in the Gloria (a notational nicety not really essential to get those notes) bespeaks a relatively advanced musical training. Yet there can be no doubt, unless his name is a cruel joke, that Madrid was authentically Spanish: he was no Urrede, come down from Bruges with a northern musical education already in place.

But such a profile, however useful, is not enough to choose among the Madrids thus far nominated. Juan Fernández de Madrid, documented at the Aragonese royal chapel from 1479 to 1482, would seem too early to be writing such modern polyphony; but then, his time there coincides with Urrede's,[55] and his music is perhaps about what we might expect from an eager and talented contemporary. Juan Ruiz de Madrid, who entered the chapel in 1493 and died in 1500 or 1501, was probably of a later generation (potentially the same age as Anchieta or even Peñalosa), and presumably this style would be well within his experience. If Ruiz was the composer, Paris 4379/D probably came from nearly the middle of his known career, and the two pieces in Chigi were copied long after his death, possibly preserved because of their unusual liturgical function and the rarity of polyphonic settings of these texts.

The Story So Far

Between them, the Cancionero de la Colombina and the related fourth portion of Paris 4379 provide some seventeen pieces of Latin church music. One, the anonymous Magnificat fragment, is probably foreign and certainly early, perhaps from the 1450s. Three by Triana and two by Urrede are likely to date from the late 1470s or early 1480s; the others are more difficult to place – Colombina was finished in the early to mid-1490s, and 4379/D cannot be much earlier or later – but on the whole it seems reasonably safe to imagine them all composed in the 1480s. We have also just seen two pieces from the Chigi codex, which round out the picture of the composer Madrid but should be kept carefully separate from the chronological scheme: they were copied many years later and cannot be dated with security.

It would once again be good to draw my conclusions from a bigger repertory. Yet there is also a coherence here that lends at least a fleeting comfort; and given that these are the best representatives that are likely to become available, they may be enough for five quick generalizations about Spanish church polyphony in their time.

First of all, they show that there was a thriving tradition of notated church polyphony in Spain at that point. This should be no surprise, but in the context of the previous chapter, which seemed to show more evidence for improvised polyphony than conventional written-out sources, it is certainly gratifying. It is, again, just hard

---

55 Stevenson, in *Spanish Music*, pp. 203–4, and Knighton, in 'Music and Musicians', vol. I, p. 301, place Urrede in the Aragonese chapel from 1477 to 1482.

to know much about the situation between the Llibre Vermell and Colombina; but by the 1470s at the latest, the practice of writing down your polyphony and singing it was clearly common in Spain as elsewhere in Europe.

Second, the church music of Colombina and 4379/D is dominated utterly by liturgical forms. Every word in this repertory can be found in the standard sources for the mass and office, and all major liturgical genres – mass ordinary, mass propers, psalms, canticles, hymns – are represented. There are no commemorative motets, no newly written texts, no Marian flights of fancy: the closest this music comes to the kind of synthetic motet text seen so often in the northern mainstream is in *Salve sancta parens*, which merely combines two liturgical items that don't normally belong together.

Third, the repertory also relies heavily on the chant tunes that go along with the liturgical texts. Normally the tunes are paraphrased and put into the superius of the polyphonic setting, where they would be clearly heard and recognized; these pieces are thus closer, in sound and function, to (if I may be forgiven a generous comparison) Du Fay's hymn cycle than to his *Missa Ecce ancilla Domini*.

Fourth, it seems to be possible to distinguish two general cleffing patterns: most of this music uses some variant of highish-medium-medium-low (say, MATB clefs), but a few pieces have two high voices contrasted with something lower (say, SST). These parallel the two types of choir in use in most European cathedrals in the fifteenth century – adult intact falsettists, tenors, and basses vs. choirboys with their master(s) – and they suggest that both kinds of ensemble are represented in the surviving polyphonic music. Little of this music would have to be moved from modern pitch levels to be comfortable for these typical choirs.

Finally, and perhaps most important: for all their striking unity of purpose, the compositions in these manuscripts fall into two broad and obvious stylistic categories. The anonymi are in general relatively homophonic and relatively simple – not simplistic necessarily, but with an open and direct aesthetic, concerned with clear text declamation and harmonic support to the paraphrased chant. The kind of active, vigorous counterpoint that attracts our attention more reliably is confined to the northern Magnificat and to the works ascribed to Triana, Madrid, and (as we shall see next) Urrede. This parallel between ambition and attribution is, I submit, no coincidence: I believe we may be seeing here an early phase in the rise of self-consciousness among composers of church music – a self-consciousness that had a long tradition in the north, but that in Spain may have been rare before the end of the fifteenth century. Works like the ferial mass in Colombina are everyone's property and no one's, like the chant they set; but something like the Madrid Gloria is a personal contribution in a very different sense.

With this in mind we can turn to the works of two very eminent composers: Johannes Cornago and Juan de Urrede.

5

Cornago and Urrede

To back up and broaden out for just a moment: anyone unreeling a microfilm of the first layer of the Cancionero de la Colombina after spending a few days among the French chansonniers of the same period would surely be struck by a disconcerting lack of human personalities. Of the thirty-one pieces I count in this layer, sixteen are anonymous; eight (actually seven and a half) are attributed to Juan de Triana, a composer of some gifts but with an evidently feeble claim to the attention of history in his time and ours; and the rest are distributed among a group of composers with one or two (in one case two and a half) ascriptions each.[1]

Yet Spain in this period – say, the 1460s through the early 1480s – had at least two musical celebrities, composers who achieved a considerable fame within the peninsula and were even fairly well known without. They were Johannes Cornago (fl. 1420–75) and Juan de Urrede (fl. 1451–82). Cornago and Urrede are major characters in our story here, but their actual positions in that story remain ambiguous. Both composers wrote some church music, but were and are better known for their courtly songs. And both have, as it were, immigration problems: Cornago seems to have been authentically Spanish, but all his church music was evidently written during a period in Naples and none of it is preserved in any Iberian source, and Urrede, though he spent almost his entire career in Spain and wrote all his songs in Spanish, was a native of Flanders who came to Spain as a young man and stayed. So for all their probable influence on Spanish musicians of the next few generations, neither of them is quite a fair representative of his own.

Cornago

In 1420, 1421, and 1429, a certain 'Iohannes Eximii de Cornago', of the diocese of Calahorra, petitioned Pope Martin V for various benefices. If this was Johannes (or Juan) Cornago the composer, then he would be about Du Fay's age, which is not altogether implausible, but at the moment it is hard to be sure: Cornago has not turned up among the known singers of the house of Aragón around this time,[2] but he

---

[1] For details on the structure of Colombina, see above, pp. 42–3. My half-ascriptions refer to number 22, *Señora qual soy venido*, which is attributed to both Cornago and Triana in the manuscript and may represent Triana's addition of a contratenor to a pre-existing Cornago song.

[2] See M.ª del Carmen Gómez Muntané, *La música en la casa real catalano-aragonesa durante los años 1336–1432* (Barcelona, 1977), vol. I, pp. 104–8 et passim, and Alejandro Planchart, 'Music in

may well have been working for a Spanish cathedral or parish church and thus have slipped under our radar.

In 1449 Cornago received a bachelor's degree in sacred scripture from the University of Paris, and by 1453 he was at the royal court of Alfonso the Magnanimous, the Aragonese king then living in Naples. Cornago was exceptionally well paid, suggesting that he was already established in his profession. Unlike some of the Spanish chapel musicians in Naples, he stayed there after Alfonso died in 1458; in 1466 he was still serving Alfonso's Neapolitan heir Ferrante I, and in 1475 he was back in Spain, paid just once by Ferdinand (who was at that time king regent of Castile and primogenitor of Aragón). This is the last we hear of Cornago, and it is probable though not certain that he died shortly thereafter – in his mid-seventies if the early references are right.[3]

A number of efforts have been made to lay Cornago's eleven surviving songs (two in Italian and nine in Castilian) onto this biographical framework;[4] but there can be little doubt that both of his known sacred compositions, a mass and a Lamentation, are from his Neapolitan period and thus of some interest, but only limited use, to us here (though we should not forget that more of this Neapolitan-Aragonese music may have come back to mainland Spain than we can now see).

The **Missa Ayo visto lo mappamundi** is Cornago's longest work; it is, in fact, the only complete mass ordinary by any Spanish composer before the late 1490s at least. It is preserved in Trent 88, a manuscript mostly of sacred music copied in Trent around 1460, and its Kyrie and Gloria are also contained, anonymously, in the Strahov codex, an eastern-European source from the sixties or seventies.[5] The mass is in three voices, the top in mezzo-soprano clef and the others mixing tenor and baritone; all five

the Christian Courts of Spain', in *Musical Repercussions of 1492*, ed. Carol E. Robertson (Washington, 1992), pp. 149–66.

3 Biography assembled from Robert Stevenson, *Spanish Music in the Age of Columbus* (The Hague, 1960), p. 121; Isabel Pope and Masakata Kanazawa, eds., *The Music Manuscript Montecassino 871: A Neapolitan Repertory of Sacred and Secular Music of the Late Fifteenth Century* (Oxford, 1978), pp. 69–71; *New Grove 1980*, s.v. 'Cornago, Johannes', by Isabel Pope; Tessa Wendy Knighton, 'Music and Musicians at the Court of Fernando of Aragon, 1474–1515' (Ph.D. diss., Cambridge University, 1983), vol. I, p. 261 and vol. II, p. 6 (later translated as Tess Knighton, *Música y músicos en la Corte de Fernando el Católico 1474–1516*, trans. Luis Gago [Zaragoza, 2001], pp. 168 and 327); Rebecca Gerber, ed., *Johannes Cornago: Complete Works*, Recent Researches in the Music of the Middle Ages and Early Renaissance XV (Madison, 1984), pp. vii–viii; Allan W. Atlas, *Music at the Aragonese Court of Naples* (Cambridge, 1985), pp. 62–9; Robert Stevenson, 'Spanish Musical Impact beyond the Pyrenees (1250–1500)', in *España en la música de occidente*, ed. Emilio Casares Rodicio, Ismael Fernández de la Cuesta, and José López-Calo (Madrid, 1987), vol. I, pp. 115–64, especially pp. 139–46; Planchart, 'Music in the Christian Courts', pp. 156–9; *MGG-P*, s.v. 'Cornago, Joan', by Allan Atlas; and *New Grove 2001*, s.v. 'Cornago, Johannes', by Rebecca Gerber.

4 Stevenson, *Spanish Music*, pp. 216–25; Pope and Kanazawa, *Manuscript Montecassino 871*, pp. 84–8; David Fallows, 'A Glimpse of the Lost Years: Spanish Polyphonic Song, 1450–70', in Josephine Wright and Samuel A. Floyd, Jr., eds., *New Perspectives in Music: Essays in Honor of Eileen Southern*, Detroit Monographs in Musicology/ Studies in Music XI (Warren, Michigan, 1992), pp. 19–36, especially pp. 24–5.

5 For a summaries of the literature on these sources see *Census-Catalogue*, vol. III, pp. 224–5 and 60–1; the entry on Trent 88 is updated by Rebecca Lynn Gerber, 'The Manuscript Trent, Castello del Buonconsiglio, 88: A Study of Fifteenth-Century Manuscript Transmission and Repertory' (Ph.D. diss., University of California, Santa Barbara, 1984), and Planchart, 'Music in the Christian Courts', pp. 163–4 n. 5.

movements begin in triple meter but have sections in duple; there are three duo sections, about where we expect them (Pleni, Benedictus, Agnus II).[6]

It is based on a song in Italian, evidently of Sicilian origin (its theme: I have seen the map of the world, and Sicily is the best place of all),[7] which becomes a cantus firmus, sometimes with its Italian words written into the manuscript, in the tenor voice (on the bottom line in the example). In the longer movements its note values are stretched out (though not rigidly, nor are there any quasi-isorhythmic manipulations); in the shorter ones – as in Example 5.1, the opening of the Agnus – it is more loosely paraphrased and goes only a little slower than the other voices. All five movements begin with a head-motive in the superius and contratenor, the tenor entering a few bars later. All the movements are written in free counterpoint, fueled by neither homophony nor imitation. The lowish pitch and densely packed ranges of the mass give it a curious energy and power, particularly in the triple-meter sections, as here.

Ex. 5.1 Cornago, *Missa Ayo visto*, Agnus Dei, bb. 1–3

Alejandro Planchart has speculated that this was among the many masses presented to Pope Calixtus III (a Catalan and a friend and ally of Alfonso) on his election in 1455, and thus probably datable to the early 1450s;[8] but at the very least, if only from its cantus firmus, it must have originated during Cornago's Neapolitan period. From its distribution it seems likely that the piece was never brought back to Spain. Its style has been compared to that of the English masses of the early and middle part of the century,[9] but perhaps more to the point for the present purpose, there is just

6   The best modern edition is Gerber's in *Cornago: Complete Works*, pp. 1–35; see also her commentary, pp. viii–x.

7   See ibid., and Allan W. Atlas, 'Aggio visto lo mappamundo: A New Reconstruction', in *Studies in Musical Sources and Style: Essays in Honor of Jan LaRue*, ed. Eugene K. Wolf and Edward H. Roesner (Madison, 1990), pp. 109–20.

8   Planchart, 'Music in the Christian Courts', pp. 157–8.

9   Gerber, *Cornago: Complete Works*, p. x; idem, 'Manuscript Trent', p. 115–16; Planchart, 'Music in the Christian Courts', p. 159.

nothing the least bit like it, either structurally or stylistically, among the sacred music preserved in Spain. So, as attractive as it may be to claim Cornago's mass as part of the Spanish tradition, and as legitimate as his Iberian roots appear to be, it is probably more helpful to see this piece as a vivid counterexample – a lesson in what a Spanish composer could accomplish when presented with a cosmopolitan audience at a more 'international' court, but may never have had cause to do back home.

Patres nostri peccaverunt, Cornago's only other Latin piece and his only composition in four voices, is an unicum in the Neapolitan source Montecassino 871.[10] It sets Lamentations 5:7 but is very distinct in style from the other two Lamentations in the manuscript (sole survivors, both anonymous, of a large clump of such pieces), which have a clear chant cantus firmus in the top voice and lower voices that harmonize it quite rigidly during the wordy portions and more contrapuntally over the Hebrew letters.[11] Isabel Pope and Masakata Kanazawa, editors of Montecassino, have suggested that these anonymous Lamentations represent the central liturgical tradition and Cornago's is part of a custom of Passiontide celebrations held outside the church in Aragonese Naples.[12] The opening phrase (Example 5.2) will give a fair notion of Cornago's short piece: more homophonic than the mass, to be sure, with at least two voices singing the same rhythm most of the time, but nothing like the fabordón-like homophony of the other Lamentations in Montecassino. It would not be out of place among the motets of the Cancionero de la Colombina.

Ex. 5.2 Cornago, *Patres nostri*, bb. 1–9

[10] It is edited in ibid., pp. 36–7, and Pope and Kanazawa, *Musical Manuscript Montecassino 871*, pp. 108–10.

[11] They are edited in ibid., pp. 343–64 and 365–75; see also the commentary, p. 35.

[12] Ibid., pp. 44–6.

Neapolitan Manuscripts and Spanish Music: An Excursus

Patres nostri brings us uncomfortably close to one of the edges of my topic. For if this Lamentation was written by a Spaniard, in a basic style more or less established in Spain, for a mixed audience of Spaniards and Italians attending a local ceremony in Italy, is it really possible or useful to distinguish Spanish church music from its neighbors at all?

The story of the Aragonese monarchy in Naples is a complicated one, and well told elsewhere.[13] In 1442 Alfonso the Magnanimous, king of Aragón since 1416, added the Kingdom of Naples to his realm after many years of diplomatic negotiations and military threats. He moved his court from Barcelona to Naples almost immediately, built up an extraordinary international humanistic intellectual circle there, and stayed for the rest of his life. When Alfonso died in 1458, the new empire was disassembled: the Italian portions went to his illegitimate son Ferrante (not to be confused with his nephew Ferdinand, later Ferdinand the Catholic) and the Iberian part, the old Kingdom of Aragón, to his younger brother Juan II (father of Ferdinand, uncle of Ferrante), so that things were more or less back where they had been.

In short, for most of the 1440s and 1450s, the musical center of the Aragonese orbit was not even on the Iberian peninsula: it was in Naples, with a distinguished polyglot chapel of singers from Spain, Italy, and the north. Though no musical sources are known to date from the court of Alfonso,[14] it is clear that a good many Spanish musicians remained in Naples (like Cornago) after the king's death, and that there was a strong Spanish presence there throughout the reign of Ferrante.[15] And this raises the question: among all the sources traced to Ferrante's vicinity,[16] is it possible that Spanish composers are responsible for a fair amount of the sacred music?

Biographies parallel to Cornago's, though on a smaller scale perhaps, can be proposed for two figures, Pere Oriola and Bernardus Ycart; this would give Oriola's one and Ycart's six pieces of church music stories more or less like that of *Patres nostri*.[17] And Neapolitan manuscripts of the 1460s through the 1480s are full of pieces with no, fragmentary, or ambiguous attributions: in only the two largest, Montecassino 871 and Perugia 431, I count almost sixty Latin compositions that could conceivably belong to Spaniards and thereby on our list.[18]

But clearly this is an unreliable way to proceed. There are two pieces in

---

13 For two recent discussions in the musicological literature, see Atlas, *Music at the Aragonese Court*, pp. 1–22 et passim, and Maricarmen Gómez Muntané, *La música medieval en España* (Kassel, 2001), pp. 296–304.

14 Atlas, *Music at the Aragonese Court*, p. 118 n. 11.

15 On these chapels, see ibid., pp. 23–97 et passim.

16 Ibid., pp. 114–25.

17 For biographical and bibliographical data on Oriola and Ycart, see ibid., pp. 60–72 and pp. 77–80 respectively, and Stevenson, 'Spanish Musical Impact', pp. 146–8 and pp. 148–51.

18 From the inventory in Pope and Kanazawa, *Musical Manuscript Montecassino 871*, pp. xi–xv, this would include numbers 4, 8, 30–36, 38, 42–45, 48–50, 52–61, 63–64, 66–68, 71, 76–80, 92–93, 106, 116, 120–21, 124, 137–38. On Perugia 431, see especially Allan W. Atlas, 'On the Neapolitan Provenance of the Manuscript Perugia, Biblioteca Comunale Augusta, 431 (G 20)', *Musica Disciplina* xxxi (1977), pp. 45–105; from Atlas's inventory (pp. 78–105), I count as potentially Spanish numbers 1 (concordant to Montecassino 871 number 78), 2–8, and 10–14. Several pieces in both manuscripts are fragmentary or otherwise problematic.

Montecassino 871 that do pique my interest: Oriola's *In exitu Israel* is a falsobordone, which may tie it in with the fabordones in Colombina and elsewhere, and there is an anonymous *Pange lingua* that appears to use a tune imported from Spain; we shall return to it shortly.[19] Otherwise, however, church music produced in – or preserved only in – Naples has got to be a very risky bet for our purposes. It is probably safest on the whole to think of the Neapolitan repertory as fundamentally separate, nourished perhaps by the Spanish tradition but not necessarily giving anything back to it, and not fairly representing it, even in music written by composers of Spanish birth.

Urrede

Juan de Urrede was born in Bruges with a name like Johannes de Wreede; he was the son of Rolandus de Wreede, who was organist at St. Donatian in Bruges from 1447 till his death in 1485. In 1451, Johannes was refused a clerkship at St. Donatian for reasons of nepotism; this means he was an adult by that time, and if (as seems logical) it was his first such application, that would have him born in the early 1430s. He became a clerk at another Bruges church in 1457 and remained there until 1460. It is not clear exactly when or why he went to Spain: he is next seen working for the Duke of Alba from 1475 to 1477, but there is one Alba document describing him as a former 'singer of the king, our lord', which must mean Ferdinand even though Ferdinand was at that point still king regent of Castile, not yet king of Aragón. Later in 1477 he became chapelmaster at Ferdinand's court; in 1479 he tried and failed to secure a position on the music faculty of the University of Salamanca; and he remained at Ferdinand's court till 1482. He may have died shortly thereafter, though there is a puzzling and inconclusive piece of testimony to the contrary. A handwritten chart of intervals, with Spanish words, under the name 'Joannes vrred.', is bound with a copy of Franchinus Gaffurius's *Practica Musica*, published in 1497, and some other undated manuscript items in the library of the University of Salamanca;[20] and while we cannot currently prove that this list was written by Urrede himself or that it is contemporaneous with the print, it is well to remember that we have no real evidence of the composer's death. If he did die in the early 1480s, he died relatively young, predeceasing his father.[21]

As best it can be reconstructed, and with a minimum of speculation, it sounds like a variant of the classic *oltremontano* story: the boy born to a musical family in the north, raised in a city with ample musical influences and opportunities, coming into a modest local position in his twenties, accomplishing something (a Kyrie-Gloria pair

---

[19] Edited in Pope and Kanazawa, *Musical Manuscript Montecassino 871*, pp. 123–4 and pp. 244–5.

[20] Biblioteca Universitaria de Salamanca, shelfmark incunab. 155; I am grateful to Tess Knighton for drawing my attention to this book and Juan Carlos Asensio for helping me see it.

[21] Biographical details assembled from Stevenson, *Spanish Music*, pp. 203–4; *New Grove 1980*, s.v. 'Urreda, Johannes', by Isabel Pope; Knighton, 'Music and Musicians', vol. I, p. 301 (*Música y músicos*, p. 346); Reinhard Strohm, *Music in Late Medieval Bruges* (Oxford, 1985), pp. 43, 142, 189–90 (for Juan) and pp. 25–6, 30–2, 184–5, 190 (for Rolandus); Dámaso García Fraile, 'La cátedra de música de la Universidad de Salamanca durante diecisiete años del siglo XV (1464–1481)', *Anuario Musical* xlvi (1991), pp. 57–101, especially pp. 78–9 and 100–1 (doc. 1287); Roberta Freund Schwartz, '*En busca de liberalidad*: Music and Musicians in the Courts of the Spanish Nobility, 1470–1640' (Ph.D. diss., University of Illinois, 2001), pp. 36–40; and *New Grove* 2001, s.v. 'Urrede, Juan de', by Tess Knighton.

under his name in Cappella Sistina 14 must date from the Bruges years[22]), taking a job in the south around thirty, and working his way up to possibly the highest musical post in the land. Whether Urrede was thoroughly naturalized like Isaac and planned to stay in Spain forever, or whether, like Obrecht, he died before he could go back north, is hard to say: he was in his fifties or thereabouts when he disappeared, about the age when Du Fay finally went back to Cambrai and Josquin to Condé. In any case it is clear that, apart from the one early mass pair, all his music belongs firmly in the Spanish years. His three songs are all in Castilian, and all the other sacred music is preserved in Iberian sources only. For us, Urrede belongs to Spain – hence my use of the hispanized version of his Flemish name.

Urrede's international fame was the product of one very successful song. *Nunca fue pena mayor* was copied into all three of the major manuscripts of Spanish songs, Colombina, Segovia, and Palacio (which it opens). It appears, with slight variants and the occasional added voice, in some twelve manuscript sources outside Spain, and Ottaviano Petrucci published it three times: with a *si placet* altus in the *Odhecaton* of 1501, in an anonymous arrangement in *Canti C* of 1504, and in a lute intabulation by Francesco Spinacino in 1507. Its superius was used as a tenor in a song by Belmonte in Colombina, its opening was parodied by Tromboncino, and it was the subject of masses by Peñalosa and La Rue.[23] Oddly, *Nunca fue* is one of only three songs he has left; the other two, also with Castilian text, are in both Colombina and Palacio, and one is also in Bologna Q16.[24]

His church music requires more disentangling. Five Latin sacred works are preserved under Urrede's name: the aforementioned Kyrie-Gloria pair, which we can set aside as written before he came to Spain; a Magnificat appearing in several different guises; two distinct – sort of – settings of the hymn *Pange lingua*; and just one unproblematic piece, the *Nunc dimittis*.

Nunc dimittis (handlist 51) is an unicum in the Spanish section of Paris 4379, in three voices, STT clefs; it sets the well-known Canticle of Simeon, used Sundays at Compline (among other times) in the modern liturgy; the canticle has a number of similar formulae,[25] all of which divide the text into four verses plus two verses of doxology, each subdivided into half-verses. Urrede follows this structure: he omits the intonation 'Nunc dimittis servum tuum Domine', probably reserved for the cantor,

[22] Strohm, *Music in Late Medieval Bruges*, p. 142. See also the edition in Nors F. Josephson, ed., *Early Sixteenth-Century Sacred Music from the Papal Chapel*, Corpus Mensurabilis Musicæ XCV (n.p., 1982), vol. II, pp. 139–46, which for some reason is incomplete; and the references in Adalbert Roth, *Studien zum frühen repertoire der päpstlichen Kapelle unter dem Pontifikat Sixtus' IV. (1471–1484): Die Chorbücher 14 und 51 des Fondo Cappella Sistina der Biblioteca Apostolica Vaticana* (Vatican City, 1991), frontispiece, pp. 294–5, pp. 472–3.

[23] For details of these versions, plus modern publications, see David Fallows, *A Catalogue of Polyphonic Song, 1450–1480* (Oxford, 1999), pp. 624–5, and Kenneth Kreitner, 'The Musical Warhorses of Juan de Urrede', paper read at the conference Legacies: 500 Years of Printed Music (Denton, October 2001). The most accessible editions of the song are in Miguel Querol Gavaldá, ed., *Cancionero musical de la Colombina (siglo XV)*, MME XXXIII (Barcelona, 1971), no. 9; Higinio Anglés ed., *La música en la corte de los Reyes Católicos: Cancionero Musical de Palacio (siglos XV–XVI)*, MME V (Barcelona, 1947), no. 1; and Helen Hewitt, with Isabel Pope, eds., *Petrucci: Harmonice Musices Odhecaton A* (Cambridge, 1942), pp. 226–7.

[24] See Fallows, *Catalogue*, pp. 613 and 620–1.

[25] *Liber Usualis*, pp. 271, 764, 784, and 1735.

and puts verse 1b, 'secundum verbum tuum in pace', in polyphony; verse 2a, 'Quia viderunt oculi mei', is written monophonically, in black mensural notation, in the superius voice; 2b, 'salutare tuum', is polyphonic again; verses 3, 4, and 5 follow the same pattern; and the last verse is given entirely in polyphony, for an alternatim pattern with a big ending. Example 5.3 shows the first and last verses, with the initial intonation restored from the *Liber Usualis*.

Urrede's six polyphonic sections show subtly contrasting contrapuntal approaches. The first has a fast superius with slower lower voices, the second begins in imitation in all three parts, the third reverses the first with a slow monotonic superius and more active lower voices, the fourth is generally full and homophonic, the fifth

Ex. 5.3 Urrede, *Nunc dimittis*, bb. 1–19, 76–97

Ex. 5.3 (cont.) Urrede, *Nunc dimittis*, bb. 1–19, 76–97

begins with two-voice imitation, and the last has alternating voice pairs and full-texture imitation. Yet they are unified too: all are firmly in G, and all pay audible homage in the superius to the C reciting tone of the chant. It is not Urrede's master-piece by any means – in fact it may be his only work to survive in just one Iberian source and may represent an early piece later abandoned. Yet it is appropriate to the restrained joy of its text, and the composer does get a surprising degree of variety from the three-voice texture.

The Magnificat

Directly after *Nunc dimittis* in Paris 4379 is a setting of the even verses of the **Magnificat** (handlist 47). It is anonymous there, as are verses 4 and 8 where they appear in Lisbon 60. In Coimbra 12, however, the piece is attributed to 'Joannes Utreda', and verses 4 and 8 appear in keyboard tablature under the name 'Urrede' in in Gonzalo de Baena's *Arte nouamente inuentada pera aprender a tanger*, a keyboard-tablature source published at Lisbon in 1540.[26] These latter sources are admittedly not only Portuguese but late (Lisbon 60 has been dated sometime after 1521 and Coimbra 12 to the 1540s[27]), but the earlier Paris version is corrupt: the fourth verse has an added altus part which doesn't work, and the twelfth has an added superius which works, more or less, but is clearly superfluous.[28] The version in Coimbra 12 has its own curious

---

[26] Tess Knighton, 'A Newly Discovered Keyboard Source (Gonzalo de Baena's *Arte nouamente inuentada pera aprender a tanger*, Lisbon, 1540): A Preliminary Report', *Plainsong and Medieval Music* v (1996), pp. 81–112; in her inventory, pp. 92–4, the two Magnificat movements are numbers 15 and 16.

[27] Owen Rees, *Polyphony in Portugal, c. 1530–c. 1620: Sources from the Monastery of Santa Cruz, Coimbra* (New York, 1995), pp. 431–6 (for Lisbon 60) and pp. 185–94 (for Coimbra 12).

[28] Ibid., p. 417. Verse 12 is a tenor-bass duo with several cadential structures where the tenor takes the role of a superius.

appendage – an extra last verse, also attributed to 'Joannes Utreda' but with the smaller annotations 'nõ est vere' and 'Penhalosa', which proves indeed to be extracted from a Peñalosa Magnificat in Tarazona 2/3.[29] The Coimbra reading has fewer problems overall, but Example 5.4, showing the first verse, is taken from Paris 4379.

The Magnificat has an exceptionally orderly architecture: all six verses are carefully divided into half-verses by longs or the equivalent; verses 2, 6, and 10 are in triple meter and four voices (and all begin with two voices expanding soon to four), and verses 4, 8, and 12 are duos in duple meter. The style throughout is a vigorous imitative counterpoint with a few moments of striking homophony (e.g. b. 6), residue of a reciting tone. Its fifteenth-century origin, even if it were not proven by its presence in Paris 4379, is attested to by the underthird cadences, and there seems no good reason,

Ex. 5.4 Urrede, Magnificat, verse 2

Ex. 5.4 (cont.) Urrede, Magnificat, verse 2

despite their distance from Urrede himself, to doubt the attributions in Coimbra and Baena. It is a very substantial and advanced composition for its time and place – which may explain its evident currency in Portugal more than half a century after the composer's death.

The Pange Lingua(s)

Two settings of the Corpus Christi hymn *Pange lingua gloriosi* survive under Urrede's name. One is in Tarazona 2/3, Barcelona 454, and at least seventeen later sources from Spain, Guatemala, and Mexico;[30] it is thus Urrede's greatest hit within the Iberian

---

[30] See Tom Ward, *The Polyphonic Office Hymn from 1400–1520: A Descriptive Inventory*, Renaissance Manuscript Studies III (Neuhausen-Stuttgart, 1979), p. 224 (no. 489); Ward has confirmed the piece's presence in these 21 manuscripts (several times in a few of them) and points out that a few further reports of concordances could not be confirmed.

Ex. 5.5 Urrede, *Pange lingua* [T], bb. 1–11

sphere, and we can call it **Pange lingua [T]** (handlist 57) after its most familiar form in Tarazona, whence it was published by Rudolf Gerber in 1957.[31] Example 5.5 shows its first eleven bars in the Tarazona reading.

The other version is in only one source, the manuscript Segovia s.s., near the very end in a hand later than the rest; it was published by Higini Anglès in 1952, and we can call it **Pange lingua [S]** (handlist 58).[32] This is an unusual state of affairs; for a

31 Rudolf Gerber, ed., *Spanisches Hymnar um 1500*, Das Chorwerk LX (Wolfenbüttel, 1957), pp. 17–19.

32 Higinio Anglés, 'El "Pange Lingua" de Johannes Urreda, maestro de capilla del Rey Fernando el Católico', *Anuario Musical* vii (1952), pp. 193–200, edn. pp. 199–200. Oddly, Anglès mentions the piece's presence in Tarazona 2/3 and Barcelona 454, but not Segovia, even though Segovia is the source for his edition. (He may not have been aware that the manuscripts present two versions.) See also Ward, *Polyphonic Office Hymn*, p. 223 (no. 488), and Kreitner, 'Musical Warhorses'. On the hands in Segovia, see Norma Klein Baker, 'An Unnumbered Manuscript of

composer to have only eight known pieces, and two of them on the same hymn text, should excite at least a little mistrust. Nor are things helped by the manuscripts: all of Urrede's other works are preserved in sources reasonably close to his lifetime, but even the earliest of the *Pange lingua* sources were copied some twenty years after his last appearance in the historical record – this section of Barcelona 454 has been dated 1500–20,[33] the last layer of Segovia is hard to date but contains a work of Alonso de Mondéjar (fl. 1502–16[34]), and Tarazona 2/3 is probably from the 1520s at the earliest.

Two explanations suggest themselves right away. It is possible that the Segovia attribution is just wrong: the scribe copied a *Pange lingua* that he thought was Urrede's, but it wasn't. Or it could be that they are both right, that Urrede really did write two settings at different times, or even at the same time for variety in an alternatim performance. Neither of these possibilities can be ruled out; but a look at the music itself adds yet another layer of complexity to the story.

Example 5.6 shows the same passage in both the Tarazona and Segovia readings, with the words removed and the voice parts interleaved for easier comparison.[35] Clearly the tenors, which carry the cantus firmus, are almost identical; the Tarazona version has a few ornamental figures that Segovia does plain (b. 6), and the Segovia fills in feminine endings where Tarazona has rests (bb. 7, 11), patterns which continue for the rest of the tune. And the other voices do start very differently, Segovia with alto and bass, Tarazona with alto and superius. All of this we should probably expect if these are genuinely separate pieces of music.

That impression is interrupted, however, by bar 3, where a very striking E-flat in the bass appears in both versions. This would be a strange thing for a composer to do if he really wanted to create two more or less distinct settings (or, taking the mistaken-attribution scenario, for Urrede and somebody else to hit upon independently), and it lures the eye to the other voices; there I have drawn lines between notes that may also represent significant parallels. Some of these seem to be reinforcements of the harmonic structure (b. 7 in all four voices, or 8 in three); some are better described as ornamentations or simplifications (5–6, bass); others I would call displacements of a contrapuntal figure (3–4, superius, or 4, alto).

These points of similarity are hard to quantify precisely and declare dogmatically, but my subjective impression is that they fade toward the middle of the pieces but pick up again at the end, with another E-flat passage in b. 30 and nearly identical final cadences. It is almost as though someone were recreating Urrede's *Pange lingua* after having heard it, but not seen it.

Is that so implausible? Such cases are well established in the popular music of later times,[36] and it may be worth remembering that *Pange lingua* is a hymn for Corpus

Polyphony in the Archives of the Cathedral of Segovia: Its Provenance and History' (Ph.D. diss., University of Maryland, 1978), especially pp. 106–7.

[33] Emilio Ros-Fábregas, 'The Manuscript Barcelona, Biblioteca de Catalunya, M. 454: Study and Edition in the Context of the Iberian and Continental Manuscript Traditions' (Ph.D. diss., City University of New York, 1992), vol. I, pp. 100–2; Ros-Fábregas's account of the *Pange lingua* is on pp. 157–8.

[34] Knighton, 'Music and Musicians', vol. I, p. 285 (*Música y músicos*, p. 338).

[35] The example incorporates a correction to the Segovia version suggested by Bruno Turner in 'Spanish Liturgical Hymns: A Matter of Time', *Early Music* xxiii (1995), pp. 473–82; see also idem, ed., *Five Spanish Liturgical Hymns* (Marvig, 1996), p. 22.

[36] See, for example, John Spitzer, ' "Oh! Susanna": Oral Transmission and Tune Transformation', *Journal of the American Musicological Society* xlvii (1994), pp. 90–136.

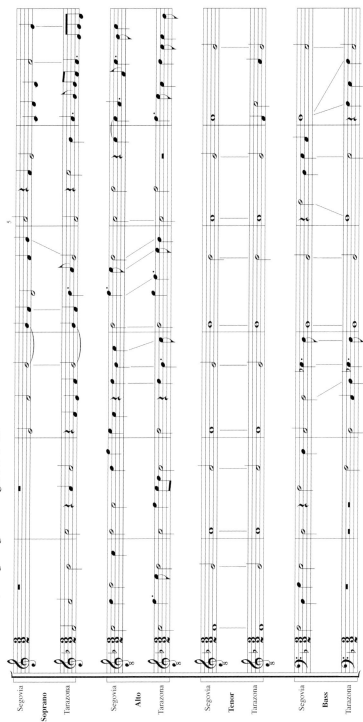

Ex. 5.6 Urrede, *Pange lingua* settings, bb. 1–11

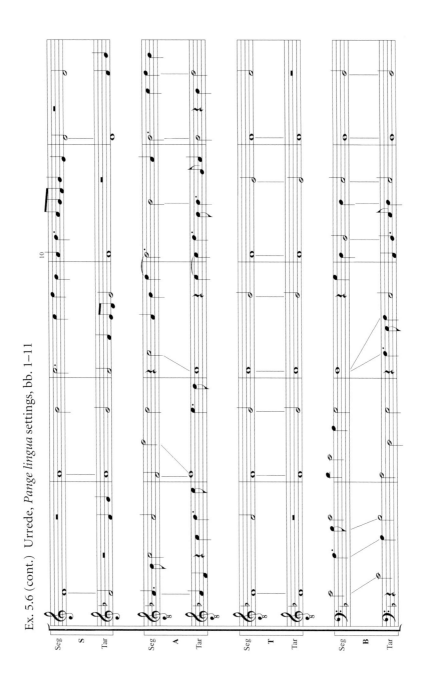

Ex. 5.6 (cont.) Urrede, *Pange lingua* settings, bb. 1–11

Christi, a feast which in fifteenth-century Spain had a decidedly popular character, with elaborate parades and festivities all day and with a powerful grip on the attention of the urban community outside the church.[37] And this may be exactly the kind of situation where the normal rules of sacred-music transmission don't quite apply.

I believe *Pange lingua* [T] represents Urrede's work or something close to it. Its wide distribution shows its priority in the consciousness of sixteenth-century Spain at least, and the underthird cadence in bar 6 gives it an air of antiquity that stands out among the nineteen other hymns, by later composers, that open Tarazona 2/3.[38] *Pange lingua* [S] is harder to account for. It may genuinely have been intended (by Urrede or someone else) as a companion to *Pange lingua* [T], for use in an alternatim performance, like Escobar's two settings of verses 2 and 4 of *Ave maris stella* in that same clump of hymns in Tarazona.[39] The first of these does show an intriguing similarity, especially in the superius line, between its two verses – the kind of unifying device that is easy to imagine being effective with *Pange lingua* too. But remember: there is no source that has both versions [T] and [S]; the evidence seems to be that they never circulated together. More likely, I think, *Pange lingua* [S] is a somewhat later creation by someone who knew Urrede's famous hymn. Whether it is best described as a modernization of the old setting – a mansard roof added to a Greek-revival house – or as an hommage, or a semiconscious plagiarism, or a pupil's imitation of a master, or a smoothing-out on the rocks of popular performance, I shall not pronounce. I continue to count [S] among the works of the fifteenth century, if only because so many of the old structural members seem to be intact, and I persist in a skeptical respect for the attribution to Urrede, who still, after all, could have been responsible for both.

The tenor is not the *Pange lingua* tune familiar today, the basis of Josquin's mass, but another melody widely copied in Spanish chant sources and included, with a few changes, in the *Liber Usualis* in our time with the label 'Spanish Chant'.[40] (Nor, incidentally, is Urrede's necessarily the earliest known setting of this tune: it is paraphrased in the superius of an anonymous *Pange lingua*, mentioned earlier in this chapter, in Montecassino 871.[41]) In the Urrede settings the tune is put into triple meter, following many of the contemporary mensural sources of Spanish hymns.[42] And the three new voices, in both versions, are examples of good strong non-imitative counterpoint – closer to the mainstream of northern sacred polyphony in the Ockeghem era than to the homophonic, superius-dominated style common in Spain

---

37 For a recent survey of this tradition see Gómez, *Música medieval en España*, pp. 95–100 and her bibliography on pp. 109–10; my own essay on Corpus Christi appears as Kenneth Kreitner, 'Music in the Corpus Christi Procession of Fifteenth-Century Barcelona', *Early Music History* xiv (1995), pp. 153–204.

38 Edited, in order, by Gerber in *Spanisches Hymnar*.

39 Ibid., pp. 28–31 and 32–4.

40 *Liber Usualis*, p. 1852; Anglés, ' "Pange lingua" de Johannes Urreda', especially pp. 194–6. For an edition from a Toledo print of 1515, see Turner, 'Spanish Liturgical Hymns', p. 476, and *Five Spanish Liturgical Hymns*, p. 18. For some other variants in the monophonic tradition of fifteenth-century Spain, see Màrius Bernadó i Tarragona, 'El repertori himnòdic del Cantorale Sancti Ieronimi (Barcelona: Biblioteca de Catalunya, M 251)' (Licenciado thesis, Universitat Autònoma de Barcelona, 1993), pp. 108–9, 128, 145, 192.

41 Edited in Pope and Kanazawa, *Musical Manuscript Montecassino 871*, pp. 244–5.

42 Turner, 'Spanish Liturgical Hymns' and *Five Spanish Liturgical Hymns*.

at this time. Yet clearly, from the local tune, the settings originated in Spain and had not been brought down.

The later fame of this piece is not our immediate concern here, except perhaps to observe that the Tarazona version, written presumably before 1485, remained fashionable through the Peñalosa era and far beyond. In the mid-sixteenth century it still had surprising prestige; the two biggest collections of Antonio de Cabezón's keyboard intabulations, published by Luis Venegas de Henestrosa in 1557 and by the composer's son Hernando posthumously in 1578, both have long series of *Pange lingua* settings, and each series is proudly finished with an intabulation of Urrede's polyphonic hymn.[43] And the fifteenth-century hymn was still being copied into the manuscript Burgos s.s. around 1710, into Plasencia 4 (still attributed to Urrede) around 1732, and into Valencia 173 around 1801.[44] This piece kept his name alive for a very long time.

The Story So Far

At the beginning of this chapter I referred to Cornago and Urrede as musical celebrities. It is, I now reflect, a term that must be understood within strict boundaries – apart from Ferdinand, Isabella, and Columbus, nobody from this era is really a celebrity by any normal standard – but still there can be little doubt that Cornago and Urrede are Names in a way that, for example, Triana and Madrid, composers of arguably comparable output and skill, are not. Nor, so far as we can tell, is this just history's whimsical illusion: the presence of Cornago in the Strahov codex shows that his music was known far away from Spain and Naples, and some of the scribes copying Urrede into Spanish cathedral manuscripts were contemporaries of Beethoven.

Cornago and Urrede stand apart from their companions, and the main reason is not hard to spot: they conducted their careers, one way or another, on an international stage. And if the story of the late fifteenth century is the story of Spain establishing a musical identity distinct from, but not lower than, the rest of the world, inevitably it was careers like theirs that made the difference.

Of the two biographies it is Urrede's that is the more conventional. Urrede was born in an important musical Flemish city, son of the organist of its most prestigious church; whether he was educated in the church school or taught the trade at home is not currently known, but clearly he had access to the kind of education for which northern musicians were prized. He established a career in Bruges and wrote at least

[43] For the Venegas version, see Higinio Anglés, ed., *La música en la Corte de Carlos V*, MME II (Barcelona, 1944, 2/1965), part 2, pp. 119–20; for Cabezón's own print, see Higinio Anglés, ed., *Antonio de Cabezón (1510–1566): Obras de música para tecla, arpa y vihuela . . .*, MME XXVII–XXVIII (Barcelona, 1966), vol. XXVIII, pp. 4–7. The two settings, incidentally, are quite different, the Venegas fancier than the later print; see P. Samuel Rubio, 'Las glosas de Antonio de Cabezón y de otros autores sobre el "Pange lingua" de Juan de Urreda', *Anuario Musical* xxi (1966), pp. 45–59.

[44] Dates from *Census-Catalogue* and the card catalogue kept by the Renaissance Manuscript Archive at the University of Illinois. Many of these later versions are, oddly, put into duple meter; for an edition of one such, based on Granada 3, see José López Calo, *La música en la catedral de Granada en el siglo XVI* (Granada, 1963), vol. II, pp. 151–3, commentary pp. xxi–xxii. Burgos s.s. puts the piece in ¢ meter, and Plasencia 4 in ₡, which makes no sense and may be a selfconscious antiquification. For other settings, parodies, etc., see Anglés, ' "Pange lingua" de Johannes Urreda', especially pp. 197–8, and Rubio, 'Glosas de Antonio de Cabezón'.

one substantial composition up there before – presumably – being recruited into a southern musical establishment hungry for his sort of training and talents. This, as we have known for a long time, is the way the musical world worked in the fifteenth century and one of the important means by which the northern style became an international standard for church music. And even if Spain is a less famous part of this story than Italy, we at least know that the Aragonese monarchy had been hiring northern musicians, and sending some of its native musicians for northern training, for many years before Urrede's arrival.[45]

The three (or four, depending how you count *Pange lingua*) pieces of church music left by Urrede in Spanish sources may not be enough to establish a distinctive artistic fingerprint, but they do support the wisdom of whoever brought him down from Bruges. Among their musical surroundings – and remember that the composer had likely been dead ten years before the earliest of their extant sources was copied – they stand out for an unusual combination of contrapuntal sophistication and rhythmic vigor. They strike our ear as exceptionally modern, and they seem to have struck Spanish ears back then the same way: the Magnificat and *Pange lingua*, for all their quaint underthird cadences, seem to have had in Iberian churches the kind of longevity that we usually associate with Josquin and only Josquin.

Cornago's biography, however, seems to be more or less the opposite story. We know nothing of his musical education, but have no reason to believe that it took place off the Iberian peninsula – he was probably in his forties when he began work at the University of Paris.[46] When he came to cosmopolitan Italy, and to wealth and fame, it was as a voice from home at a court in self-imposed exile, part of Alfonso's practice of staffing his musical chapel largely with Spanish singers.[47] Possibly Cornago's Castilian songs, at least some of which must have been written during the Neapolitan years, were the sort of thing to inspire nostalgia in the Castilian-speaking expatriates of that audience, but the anglophilic mass registers as, if anything, a gesture in the other direction. So far as we can tell from what survives, no one back in Spain ever heard it, no other Spaniard wrote a complete mass ordinary for forty, perhaps fifty years, and the next to base one on a secular tune would be Peñalosa. Cornago's case, then, shows something that we might have surmised, but which is good to see confirmed: that northern training was not so indispensible after all, and that a talented musician from the periphery, given some exposure to northern music and an audience that appreciated it, could produce sacred music in the most advanced international styles of the day.

In the end, they did not doublehandedly change the world. Cornago's music may have been distributed far and wide, and Urrede's was certainly sung for a long time, but their influence is hard to see for perhaps twenty years after Urrede's death. When we next pick up the story, in the mid-1490s with the Segovia manuscript, the mainstream of Spanish sacred music still appears to be much simpler and more homophonic than anything Urrede wrote, but the northern style now has a genuinely influential champion in Juan de Anchieta.

[45] Gómez, *Música en la casa real*, passim.
[46] Planchart, in 'Music in the Christian Courts', p. 158, speculates that, as a Calahorran, Cornago may have been educated at the cathedral of Tarazona.
[47] Atlas, *Music at the Aragonese Court*, pp. 29–30.

6

The Segovia Manuscript

Segovia s.s. may be the most famous Spanish source from this period, largely because it contains many pieces by eminent northern composers of the Josquin era. Its discovery by Higini Anglès in 1922[1] dramatically changed the worklists of some very familiar figures, and some of its attributions have continued to be at the center of active debate in the larger musicological community.[2] In all the excitement, its local repertory has so far taken quite a distant second place; but in fact Segovia is the largest source of Spanish church polyphony for the entire century.

The Segovia manuscript has never been published in a comprehensive edition. But a number of its pieces, particularly those of the northern composers, trickled into print in the several decades after its discovery, a facsimile of the entire manuscript appeared in 1977,[3] and the works still unpublished were edited in Norma Baker's doctoral dissertation of 1978.[4]

Segovia: Contents and Origins

The standard inventories of Segovia by Anglès and Baker[5] both list 204 compositions. A glance over either will reveal the manuscript to have been carefully planned: it is divided broadly into four- and three-voice works, and each big section is further subdivided along sacred/secular and northern/Spanish lines.[6] Its northern works are

---

[1]   Segovia, Archivo Capitular de la Catedral, MS s.s. (*Census-Catalogue* SegC s.s.). Anglès's first published description of the manuscript is found in Higinio Anglés, 'Die spanische Liedkunst im 15. und Amfang des 16. Jahrhunderts', in *Theodor Kroyer: Festschrift zum sechzigsten Geburtstage am 9. September 1933*, ed. Hermann Zenck, Helmut Schultz, and Walter Gerstenberg (Regensburg, 1933), pp. 62–8; a fuller account (though now unreliable) appeared in Higinio Anglés, 'Un manuscrit inconnu avec polyphonie du XVe siècle conservé à la cathédrale de Ségovie (Espagne)', *Acta Musicologica* viii (1936), pp. 3–17.

[2]   For two recent specimens, see Honey Meconi, 'Poliziano, *Primavera*, and Perugia 431: New Light on *Fortuna desperata*', and Joshua Rifkin, 'Busnoys and Italy: The Evidence of Two Songs', both in *Antoine Busnoys: Method, Meaning, and Context in Late Medieval Music*, ed. Paula Higgins (Oxford, 1999), pp. 463–503 and 505–71.

[3]   Ramon Perales de la Cal, F. Albertos, and Hilario Sanz, eds., *Cancionero de la Catedral de Segovia* (Segovia, 1977).

[4]   Norma Klein Baker, 'Unnumbered Manuscript of Polyphony in the Archives of the Cathedral of Segovia: Its Provenance and History' (Ph.D. diss., University of Maryland, 1978).

[5]   Higinio Anglés, *La música en la corte de los Reyes Catolicos I: Polifonía religiosa*, MME I (Madrid, 1941), pp. 107–12; Baker, 'Unnumbered Manuscript', pp. 240–559.

[6]   For details, see ibid., pp. 83–4.

dominated by Obrecht, with respectable showings by Agricola, Isaac, and Compère, and its Spanish compositions by Juan de Anchieta.[7] It contains a remarkable variety of music, from large complex masses by Josquin and Obrecht down through shorter Latin church music, to songs in French, Flemish, Italian, and Castilian, to proportional duos and other pieces more at home in the classroom than the chapel. Baker identifies three scribes: a main scribe, A, who is responsible for 90 per cent of the manuscript, including almost all of the sacred music and all of the foreign secular music; B, who copied the section of Spanish songs; and C, who did just the last three pieces.[8] The work of scribe C is presumably later than that of the others, but A and B may have been copying at more or less the same time.

The origins of Segovia have, as one might imagine, been more intensely debated than those of any other Spanish source of this era. For a long time it was generally agreed that the manuscript was copied either for the court of Queen Isabella between 1500 and her death in 1504, or for that of her daughter Juana the Mad, who was in Flanders from 1504 to 1506 and back in Spain from 1506 to 1508;[9] more recently, however, Emilio Ros-Fábregas has made a persuasive case for a considerably earlier date, 1495–97, and for the possibility (among several) that it may have belonged to Prince Juan, eldest son of Ferdinand and Isabella, who was an enthusiastic amateur musician and had Anchieta as his chapelmaster – and probably his teacher – before dying young in 1497.[10] If Ros-Fábregas is right, then Segovia should be considered almost contemporaneous with the second layer of Colombina; but even the later dates would place most of its repertory firmly into the fifteenth century.

Obviously, however, most of this music does not figure immediately into our story here. So: when northern, Castilian-texted, textless, and fragmentary works are removed from the list, we are left with twenty-seven pieces of Latin sacred music[11] either attributed to Spaniards or anonymous, and with some assurance, from their placement in the order of the manuscript and their peculiar style, that the anonymi can safely be called Spanish. The three pieces at the end, added later by scribe C, need a bit of skepticism, and indeed one of them, Mondéjar's *Ave rex noster*, does have to be set aside because its composer is documented only after 1500.[12] The others are Urrede's *Pange lingua* [S], handlist 58, which we saw in the previous chapter, and a setting of *Ne recorderis*, handlist 50, unfinished and anonymous here but intact elsewhere; it too is almost certainly from the fifteenth century, but is best left for

---

7   See *Census-Catalogue*, vol. III, pp. 137–8; though exact numbers are impossible because of conflicting attributions, the *Census-Catalogue* counts 28 undisputed Obrecht works, 16 for Agricola and Isaac, and 10 for Compère. The *Census-Catalogue* gives Anchieta 7 (separating the disputed *O bone Jesu*).

8   Baker, 'Unnumbered Manuscript', pp. 92–108.

9   The case for each of the various hypotheses is summarized well in in Emilio Ros-Fábregas, 'The Manuscript Barcelona, Biblioteca de Catalunya, M. 454: Study and Edition in the Context of the Iberian and Continental Manuscript Traditions' (Ph.D. diss., City University of New York, 1992), vol. I, pp. 207–8; for more detail, see also Baker, 'Unnumbered Manuscript', especially pp. 192–239.

10 Ros-Fábregas, 'Manuscript Barcelona', vol. I, pp. 208–23.

11 These figures count Anchieta's Gloria and Credo, handlist numbers 4 and 6, as separate pieces even though they are grouped as a possible pair here and elsewhere.

12 Mondéjar is currently documented only from 1502 to 1516; see below, pp. 132–3.

chapter 9. This leaves twenty-six pieces for our present consideration – more than a third of the music in my handlist.

Segovia and Anchieta

With nine attributed pieces, and no other Spanish composer given more than one,[13] Juan de Anchieta must be somewhere near the center of Segovia's mysteries. He was probably not the main scribe – Scribe A appears to have been a Castilian, but one fluent in Flemish and not French[14] – but the manuscript almost has to have come out of a time and place where Anchieta was the most eminent musician, and in fact Anchieta was closely connected, at various points, with Isabella, Juan, and Juana.[15] I find it tempting to see Segovia as commissioned by Anchieta, either for himself as a collection of his own stuff, that of his contemporaries, and study-scores from the Franco-Flemish masters,[16] or for Juan as a kind of teaching anthology, perhaps during the time of his engagement to Marguerite of Austria.

We can return to these possibilities, and to the life and personality of the Segovia manuscript, after we have seen some music; for now, two more general observations. First, seven of the Spanish sacred pieces in Segovia appear also in the much later manuscript Tarazona 2/3, and four of those appear in other Spanish and Portuguese sources as well; the Segovia repertory, then, was apparently much better connected to the later mainstream than the sacred music in Colombina, Paris 4379, and the other early sources. And second, of those seven pieces with concordances, six are attributed to Anchieta himself: clearly Anchieta represents not only the origins of the Segovia manuscript but its main link to the future of Spanish sacred music. And indeed, his compositions here are distinctly more advanced in style than most of their companions. In short, Anchieta deserves a chapter to himself, and he shall have it next, after we have studied the more traditional repertory of Segovia s.s.

Alba, Marturià, and Binchois

Three other Spanish sacred pieces in Segovia have attributions, there or elsewhere.

On folio 99 is a four-voice piece (handlist 64, Anglès and Baker no. 30), STAT clefs and ¢ meter, with no composer's name and with the text incipit 'Veni sancte spiritus' in three voices and 'Veni creator spiritus' in the other. This textual puzzle is easily cleared up: the superius paraphrases the familiar hymn for Pentecost, *Veni creator spiritus*, while no voice makes reference to *Veni sancte spiritus*, the sequence for the

---

[13] All the Castilian-texted pieces in the manuscript, incidentally, are anonymous, though many (including eight by Encina) can be identified through concordances.

[14] See Baker, 'Unnumbered Manuscript', pp. 95–9 and 225–6, and Rifkin, 'Busnoys and Italy', p. 528, especially n. 101, where he imagines the scribe as 'either a Netherlander who emigrated early to Spain or as the Castilian-born child of a Flemish parent', and wonders aloud if Urrede could have had a son.

[15] For details of Anchieta's life, see below, chapter 7, and its bibliography.

[16] See also Ros-Fábregas, 'Manuscript Barcelona', vol. I, p. 223.

same day,[17] and in fact this piece appears in Tarazona 2/3 with the hymn text in all four voices and a few very minor musical changes. Clearly, then, **Veni creator spiritus** is right, and 'Veni sancte' is a scribal error.[18] In Tarazona the piece appears as part of a four-voice hymn cycle covering the entire church year, and there it is attributed to 'Alonso Dalua'.

Alonso de Alba was, or would become, a major figure in this world – he has some twenty sacred compositions in Tarazona 2/3 and a song in Palacio – but his biography is in doubt. Alba is a Doppelmeister, one of whose identities was chapelmaster of the Seville cathedral and died before 1504, and the other served the chapels of Isabella and Juana (though not necessarily as a singer) from sometime before 1497 and died between 1516 and 1527.[19] Either one would seem to have a reasonable claim to being the composer, the Seville Alba for his proven musicianship and the royal Alba for his dates closer to those of the other Tarazona composers; but even the royal Alba, if he was working for Isabella or one of her children in the mid-1490s, could easily have contributed this hymn to the Segovia collection. In any case, *Veni creator spiritus* is quite an advanced composition: the chant is paraphrased and ornamented, not quoted literally, in the superius; the other parts move gracefully beneath it in non-imitative polyphony; and the intricate rhythms at the end of the superius and the long hanging-over of the altus into the final cadence are both more characteristic of the early sixteenth than the late fifteenth century in Spain – all of which may tip the balance toward the royal Alba, appearing in this manuscript as a capable up-and-comer and fulfilling his early promise over the next few decades.

On folio 169 are two settings of the Advent hymn[20] **Conditor alme siderum,** one (handlist 26, AB 100) attributed to Anchieta and the other (handlist 27, AB 101, also marked 'alius' in the margin) to 'Marturia',who is probably Marturià Prats of Barcelona (also the composer of a textless piece in Barcelona 5), a singer, abbot, and organ-builder who can be traced in various parts of the Aragonese realm from 1466 to 1514, with a stint at the papal chapel in Rome from 1501 to 1503.[21] Especially convenient for us, the 1466 document has him as a boy singer (*fadrin chantre*), which would

---

[17] *Liber Usualis*, pp. 885–6, 880.

[18] Baker, 'Unnumbered Manuscript', pp. 347–8. Baker does not edit the Segovia version, since the Tarazona version had already been published by Rudolf Gerber in *Spanisches Hymnar um 1500*, Das Chorwerk LX (Wolfenbüttel, 1957). To adapt Gerber's Tarazona edition (which uses quartered note values) to Segovia's reading, only three changes are needed:

   bb. 4–5, tenor: half C becomes dotted-quarter C, 16th B, A

   b. 7, superius: 8th B becomes 16th B, A

   bb. 7–8, altus: half E's tied together.

[19] Robert Stevenson, *Spanish Music in the Age of Columbus* (The Hague, 1960), pp. 164–7, conflates the two Albas; *New Grove* 1980, s.v. 'Alba, Alonso Perez de', by José M. Llorens, separates them and favors the royal; Tessa Wendy Knighton, 'Music and Musicians at the Court of Fernando of Aragon, 1474–1516' (Ph.D. diss., Cambridge University, 1983), vol. I, pp. 249–50 (later translated as Tess Knighton, *Música y músicos en la Corte de Fernando el Católico 1474–1516*, trans. Luis Gago [Zaragoza, 2001], pp. 322–3); *MGG-P*, s.v. 'Alba, Alonso', by Tess W. Knighton; *DMEH*, s.v. 'Alba, Alonso de', by Tess Knighton, and *New Grove* 2001, s.v. 'Alba, Alonso (Pérez) de', by Tess Knighton, make a strong case for both candidates.

[20] *Liber Usualis*, pp. 324–6, with the text *Creator alme siderum* and a few other minor changes; this is the hymn for the first Sunday of Advent. Marturià's and Anchieta's both have the same text.

[21] Knighton, 'Music and Musicians', vol. I, pp. 280–1 (*Música y músicos*, p. 336).

put his birth in the 1450s and make him perhaps fortyish at the time of Segovia's compilation.

How this piece would have got to the Castilian courts is another question, but of course it would have been easy for Ferdinand's musicians to bring something like this to Castile on one of their visits, and there may even be reason to suspect that Anchieta took a particular interest in Marturià's piece. Example 6.1 shows that their two settings are strikingly alike, with identical MAR clefs, similar (and in this context rare) imitative openings, and especially the very unusual adaptation of the triple-meter hymn to ¢ mensuration in the top voice. So possibly Anchieta saw the elder Catalan's setting and was inspired to try one of his own, or perhaps they were placed in the manuscript together for ease of study or alternation in performance.

Ex. 6.1 Anchieta and Marturià, *Conditor alme siderum* settings, bb. 1–12

On folios 101v–102 is an anonymous four-voice piece, SATT clefs and ○ meter, with the text *Te Dominum confitemur* (handlist 63, AB 34), which Baker identified as a version of the **Te Deum** of Gilles Binchois.[22] She describes it as a fourth, bass voice added to an existing three-voice composition; but in fact the situation is a little more problematic and the relationship a little more complex and interesting than that.

Example 6.2 juxtaposes the opening section of the Binchois *Te Deum*[23] with my best effort to interpret the Segovia version on the scribe's own terms.[24] And this little passage makes it clear, I think, that the anonymous Spanish composer – for there is no doubt, from its position in the manuscript, that the scribe thought of this piece as a local product – has not only added a bassus but replaced the old fauxbourdon-derived altus with a new contrapuntal part and made significant changes in the rhythm of the old superius and tenor as well. So it is not quite right to think of this piece as Binchois-plus-a-bit-more.

I prefer to see it not as a conscious reworking of a French composition, but as a sign of the broad informal circulation of pieces like Binchois's in fifteenth-century Europe.[25] The *Te Deum* is listed in the *Liber Usualis* today as a Hymn of Thanksgiving,[26] and in fifteenth-century Spain (as elsewhere) it was frequently used on important celebratory occasions of the kind where polyphony might well be appropriate and where a celebration often had to be put together in a hurry.[27] This is an argument, and a situation, similar to those I earlier suggested for the two Urrede *Pange lingua* settings: it is not hard to imagine, in these circumstances, a piece like the Binchois becoming a kind of local standard and fading gradually into the public domain, with its origins forgotten, to reëmerge in forms such as it takes in Segovia.

---

22 Baker, 'Unnumbered Manuscript', pp. 352–3; for an earlier but less detailed notice of this piece, see also Winfried Kirsch, *Die Quellen der mehrstimmigen Magnificat- und Te Deum-Vertonungun bis zur Mitte des 16. Jahrhunderts* (Tutzing, 1966), p. 287, item 621.

23 After Philip Kaye, ed., *The Sacred Music of Gilles Binchois* (Oxford, 1992), pp. 243–53.

24 I say 'my best effort' because it has required some fairly heavy repairs to make even these seven bars work and because the existing editions of the piece come up with very different solutions to its problems. Baker edits the Segovia version in 'Unnumbered Manuscript', pp. 816–26, and Kaye in *Sacred Music*, pp. 254–6, commentary p. 319. Kaye's edition works hard to bring Segovia's readings of the superius and tenor in line with the other Binchois sources – a bit too hard, in fact, for my taste. For example, in our specimen he has added rests in all voices at the beginning and changed the fourth note in every voice, all breves in Segovia, to semibreves: this would be a remarkable string of coincidences to be blamed on scribal error. Many sections of the piece, it should be added, are less problematic; but on the whole, Baker (who does not appear in Kaye's bibliography) seems to come closer to what the Segovia scribe must have had in mind. My Example 6.2 adds two notes to the manuscript's reading:
>   b. 3 bassus: 1st note not in ms.; breve F inserted after Baker and Kaye both.
>   b. 5 altus: 3rd note not in ms.; semibreve D inserted after Kaye.

25 Indeed, the long list of variants for the three-voice version given by Kaye in *Sacred Music*, pp. 318–19, may be further evidence that this piece got a good deal of airplay outside Spain too. My thinking on this piece has been much influenced by a correspondence with Bernadette Nelson and a paper, 'Binchois Revisited: The Segovia Te Deum and Falsobordone Practice', which she kindly shared with me in advance of publication.

26 *Liber Usualis*, pp. 1832–7; the tune set by Binchois and in Segovia is the second, pp. 1834–7.

27 For example, see Kenneth Richard Kreitner, 'Music and Civic Ceremony in Late-Fifteenth-Century Barcelona' (Ph.D. diss., Duke University, 1990), pp. 478–81, and Maricarmen Gómez, *La música medieval en España* (Kassel, 2001), pp. 100–4.

Ex. 6.2 *Te Deum*, bb. 1–7, with Binchois original

Five Anonymous Quartets

Juste judex (handlist 39, AB 35) is a setting of the same hymn text set by Triana in the Cancionero de la Colombina (Example 4.3 above) and before that by an anonymous Ars subtilior composer in Madrid 1361.[28] The settings seem to have few if any musical elements in common: while a hint of the first point of imitation in Triana's piece (A-C-B-A-G-F in the top and middle voices) may be detectable in the D-F-E opening of the superius in Segovia, the thread seems to disappear after that and may amount to nothing. The two fifteenth-century pieces are also very different in texture and sound: where Triana's was an actively contrapuntal 'song-motet' in SST clefs possibly for the choirboys, the Segovia setting is in sober STAR clefs and much more stationary (see Example 6.3).

Ex. 6.3 *Juste judex*, bb. 1–15

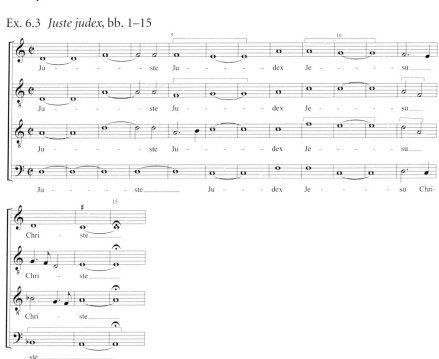

The example may exaggerate the slowness of the piece (most of which works in semibreves and breves, not breves and longs), but it does not misrepresent its stark homophony, only occasionally lightened by syncopations in the middle voices or a bit of ornamentation here and there. I would call it a descendant of the chant harmonizations found in Paris 967, and perhaps a cousin to the fabordón-influenced compositions in Colombina. For all its modesty on the page, however, in performance it has a splendid kind of austere rawness appropriate to its text, imploring mercy in divine judgement.

Ave verum corpus (handlist 21, AB 76) is a setting, in MAAR clefs, of the familiar

---

28 See above, pp. 44–7.

hymn for the sacrament,[29] a good deal more contrapuntal than *Juste judex* but with some nice moments of dramatic homophony. It is not based on the tune preserved in the *Liber Usualis*, but two pieces of evidence hint at a rich hidden past of its own. First, it has a remarkable affinity to a setting of the same text in Tarazona 2/3, anonymous on the page but with an attribution, later crossed out, to Peñalosa in the table of contents. Probably, then, the Tarazona piece is not actually by Peñalosa (nor does it sound like him); but as you can see in Example 6.4, where I have tried to line the opening passages up for comparison, its resemblances to the Segovia version are much too strong to be coincidental.[30] And second (and also visible in the example), the Segovia setting adds and subtracts a number of words from its modern text – not a particularly serious crime in itself, except that there is no good way to cram in all the manuscript's given text (full in all four voices) without omitting words and breaking ligatures and even notes.[31] All of this – the striking similarities and very significant differences in the music, the variants of text, the addition of text impossible to sing – suggests a scribe working from an aural and not only a written exemplar.

It is hard to say which of these pieces is older. Tarazona 2/3 was copied probably at least thirty years after Segovia, but we have already encountered a number of pieces from this period or earlier – Urrede's *Pange lingua*, for example, and all those early works of Anchieta – and the Tarazona *Ave verum* could well be among them. (It could, for that matter, conceivably be even an early composition of Peñalosa's, attributed correctly in Tarazona and disbelieved afterward by someone who, like us, knew only his later style.) So I am reluctant to call this a model-and-adaptation relationship, much less to speculate which is which; more likely the tight, spare, homophonic Tarazona setting and the more expansive Segovia are part of yet another sacred tradition that entered the local popular realm, like the Urrede *Pange lingua* (also for Corpus Christi) and the *Te Deum*.

Two of the quartets are Kyries tenebrarum, of the kind we saw in Paris 967. **Kyrie**

---

29 *Liber Usualis*, p. 1856

30 See Kenneth Kreitner, 'Peñalosa on Record', *Early Music* xxii (1994), pp. 309–18, especially p. 312 and p. 318 n. 12, and Dionisio Preciado, ed., *Francisco de Peñalosa (ca. 1470–1528): Opera Omnia* (Madrid, 1986–), vol. I, p. 40 n. 27. For further similarities compare Baker's edition of the Segovia version in 'Unnumbered Manuscript', pp. 923–32 with Martyn Imrie's of the Tarazona in *Francisco de Peñalosa, Motets for 4 & 5 Voices* (London, 1990), pp. 19–21, as follows:

Segovia bb. 28–32 ~ Tarazona mm. 21–25 ('immolatum');
Segovia bb. 42–50 ~ Tarazona mm. 35–41 (dropping-out of superius on 'cuius latus');
Segovia bb. 70–75 ~ Tarazona mm. 48–52 ('mortis').

31 For comparison (changes from the *Liber Usualis* text in italics):

LIBER	SEGOVIA	TARAZONA
Ave verum Corpus natum	Ave verum corpus *Domini nostri Jesu Christi*	Ave verum corpus natum
de Maria Virgine:	*natum ex* Maria Virgine	de Maria Virgine
Vere Passum, immolatum	vere passum *et* immolatum	vere passum immolatum
in cruce pro homine:	in cruce pro homine	in cruce pro homine
Cujus latus perforatum	cuius latus perforatum	cuius latus perforatum
fluxit aqua et sanguine:	*vere fluxit* sanguine	*vere fluxit* sanguine
Esto nobis praegustatum	esto nobis praegustatum	[. . .] praegustatum
mortis in examine.	*in mortis* examine	mortis in examine
O Jesu dulcis!		*O clemens*
O Jesu pie!	[. . .]	*O pie*
O Jesu fili Mariae.		O Jesu fili Marie
		miserere nobis

Ex. 6.4 *Ave verum corpus*, bb. 1–21, with Tarazona 2/3 setting, bb. 1–14

Ex. 6.4 (cont.) *Ave verum corpus*, bb. 1–21, with Tarazona 2/3 setting, bb. 1–14

. . . **Qui passurus** (handlist 42, AB 32) is the longer of the two; it is in four sections, setting the 'Kyrie' and the three 'Qui' phrases of the chant, with a cantus firmus in the superius, not the tenor as in Paris 967.[32] Its clefs are MATB. The manuscript presents it in white mensural notation, but gives the impression that the new notation is being adapted to a very old purpose: as Example 6.5 shows, every note in every voice is a breve except for final longs at the end of each phrase.[33] Probably, then, this was intended not to be performed mensurally but to be sung in harmony at the normal chant rhythm.

Ex. 6.5 *Kyrie . . . Qui passurus*, sections 1–2

The other, **Kyrie . . . Qui expansis** (handlist 40, AB 29), sets only the Kyrie and one of the verses; the superius of the Kyrie paraphrases the tune published by Anglès in 1935, and that of the verse is related but not identical to some of the verse figures in the same chant.[34] Like *Kyrie . . . Qui passurus*, it is also in MATB clefs and white notation, but here the notation takes its usual mensural significance and the polyphony (Example 6.6) is much more active and modern-sounding. I am inclined to imagine these two sections written as essentially substitute clausulae, to be fitted into a performance otherwise made up of pure chant and old-style harmonized chant.

If *Kyrie . . . Qui passurus* is the most backward-looking of the anonymous quartets in the Segovia manuscript, **O crux ave** (handlist 54, AB 31) is arguably the most advanced. It is in low clefs, ARTB, with text incipits only. The given text can be found in the modern Gregorian liturgy at the beginning of the sixth verse of *Vexilla regis*, the hymn for Passion Sunday (among other occasions),[35] but Barcelona 251 includes it also by itself as a hymn for vespers and lauds on the feast of the Exaltation of the Holy Cross.[36] Probably the Segovia setting was meant for a cross-related feast, though its

---

[32] See above, Chapter 3, pp. 34–40; our touchstone for the chant to the Kyries tenebrarum there was a setting published by Higini Anglès in *La música a Catalunya fins al segle XIII* (Barcelona, 1935), p. 240. Segovia sets text lines 1, 3, 11, and 7 of this version, and uses the same tune for all but the 'Qui expansis' verse.

[33] In the example I have violated my usual conventions, transcribing breves as half notes and longs as whole notes.

[34] See ibid. The cantus firmus to the Kyrie is closer to a slightly more elaborate tune published by Jane Morlet Hardie in 'Kyries tenebrarum in Sixteenth-Century Spain', *Nassarre* iv (1988), pp. 161–94, especially p. 190.

[35] *Liber Usualis*, pp. 575–6; but see also p. 1461 (Finding of the Holy Cross) and possibly others.

[36] Barcelona 251, f. 66v.

Ex. 6.6 *Kyrie . . . Qui expansis*, bb. 1–16

music seems to owe a little something to *Vexilla regis* and nothing to the Barcelona hymn tune.

O crux ave hits the ear instantly as something very different from its neighbors: the opening gesture (Example 6.7) is a point of imitation, and it registers that way, but its note values are so long and the rhythms thus so slow as to avoid the busy quality of the typical imitative beginning of this era, and it quickly and subtly fades into an overall homophonic texture. It seems to crystallize a kind of transitional moment in the history of Spanish sacred music – a composer who saw, and wished to exploit, the ability of imitation to create a sense of structure and growth, but at the same time wanted to preserve the dignity, the pure gorgeous sound, of the traditional chant harmonization. It is one of the most effective pieces in the manuscript.

Two Lamentations

As we saw in chapter 3, Paris 967 contains some of the earliest surviving polyphonic Lamentations in all of Europe. This tradition continues in the Segovia manuscript with two anonymous compositions: **Aleph. Quomodo obscuratum est** (handlist 11, AB 74) sets Lamentations 4: 1–2 (the beginning of Lesson II for Holy Saturday[37]), and **Aleph. Viæ Sion lugent** (handlist 13, AB 75) sets Lamentations 1: 4–5 (the end of Lesson I for Maundy Thursday[38]), but gets the Hebrew letters wrong – has 'Aleph' and

---

[37] *Liber Usualis*, p. 717.
[38] Ibid., p. 627.

Ex. 6.7 *O crux ave*, bb. 1–19

'Beth' for 'Daleth' and 'He'. Probably this is an honest mistake made by a scribe who didn't quite understand the system or heard something wrong; for now, I shall sidestep the confusion by referring to the pieces as *Quomodo obscuratum* and *Viæ Sion*. They are grouped together at the end of a section of Spanish sacred trios, and indeed they have a lot in common: they are the longest pieces we shall be discussing in this chapter; they are both oddly incomplete;[39] they are both in low clefs (TRB, ARB); they both have a cantus firmus, mostly in breves and semibreves but with a bit of ornamentation, in the middle voice; and both add outer voices that move faster in a mixture of non-imitative counterpoint and declamatory homophony, as in Example 6.8.

Clearly the Segovia scribe saw these two pieces as a pair, and clearly they come out of the same stylistic world; yet they cannot quite belong together, for the superius of *Viæ Sion* is about a fourth higher than that of *Quomodo obscuratum*. So probably they are not here together because they were performed together, by the same ensemble, on two days of the same Holy Week: rather, their grouping and musical similarity should be seen as a sign that by the mid-1490s the Spanish Lamentation had evolved into a distinct genre, seen as such by the Segovia scribe, and a genre that may already have developed its own stereotyped musical style.

---

[39] *Quomodo obscuratum* begins at the beginning of the lesson and breaks off about a quarter of the way through, without any 'Jerusalem . . .' passage at the end; *Viæ Sion*, in contrast, starts in the middle but gets all the way to the end, with a 'Jerusalem . . .' passage.

Ex. 6.8 *Aleph. Quomodo obscuratum*, bb. 1–26

Two Alleluias

Right before the Lamentations in the manuscript are two Alleluias – the only mass propers in the whole source. Like the Lamentations, they are paired by the scribe and basically parallel in style, but separated in sound and practice by their cleffing.

Alleluia. Salve Virgo (handlist 16, AB 73) is a Marian Alleluia and verse, in conventional MTR clefs, based on an Alleluia that survives in the Vatican editions today, though with a different verse text and some important musical divergences.[40] Example 6.9 shows the opening, with chant added from the *Liber Usualis*.

The texture of this piece is more or less what we have come to expect from anonymi of the period: the chant is made into a rigid cantus firmus in the middle voice, all in breves, and the other voices are woven around it in a way that mixes styles and slips among them easily. Both the Alleluia and the verse begin with big block chords in the spirit of the chant harmonization, but the Alleluia fades into a chant-accompaniment style, with the outer voices moving in semibreves and minims but following each other's rhythm rather than the tenor's, and the verse, where the words need to be more distinct, is done with a lightly elaborated homophony: here, at any given

---

40 *Liber Usualis*, p. 1456, for 3 May, the feast of the Finding of the Holy Cross; the verse in the *Liber* begins 'Dulce lignum, dulces clavos'. The cantus firmus in Segovia sticks fairly close to the tune through the phrase 'dulcia ferens', almost halfway through, before diverging.

Ex. 6.9 *Alleluia. Salve Virgo*, bb. 1–24

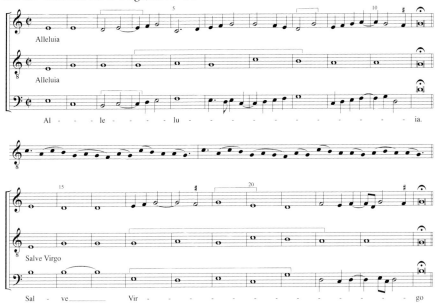

moment, there is usually one outer voice reinforcing the tenor's breve, but there is enough activity in both that the piece (which continues in this vein) registers as closer to conventional polyphony than to chant harmonization.

The other **Alleluia** (handlist 14, AB 72) has a similar structure, though the outside voices move faster (semibreves, minims, and semiminims) and the top voice is in tenor rather than mezzo clef, producing a darker sound. A cantus firmus is again placed in the middle voice, all in breves, but this one's tune is unidentified and the scribe provides no text beyond 'Alleluya'.

Five Anonymous Trios

The remaining anonymous trios in Segovia do not quite form a coherent unit in themselves, though there are at least a few noticeable commonalities. Three of the five are in honor of the Virgin (compared, for example, to none of the quartets); all but one begin, as almost everything so far has begun, in duple meter; and all are scored more or less like *Alleluia. Salve Virgo*, for a falsettist (S or M clef) on the top line, what we would call a tenor (A or T) in the middle, and a bass (R or B) on the bottom. I am reluctant to make too much of all this – it is, after all, rather an artificial category, anonymous Latin trios of Spanish origin in one manuscript, exclusive of Lamentations and Alleluias. But it may be that these small non-liturgical pieces came out of a performing world separable from the cathedral and royal court, that they were intended for use in confraternities or at private devotions. In any case, they seem to be the first substantial signs of what would become a very distinguished repertory in a few decades.

Hosanna salvifica (handlist 35, AB 71) has at least the outward cast of a troped

Hosanna – that is to say, it begins with 'Hosanna' and ends with 'in excelsis' – but the added material is so substantial that the piece probably functioned as an independent motet and not a mass section. It is in SAR clefs, with its top voice written entirely in white breves, doubtless a cantus firmus (though as yet unidentified). Its general texture, apart from the position of the cantus firmus, is like that of the verse section of *Alleluia. Salve Virgo*: homophonic, with at least one outer voice usually matching the superius's breve at any moment, but with plenty of passing tones and ornamental figures to soften the stiffness of the chant harmonization.

Salve sancta facies (handlist 60, AB 69) and **Ave sanctissima Maria** (handlist 18, AB 102) are settings of two non-liturgical texts popular throughout Europe; the former, in honor of St. Veronica, is attributed sometimes to Aegidius Magnus and sometimes to Pope John XXII (r. 1316–34); the latter is usually attributed to Pope Sixtus V (r. 1471–84).[41] The two motets are very similar: both begin in duple meter, in strict homophony (though neither has a strict cantus firmus like the Alleluias or *Hosanna salvifica*), both tend to speed up their note values a bit as they go on, and both have a short triple-meter section at the end – an unusual feature thus far seen only in the works of Madrid.[42] Possibly they come from the same composer, or at least out of the same milieu; Bonnie Blackburn's recent observation that *Ave sanctissima* was a prayer particularly favored by Marguerite of Austria[43] may fit in with the possibility that Segovia was compiled during Prince Juan's engagement to Marguerite. The beginning and end of *Salve sancta facies* (Example 6.10) will give the flavor of both pieces.

Only one of the Segovia anonymi is in triple meter throughout: **Imperatrix reginarum** (handlist 36, AB 70), a Marian motet in $\bigcirc$ meter, MTB clefs. Its text is related but not identical to that of an Alleluia verse still in the Vatican chant editions,[44] but is probably derived (along with the triple meter) from a medieval *cantio*.[45] The polyphonic setting is a sophisticated piece, with three largely independent voices, ragged phrase ends, moments of close imitation, and interesting syncopations (Example 6.11).

Finally, tucked into the bottom corner of folio 168, between an Isaac piece and a clump of Anchieta, is **Sancta Maria ora pro nobis** (handlist 62, AB 98), MAB clefs, only thirteen bars long. In style it fits in nicely with the rest of the anonymi, but in

---

[41] On both texts and their musical settings, see Bonnie J. Blackburn, 'For Whom Do the Singers Sing?' *Early Music* xxv (1997), 593–609; on *Ave sanctissima*, see idem, 'The Virgin in the Sun: Music and Image for a Prayer Attributed to Sixtus IV', *Journal of the Royal Musical Association* cxxxiv (1999), pp. 157–95; on *Salve sancta*, see Howard Mayer Brown, 'On Veronica and Josquin', *New Perspectives on Music: Essays in Honor of Eileen Southern*, ed. Josephine Wright with Samuel A. Floyd, Jr. (Warren, Michigan, 1992), pp. 49–61.

[42] In *Ave sanctissima* the triple section is indicated by $\bigcirc 3$, and in *Salve sancta* by $\frac{\bigcirc}{3}$; both symbols appear to amount to the same thing. On Madrid's pieces, see Chapter 3 above.

[43] See Blackburn, 'For Whom', pp. 594–7, and 'Virgin in the Sun', pp. 187–9.

[44] *Variæ Preces* (Solesmes, 1901), pp. 51–2. Baker, in 'Unnumbered Manuscript', p. 410, describes the Segovia piece as paraphrasing both the text and the music; to my eye, however, the textual differences are significant and the musical similarities nonexistent.

[45] Another significantly similar text (and different musical setting) is edited in Guido Maria Dreves, ed., *Cantiones et muteti: Lieder und Motetten des Mittelalters*, Analecta Hymnica Medii Aevii XX (Leipzig, 1895), pp. 154–5 and 247; I am grateful to Màrius Bernadó for bringing it to my attention.

Ex. 6.10 *Salve sancta facies*, bb. 1–22, 74–89

length it is reminiscent of the curious miniatures of Colombina. It was probably used as a polyphonic response in an otherwise monophonic litany for the Virgin (Example 6.12).

The Story So Far

Segovia is a difficult manuscript to get into perspective: it is like a house whose contents can be seen only by peering into one window or another. For a long time it has been treated principally as a peripheral but important source of northern polyphony by Obrecht and his contemporaries, and as the scene of a number of longed-for but debatable attributions in that repertory.[46] Closer to home, the manu-

---

46 See, for example, Baker, 'Unnumbered Manuscript', pp. 34–62; also note 2 above.

Ex. 6.11 *Imperatrix reginarum*, bb. 1–20

script has attracted some attention as a source of Spanish songs: the title page to the facsimile edition of 1977 even calls it *Cancionero de la Catedral de Segovia*, deliberately placing it alongside Palacio, Colombina, and the other 'songbooks' in the reader's mind. And of course the present chapter, focusing on Latin music of Spanish origin but saving its most important composer Anchieta for later, uses the smallest, murkiest porthole of all.

Yet there is some interesting furniture to be seen. If it was really copied in 1495–97 or thereabouts, then Segovia is actually about the same age as the later layer of the Cancionero de la Colombina. And indeed, most of the music we have seen in this chapter fits comfortably into the basic style observed in Colombina: liturgical, chant-based, cantus firmus often in the top voice, an essentially homophonic accompaniment below. There are a few throwbacks (*Kyrie... Qui passurus*) and glimpses of the future (*Imperatrix reginarum*), which is about what we should expect. And in general, as in Colombina, pieces with attributions tend to be more complex and

Ex. 6.12 *Sancta Maria ora pro nobis*

ambitious than anonymi – a distinction that will be made even more dramatic in the next chapter when we add the works of Anchieta into the mix. The style of Segovia's Spanish sacred music, in other words, supports Ros-Fábregas's more circumstantial hypothesis about its date.

Three important differences may be worth noting, however. First, where in Colombina everything stuck close to the liturgical texts, Segovia departs from the liturgy in a number of conspicuous cases: *Ave sanctissima Maria* and *Salve sancta facies* are both on the kind of devotional texts found in books of hours and without preëxisting chant models. Spanish composers in the early to mid-1490s seem, in other words, to have begun to write true motets. Second, where the cantus firmi in Colombina tended to be in the top voice, there are a fair number of Segovia pieces with evident cantus firmi in the tenor. And third, where in Colombina there were two cleffing patterns, high (for the choirboys?) and medium (for the adult choir?), in Segovia there are medium and low: four of its pieces have alto or tenor clef on the top line, using a subgroup of the normal choir for special effect (and it is probably significant that two of the pieces are Lamentations and one a hymn to the Holy Cross). All of these differences seem to suggest, at least tentatively, that Segovia is farther ahead than Colombina, closer somehow to Josquin and La Rue; yet they need not be the result of mere chronology. The important difference may lie in the external circumstances of the two manuscripts and their exemplars, and with the difference between the situation at a local cathedral (even a cathedral as important as Seville or Toledo) and an international court.

It is possible, considering all these pieces together and blurring the eyes only slightly, to come up with a composite 'Segovia style'. The archetypal Spanish Latin Segovia piece would have a cantus firmus in the top or tenor voice, in steady breves. It would be for falsettist, one or two tenors, and bass. It would begin with big block chords: of the seventeen pieces covered here, eight open with breves and/or longs in all voices, and five more with one running part and breves or longs in all the others. And within the first few bars, this dramatic opening would give way to a style basically homophonic, but with its square corners softened by ornamentation or syncopation in some of the accompanying lines. Of the examples already given, 6.9, *Alleluia. Salve Virgo*, comes perhaps closest to the archetype, but all the anonymi share at least some of its features.

I have avoided using the word *simple* to describe the Segovia style. This kind of craftsmanship is never as simple as it looks, and as I have tried to stress, at its best the vigor and directness of this music has a very genuine appeal. But there is no denying that it is not quite what comes to mind first when most of us think of the 1490s. Nor is this a mere illusion of our modern perspective: such thoughts must have occurred just as readily to the users of Segovia in its own time. It is just hard somehow to imagine the Segovia scribe, after copying out Josquin's *Missa L'homme armé sexti toni* over seven folios at the beginning of the manuscript, being much impressed by *Alleluia. Salve Virgo* later on. Yet there it is, and that is all the evidence we need to know that we are wrong: evidently he thought the native Spanish style deserved to be there between the same covers as Josquin, Isaac, and Obrecht – which brings us back once again to the question: what was Segovia for?

Prince Juan, first son of Ferdinand and Isabella, was born in 1478 and raised mostly at the Castilian court of his mother, where he is said to have received musical instruction from Anchieta.[47] In January 1495 he was betrothed to Marguerite of Austria (born 1480, granddaughter of Charles the Bold and sister of Philip the Fair of Burgundy). At some point in that year, Anchieta moved over to become chapelmaster in the prince's household.[48] Juan and Marguerite were married in April 1497, and the following October Juan died. Marguerite went back north in 1499 to a life of personal tragedy and musical patronage.[49]

It is thus to the eventful last three years of the prince's life, 1495–97, when he was seventeen through nineteen, that Gonzalo Fernández de Oviedo's famous description of the musical life at Juan's court must refer:

> Prince Juan, my lord, was naturally inclined to music, and understood it very well, even though his voice was not equal to his persistence in singing. And so, during the siesta, especially in summer, Juan de Anchieta, his chapelmaster, came to the palace, along with four or five youths, choirboys with beautiful voices, among whom was one Corral, a beautiful treble; and the prince would sing with them for two hours, or as long as he wanted to, and he took the tenor, and was very skillful in the art.[50]

---

[47] The assertion that Anchieta had been Juan's music teacher before becoming his chapelmaster is made by a number of biographical surveys but is not, so far as I can see, clearly attested to in the Castilian documents; the best evidence I have found is a reference from the Burgundian account books describing him as 'nagaires maistre d'escole de monseigneur le prince de Castille'; see Mary Kay Duggan, 'Queen Joanna and Her Musicians', *Musica Disciplina* xxx (1976), pp. 71–95, quotation p. 85.

[48] Adolphe Coster, 'Juan de Anchieta et la famille de Loyola', *Revue Hispanique* lxxix (1930), pp. 1–322, especially p. 67; throughout his service to the prince, Anchieta remained on the queen's payroll; see Knighton, 'Music and Musicians', vol. II, pp. 48–51 (*Música y músicos*, pp. 193–4). See also below, Chapter 7.

[49] Martin Picker, *The Chanson Albums of Marguerite of Austria* (Berkeley, 1965); for a summary of Marguerite's biography, see especially pp. 9–20.

[50] Jon Vincent Blake, '*Libro de la cámara real del Príncipe don Juan e officios de su casa e servicio ordinario* de Gonzalo Fernández de Oviedo y Valdés – según el manuscrito autógrafo Escorial

This image of the young prince, keen on music despite his mediocre voice, singing away in the afternoons with the established master and some invited choirboys, is a vivid and memorable one, and it is supported by independent evidence of Juan's musical literacy: inventories of Isabella's possessions taken in 1501 and 1503 included some of his musical exercise books.[51] When we hear also that the Segovia manuscript may have come from the Castilian orbit during these very years, the target becomes all but irresistible. Possibly for just this reason it should be resisted; but in fact a connection with Prince Juan would explain a number of Segovia's peculiarities (and it's worth remembering that Segovia is a very peculiar manuscript).

- The high proportion of northern pieces, most unusual in Iberian sources of this period, would fit in with Juan's betrothal and marriage to Marguerite. One can readily imagine him seeing the marriage to a musically astute member of the house of Burgundy as an opportunity to get exciting new northern material for his hobby, or seeing Obrecht and Isaac as a way to impress the new bride, or both.
- As I mentioned above, there is at least one locally written piece, *Ave sanctissima Maria*, whose text has been explicitly connected with Marguerite. A gift?
- Juan's ownership and Anchieta's influence would explain not only the strong presence of Anchieta in this manuscript but also its odd pattern of attributions. Nearly all the northern pieces have attributions, but the Spanish ones do not, unless they are by Anchieta or (like Marturià's hymn) paired with one of Anchieta's – and this includes the Castilian songs, which are all anonymous even when, as in several cases, they are the work of celebrities like Juan del Encina.
- If Anchieta was indeed Juan's teacher as well as chapelmaster, that would explain the unusual number of proportional duos and other pedagogical pieces.[52] Or for that matter, it is not hard to imagine Juan and Anchieta and the choirboys getting out the Tinctoris for a challenge on one of their recreational afternoons (or using it to dazzle Marguerite).[53]
- The section of Castilian songs in Segovia is curiously devoid of the kind of racy,

---

e.iv.8: Estudio, transcripción y notas' (Ph.D. diss., University of North Carolina at Chapel Hill, 1975), p. 124: 'Era el Príncipe don Johan, mj señor, naturalmente inclinado a la música, e entendíala muy bien, avnque su voz no era tal, como el era porfiado en cantar; e para eso, en las siestas, en espeçial en verano, yuan a palaçio Johanes de Anchieta, su maestro de capilla, e quatro o çinco muchachos, moços de capilla de lindas bozes, de los quales era vno Corral, lindo tiple, e el Príncipe cantaua con ellos dos oras, o lo que le plazía, e les hazía thenor, e era bien diestro en el arte.' (I have omitted some of Blake's scholarly apparatus.) See also Gonzalo Fernández de Oviedo, *Libro de la camara real del prínçipe don Juan e offiçios de su casa e seruiçio ordinario*, ed. J.M. Escudero de la Peña (Madrid, 1870), pp. 182–3; Stevenson, *Spanish Music*, p. 133; and Baker, 'Unnumbered Manuscript', pp. 202–3.

51 See Emilio Ros Fábregas, 'Libros de música en bibliotecas españolas del siglo XVI (I)', *Pliegos de bibliofilia* xv (2001), pp. 37–62, especially pp. 58–60, nos. 2/8–10; the reference is to '. . . cinco cartapacios borrados de cuando al Príncipe se mostraba latín e las cubiertas de pergamino, e dos cuadernos de papel de marca mayor de canto de órgano, e otro cuaderno de pergamino de canto llano . . .'.

52 Ros-Fábregas, 'Manuscript Barcelona', vol. I, p. 222 n. 136.

53 See also David Fallows, 'The End of the Ars Subtilior', *Basler Jahrbuch für historische Musikpraxis* xx (1996), pp. 21–40, especially pp. 37–8, where he calls these pieces 'games'; for a dissenting view which sees the duos principally as conventional instrumental repertory, see Jon Banks, 'Performing the Instrumental Music in the Segovia Codex', *Early Music* xxvii (1999), pp. 295–309.

sometimes almost pornographic material found in Palacio or especially the later layers of Colombina;[54] everything here is either courtly or devotional. Could this have been a concession to the prince's tender age, unmarried status, and/or presumed royal sensibilities?

- Segovia is the only surviving Spanish source from this time bound in parchment, and as Ros-Fábregas has observed, it may correspond to a 'libro de canto cosido en pergamino' inventoried among Anchieta's possessions at his death in 1523.[55]
- Finally, and returning to the subject of the present chapter: by the mid-1490s, Ferdinand and Isabella had already established their pattern of support for Spanish musicians and Spanish music. Juan, as primogenitor, was being groomed for the thrones of a united Castile and Aragón, and surely his musical education would have been conducted in that same spirit – which may be enough to explain why the more modest-looking motets, hymns, mass propers, and so forth that we have seen here were copied into Segovia and not obliterated by the brilliance of their more spectacular northern counterparts, and perhaps why so many of the sacred works (like the *Te Deum*, *Ave verum corpus*, and perhaps the Kyries tenebrarum) give evidence of belonging to a mostly unwritten local polyphonic tradition.[56]

There are, I admit, problems with this hypothesis. Chief among them is the nature of the northern repertory. If this came directly out of the betrothal and marriage of Juan and Marguerite, one would expect it to be thick with the works of La Rue, the most important musical figure in the Hapsburg-Burgundian sphere at that time; but it contains no La Rue at all, and its most prominent composers Obrecht, Isaac, and Agricola have only tenuous and/or later connections to that court. Joshua Rifkin has suggested that the northern music is more likely to have come from a Flemish urban center,[57] which would seem to deflect our attention from the royal embassies toward a more workaday path of transmission. Another problem is the name of Rodrigo Manrique, recently deciphered by Emilio Ros-Fábregas on the last page of the manuscript: Rodrigo Manrique was the *mayordomo mayor* of Juana the Mad on her first trip to the Low Countries, which would perhaps move the Segovia manuscript out of Juan's court and into that of his sister.[58] And a third is, as we have seen, the main scribe, who uses a very odd combination of Castilian handwriting and Flemish-

[54] For a particularly entertaining or egregious example, see Triana's multitextual song, *Non puedo dexar/ Querer vieja yo/ Que non se filar*, as edited and translated by Stevenson in *Spanish Music*, pp. 216–18.

[55] Ros-Fábregas, 'Manuscript Barcelona', vol. I, p. 223; but see n. 137 for caveats. See also idem, 'Libros de música en bibliotecas españolas del siglo XVI (II)', *Pliegos de Bibliofilia* xvi (2001), pp. 34–46, especially pp. pp. 34–6, nos. 15/1–3.

[56] For many of these insights (and some of the facts behind them) I am grateful to a correspondence with Honey Meconi; her own views on Segovia, independent from but generally agreeing with Ros-Fábregas's, can be found in 'Poliziano, *Primavera*, and Perugia 431' and 'Art-Song Reworkings: An Overview', *Journal of the Royal Musical Association* cxix (1994), pp. 1–42, especially pp. 15–16.

[57] Rifkin, 'Busnoys and Italy', especially pp. 525–33 and 542.

[58] In his dissertation ('Manuscript Barcelona', vol. I, pp. 219–21), Ros-Fábregas identified this name as that of Don Rodrigo de Mendoza and associated the manuscript with the eminent Mendoza family; he has since discarded that hypothesis upon a new reading of the name. I am grateful to Dr. Ros-Fábregas for sharing this discovery and revision with me in advance of publication.

influenced spelling; none of the people we know of seems to fit this peculiar description.

So if I want to twist the Juan hypothesis around these obstacles I shall have to suggest that somewhere in the prince's vicinity was an unusual Hispano-Flemish musical scribe who was not Anchieta but knew him; that this scribe got his northern music not via the marriage embassies between the Castilian and Burgundian courts but through some other connection to a Flemish city; and that after Juan's death the manuscript passed into the hands of one of Juana's retinue and thence, maybe, into Anchieta's possession during his own time with Juana. If these conditions seem fanciful, it must also be admitted that none is particularly implausible – and that no one has yet been able to propose a trouble-free story for Segovia s.s.[59] For now, perhaps the best thing to say is that there is nothing to disprove Ros-Fábregas's earlier suggestion that Segovia was written for Prince Juan in the mid-1490s, and that a close look at the Spanish sacred music in the manuscript appears to give support to such a notion.

At any rate, there can be little doubt that Segovia is the most plentiful surviving source of sacred music from fifteenth-century Spain; that, with so many concordances among the sacred music of later manuscripts (compared to, for example, only one in Colombina) it represents a clear connection to the continuous line that will lead to Peñalosa, Morales, and the future; and that it is dominated, one way or another, by one very strong Spanish personality: Juan de Anchieta.

[59] See especially Rifkin, 'Busnoys and Italy', pp. 519–43.

7

Anchieta

To speak, as I did a few pages ago, of a 'composite Segovia style' for Spanish sacred music without considering the works of Juan de Anchieta is a little like trying to describe New York without making reference to Manhattan. I believe it was a useful exercise; but if it allows us to see the, shall we say, outer boroughs of this repertory more clearly, it does so only at the expense of our perspective. Anchieta may or may not have had something to do with the preparation of the manuscript, and may or may not have owned it himself, but he is certainly the controlling personality of the section we are most interested in here. He is also the one figure from this period with enough surviving music and enough known biographical details to sustain a chapter on his own.[1]

Anchieta's biography has benefitted from two happenstances: first, that he was born into a family that would shortly produce an important and well-documented celebrity (his mother and St. Ignatius Loyola's paternal grandfather were brother and sister), and second, that he spent almost his entire career at the royal courts. The result is that, unlike any Iberian composer of his era, Anchieta now has no serious gaps in his résumé. His story was first outlined by Adolphe Coster in a book-length article of 1930 and has since been updated and elucidated by Robert Stevenson and Tess Knighton.[2]

Anchieta was born in the Basque country, probably in the village of Urrestilla or the larger town of Azpeitia; Coster's estimate of 1462 for his birthdate has been universally repeated and may be about right, but rests on a shaky interpolation between two secure but remote dates, the marriage of his grandparents in 1413 and his first known employment in 1489.[3] In February 1489 he entered Isabella's chapel, and

---

[1] My thinking about Anchieta over the years has drawn on discussions with two of my students, Patrick Miller, who read a paper on 'A Chronology of the Works of Juan de Anchieta' to the American Musicological Society, South-Central Chapter, in Atlanta in April 1995, and Daniel Denley, who turned in a senior paper on 'The Mystery of Anchieta's *Missa de nostra dona*' in December 1998.

[2] Adolphe Coster, 'Juan de Anchieta et la famille de Loyola', *Revue Hispanique* lxxix (1930), pp. 1–322; Robert Stevenson, *Spanish Music in the Age of Columbus* (The Hague, 1960), pp. 127–35; Tessa Wendy Knighton, 'Music and Musicians at the Court of Fernando of Aragon, 1474–1516' (Ph.D. diss., Cambridge University, 1983), vol. I, pp. 251–3 (later translated as Tess Knighton, *Música y músicos en la Corte de Fernando el Católico 1474–1516*, trans. Luis Gago [Zaragoza, 2001], pp. 323–4); *MGG-P*, s.v. 'Anchieta, Juan de', by Maricarmen Gómez; *New Grove* 1980, s.v. 'Anchieta, Juan de', by Robert Stevenson, which article appears almost unchanged, apart from an updated worklist and bibliography, in *New Grove* 2001. See also *DMEH*, s.v. 'Anchieta, Juan de', by Pedro Aizpurúa Zacalaín.

[3] Coster, 'Juan de Anchieta', pp. 51–8. Coster's argument is essentially as follows: Lope García de

he essentially remained with the royal house of Castile, through its vicissitudes, for the next thirty years. In 1495, as we have seen, he became chapelmaster to the young Prince Juan (though remaining on the regular Castilian payroll), returning to the queen's employ when Juan died in 1497; in 1504, when Isabella died, Anchieta entered the chapel of her daughter and heir, Juana the Mad (wife, soon widow, of Philip the Fair of Burgundy). With her court he travelled to Flanders and England, teaching music to her children as he had done for her late brother, and even being approached to spy for the Burgundians against Ferdinand, whom he reportedly hated.[4] In 1515 Ferdinand succeeded in having Juana declared incompetent and assigning himself as regent of Castile, and at that point, all apparently being forgiven, Anchieta came onto Ferdinand's payroll until the king's death the following year.

As early as 1500, Anchieta had secured an appointment as rector of a parish church back in Azpeitia (this through the influence of his cousin, Loyola's father), and he discharged his duties through an intermediary, only occasionally intervening in parish affairs himself, for some years. At some point in the mid-1510s he reclaimed his hometown connections in earnest (we see him physically attacked by his young cousins, including the future saint, in a bizarre incident of 1515); and when, in 1519, Charles V declared the composer too old to reside at court and provided a pension equal to his highest salary, he was back home for good. In 1520 Anchieta was reported ill in Azpeitia, and he died on July 30, 1523.

In addition to the four songs in the Cancionero de Palacio, which are not our concern here, Anchieta has left what I choose to count as thirteen pieces of sacred music.[5] A number of them have been edited in various publications over the years, but the most convenient compilation is probably Samuel Rubio's collected-works edition of 1980; it shall be my standard reference.[6]

Lazcano and Sancha Yañez de Loyola were married in 1413; Urtayzaga, the composer's mother, was their seventh daughter, therefore born c.1442; she was married probably at eighteen, therefore c.1460; Juan is their second child, born therefore c.1462; thus when we first see him appearing on the scene, entering the royal chapel of Castile in 1489, he is twenty-seven.

4   See Mary Kay Duggan, 'Queen Joanna and her Musicians', *Musica Disciplina* xxx (1976), pp. 73–95, especially pp. 84–5.

5   This possibly somewhat eccentric statistic, explained over the course of the chapter, counts the *Missa [sine nomine]* as one piece but separates the three movements of the Marian mass; includes *O bone Jesu*; and puts *Domine ne memineris* and *Domine non secundum*, which may have led a separate existence, as *partes* of a single composition.

   It excludes a number of anonymous compositions given tentatively to Anchieta by Samuel Rubio in his edition (see next note) because of their proximity to ascribed works in Segovia, and also the four passions and three psalms identified by Dioniso Preciado in *Juan de Anchieta (c. 1462–1523): Cuatro Pasiones polifónicas* (Madrid, 1995) and 'Juan de Anchieta (c. 1462–1523) y los Salmos del Códice Musical de la Parroquia de Santiago de Valladolid', *Encomium Musicæ: Essays in Memory of Robert Snow*, ed. David Crawford and G. Grayson Wagstaff (Hillsdale, 2002), pp. 209–29. These latter seven pieces are an interesting case: they are anonymous in their only source, Valladolid, Parroquia de Santiago, s.s., in a section that may be older than the main corpus of the manuscript (dated 1616 – see *Census-Catalogue*, vol. IV, p. 8) but that remains undated. Preciado's ascription is based on their position after a known and attributed Anchieta motet. Between the problems of identification and manuscript date, I have regretfully had to exclude them all from Anchieta's worklist and my handlist of fifteenth-century music.

6   Samuel Rubio, ed., *Juan de Anchieta: Opera Omnia* (Guipuzcoa, 1980).

Anchieta and Segovia

Anchieta's strong presence in the Segovia manuscript affords an opportunity so far unique in this repertory – the chance to establish at least the outlines of a chronology within a single composer's work. Of all the Iberian church musicians active during the time of Ferdinand and Isabella, only Anchieta, Escobar, Peñalosa, and Alonso de Alba have left more than, say, five pieces of church music, or enough to make personal chronology even an issue; and the worklists of the last three of these are unhelpfully limited to late sources – especially Tarazona 2/3, whose date has never been established but which was probably copied in the late 1520s, the 1530s, or even later.[7]

But for Anchieta the situation is very different. For if it is true that Segovia dates from 1495–97, then it would seem that almost two thirds of his sacred compositions were written in the first eight or nine years of his known career. This makes a convenient framework for talking about his sacred music: we can start with two pieces that appear only in Segovia, move on to the ones in both Segovia and Tarazona 2/3 (among, in some cases, other late sources), and conclude with a brief look at the works in late sources only.

Conditor alme siderum (handlist 26, Rubio number 8) we saw in the previous chapter, paired with a setting of the same tune (on the same page of Segovia) by Marturià Prats. And as we saw there, it is much like its companion: a three-voice arrangement of an Advent hymn, MAR clefs, with the hymn tune in the superius in note values lengthened so that its triple meter becomes a kind of long-term hemiola over the faster duple of the lower voices. Like Marturià's setting it begins in imitation but quickly settles into a pattern where the lower voices follow one another's rhythm rather than being truly independent (see example 6.1 above).

On folio 168v of Segovia, right before *Conditor* actually, is Anchieta's three-voice setting, TTB clefs, of the beginning of the tract for Ash Wednesday, **Domine non secundum peccata nostra** (handlist 32, R 4); it ends at the text 'retribuas nostras', but then earlier in the manuscript, on folios 97v–98, is a four-voice setting, TTTB clefs, of the next part of the tract, *Domine ne memineris*, also attributed to Anchieta. In the second voice of the former and the third of the latter they loosely paraphrase the Vatican chant tune.[8] These have sometimes been counted as two separate compositions, but surely Rubio is right to suppose that they were meant as two parts of the same piece,[9] to be combined in the manner of Madrid's *Domine non secundum*, which

---

[7]   The most convenient overview of this issue is probably still Stevenson, *Spanish Music*, pp. 121–200, though a few of Stevenson's details have of course been adjusted in the years since. My figures omit Bernardo Icart (pp. 124–5) because of doubts over his nationality and because none of his works is preserved in a peninsular source, and Pedro Fernández (pp. 176–7) for difficulties of identification. On the date of Tarazona 2/3, see Chapter 9 and its bibliography below.

[8]   *Liber Usualis*, pp. 527–8. Rubio, in *Anchieta: Opera Omnia*, p. 40, sees the relationship as being fairly distant: 'Compararla con la vaticana', he says, 'sería como mirarse en un espejo o en un modelo falso, no auténtico.' And indeed it is odd that the tune should be both paraphrased and used as a fairly rigid tenor cantus firmus; so perhaps it is possible that Anchieta is setting a local variant of the tract.

[9]   See his introduction to ibid., pp. 39–40. Stevenson counts these as separate pieces in *Spanish Music*, p. 136, and in both versions of his *New Grove* article, as does Gómez in *MGG-P*.

likewise mixes different polyphonic voicings and omits the verse, probably for mono-phonic performance.[10]

How the sections got separated in Segovia and their order reversed is hard to say for sure, especially if (as I maintain) Anchieta, who presumably knew how his own music went, was close to the manuscript's compilation. The most likely explanation may be that this is further evidence that Segovia was conceived not for liturgical use but for educational or recreational purposes: *Domine non secundum* is in a clump of three-voice Latin works and *Domine ne memineris* in one of Latin quartets, different sections, perhaps, to teach Prince Juan how to write three- and four-voice polyphony, or for different groups of afternoon choirboys.

The opening of the four-voice section (Example 7.1) will show the general char-acter of this piece: the phrase-by-phrase construction, with most lines of text ending (as here, b. 94) in a fermata in all voices; the slowly and precisely moving tenor, slightly ornamented only toward the end of a phrase; the overall homophonic quality, with at least one, but seldom all, of the new voices following the rhythm of the tenor; the somewhat fancier quality of the superius, with occasional bursts of activity in the alto and bass; and the mixture of homophonic phrase beginnings (bb. 81 ff.) and slow, incomplete imitation (bb. 95 ff., tenor and alto).[11]

These are the only Anchieta compositions that appear in Segovia and never anywhere else, and it may be fair to ask why. The temptation to assume that they represent a very early layer of his work, disavowed by the end of his life, should prob-ably be resisted as a little too glib; yet it is certainly true that both pieces are on the old-fashioned side, similar in many ways to the Segovia anonymi we examined in Chapter 6; even the imitative passages, normally a forward-looking feature, do not much conceal a basically blocky homophonic structure.

In the case of *Conditor alme siderum*, at least, I can think of a mundane practical explanation: the hymn cycle that begins Tarazona 2/3, which is our main later source for hymns, was apparently assembled from disparate sources and put in church-year order for this one manuscript, but all twenty of its hymns are in four voices, and *Conditor*, in three, would not have fit.[12] *Domine non secundum* is harder to figure: its unusual cleffing is not unknown in Tarazona, and the number of Lamentations there would seem to suggest that an Ash Wednesday tract would not have been altogether out of place. So it may be that this is one piece by Anchieta that, with its somewhat clunky structure and its infelicities of counterpoint (e.g. the unsuccessful attempt to avoid parallel fifths in bar 88 of *Domine non secundum*), had become outmoded in the age of Peñalosa.

---

[10] Neither of these Spanish pieces, incidentally, appears in a discussion of contemporaneous settings of the tract in Richard Sherr, '*Illibata Dei virgo nutrix* and Josquin's Roman Style', *Journal of the American Musicological Society* xli (1988), pp. 434–64, at pp. 455–62. Sherr posits a Roman origin to this tradition, though of course there is no reason to suspect firsthand Roman influence behind either Madrid or Anchieta. None of the settings listed by Sherr omits 'Adjuva nos'.

[11] The example incorporates a correction made by Rubio in the altus of bb. 77–8; Segovia has a B-flat dotted breve and a D dotted semibreve.

[12] See Rudolf Gerber, 'Spanische Hymnensätze um 1500', *Archiv für Musikwissenschaft* x (1953), pp. 165–84, and idem, *Spanisches Hymnar um 1500*, Das Chorwerk LX (Wolfenbüttel, 1957).

Ex. 7.1 Anchieta, *Domine non secundum*, bb. 81–107

The Marian Mass

To put it as neutrally as possible: two batches of mass music survive with Anchieta's name attached. One, which Rubio calls the *Misa [sine nomine]*, is a conventional KGCSA mass preserved only in Tarazona 2/3; it is surely a late work, and we can return to it for a moment at the end of this chapter. The other, which Rubio calls the *Misa [Rex virginum]* and I call the Marian mass, is a more confusing story. The Segovia manuscript, after a section of northern masses, has a Credo attributed to Anchieta and then a Gloria, also under Anchieta's name, with the Marian trope *Spiritus et alme*. The second

layer of Barcelona 454, copied between 1500 and 1520,[13] includes the same Marian
Gloria and fleshes it out with new introit, Kyrie (with the trope *Rex virginum*), gradual,
Alleluia, offertory, Sanctus, Agnus, and communion to make a plenary Marian mass,
called *Missa de nostra dona* in the manuscript's tabla; this is not attributed to Anchieta,
though in the tabla it is followed by his *Salve Regina*, attributed correctly.[14] Tarazona
2/3 includes the troped Kyrie from Barcelona (attributing it now to Anchieta), the now
familiar Marian Gloria, and the Credo from Segovia, and adds a Sanctus and Agnus by
Pedro de Escobar to make a complete composite mass ordinary, called *Missa de nuestra
señora* in the tabla.[15] Finally, the Credo from Segovia appears anonymously, in the
midst of other anonymous (and as yet unidentified) mass movements in Coimbra 12
(copied in the 1540s or early 1550s).[16] Table 7.1 may clarify things a little.

What we have here, then, is a mass that grew by accretion over quite a few years.
Here is my own hypothetical scenario.

- In the early 1490s Anchieta writes a troped Gloria and a Credo. They are part of an
  old-fashioned mix-and-match tradition of mass movements and are not particularly intended to be performed together: their order is reversed in Segovia,
  remember, and although their voice ranges are compatible in absolute terms, the
  tessituras of the Gloria's superius and alto are substantially lower than those of the
  Credo.
- In the mid-1490s, someone near Anchieta puts together the Segovia manuscript,
  intending to organize it in sections, genre by genre, with northern examples of each
  first and Spanish afterward. After copying a number of conventional five-
  movement masses by Obrecht et al., he is in trouble for local repertory, Spanish
  musicians not yet having quite developed the tradition of the cyclic mass. The
  Credo and Gloria are all, or the best, he can come up with, and in they go.
- Sometime afterward, say in the late nineties, Anchieta writes a Kyrie with a Marian
  trope, not necessarily meaning it to go with either the existing Gloria or Credo.
- Later still, perhaps in the first years of the sixteenth century, someone needs a
  plenary Marian mass; he starts with Anchieta's Kyrie and Gloria (leaving the Credo
  out for some reason) and adds a batch of new ordinary and proper settings for the
  occasion. At least some of these new movements are meant to go together; several
  use a head-motive derived from the Kyrie's opening (which is itself based on the
  chant, as we shall see shortly). The composer of the new material may possibly have
  been Anchieta himself,[17] but it could just as well have been any competent musician who understood a little about the sound of the Kyrie and could write other

[13] Emilio Ros-Fábregas, 'The Manuscript Barcelona, Biblioteca de Catalunya, M. 454: Study and
      Edition in the Context of the Iberian and Continental Manuscript Traditions' (Ph.D. diss., City
      University of New York, 1992), vol. I, pp. 100–14.
[14] Ibid., vol. I, p. 299 n. 96; Ros-Fábregas points out that it was common in Spain to perform the
      Salve right after a Marian mass. The plenary mass is edited in ibid., vol. II, pp. 98–138.
[15] It is published, in an edition based on Tarazona, in Higinio Anglés, *La música en la Corte de los
      Reyes Católicos I: Polifonía religiosa*, MME I (Barcelona, 1941), 35–60. The tabla to Tarazona, inci-
      dentally, gives only the name 'Jo. Ancheta' and does not mention Escobar.
[16] Owen Rees, *Polyphony in Portugal c.1530–c.1620: Sources from the Monastery of Santa Cruz,
      Coimbra* (New York, 1995), pp. 185–94; the Credo is in number 4 of his inventory.
[17] Ros-Fábregas has made this suggestion in 'Manuscript Barcelona', vol. I, p. 300.

Table 7.1 Sources for Anchieta's Marian mass

	Segovia s.s.	Barcelona 454	Tarazona 2/3	Coimbra 12
Introit		[Anon.] Salve sancta parens (Barcelona)		
Kyrie		[Anon.] Kyrie rex virginum (Barcelona)	Jo. Ancheta Kyrie rex virginum (Barcelona)	[Anon.] Kyrie (Coimbra)
Gloria	Jo. Ancheta Gloria spiritus et alme (Segovia)	[Anon.] Gloria spiritus et alme (Segovia)	[—] Gloria spiritus et alme (Segovia)	[Anon.] Gloria (Coimbra)
Credo	Johannes Anxeta Credo (Segovia)		[—] Credo (Segovia)	[Anon.] Credo (Segovia)
Gradual		[Anon.] Benedicta et venerabilis (Barcelona)		
Alleluia		[Anon.] Alleluia. Dulcis mater (Barcelona)		
Offertory		[Anon.] Felix namque (Barcelona)		
Sanctus		[Anon.] Sanctus (Barcelona)	Scobar Sanctus (Tarazona)	[Anon.] Sanctus (Coimbra)
Agnus Dei		[Anon.] Agnus Dei (Barcelona)	Escobar Agnus Dei (Tarazona)	[Anon.] Agnus Dei (Coimbra)

movements to fit, the way an architect might design an addition to match the original house's exterior. The result is copied into Barcelona 454.

• The three older movements continue to circulate semi-independently for many decades, and they are fair game for the scribes who are putting together composite masses after the fact to satisfy the sixteenth-century preference for full five-movement ordinaries: in the 1520s or 1530s they are combined in Tarazona 2/3 (or one of its exemplars) with similarly free-floating mass movements by Escobar, and in the 1540s or 1550s (by which time it has to be at least a half century old) the Credo turns up in an anonymous mass in the Portuguese source Coimbra 12.[18]

---

[18] Rees, in *Polyphony in Portugal*, pp. 413–14, points out that 'None of the three readings of Anchieta's *Credo* are particularly close, and no two readings are consistently closer to each other than they are to the third' – further confirmation, if such be needed, that the movements circulated independently.

I call this a hypothetical scenario, and I would not like to be pinned too rigidly to any of its details. There are doubtless any number of lost intermediary sources and potential confounding (or simplifying) factors that we don't know about. But surely the general outlines of the story are right: between the beginning of Anchieta's career and the end, Spanish musicians embraced the international tradition of the five-movement cyclic mass ordinary. And the music of Anchieta's Marian mass took part in both ends of this change. In any case, I consider the Kyrie, Gloria, and Credo to be authentically Anchieta's and to date from the late fifteenth century.

The **Gloria** (handlist 4, R 2) is based on Vatican Gloria IX, for feasts of the Blessed Virgin, and it incorporates a Marian trope, already common for some centuries in and out of Spain, with the text *Spiritus et alme*.[19] Like most Glorias, it begins with the monophonic intonation 'Gloria in excelsis Deo', as usual not written into the manuscripts; unusually, however, it continues in monophony through 'Et in terra pax hominibus', these words and music written in black notation in Segovia, before entering polyphonically on 'bonæ voluntatis' – all of which may suggest that the custom elsewhere in Europe was not fully formed in Spain. After the polyphony begins, the relationship with the chant is clear but relatively informal; sometimes it appears as a paraphrased cantus firmus in one voice or another (perhaps most often the superius), and sometimes it is woven into points of imitation. The **Credo** (handlist 6, R 2) is a more complex case: Anglès cannot find a chant original, Rubio believes he may see a hint of Credo I or II, and I lean very hesitantly toward Credo I.[20]

Their general styles are similar, though the Gloria, at almost 250 bars with all its interpolations, turns out to be an exceptionally long mass movement, especially for this early period. Partly as a result of this prolixity, the movements are hard to encapsulate in a short excerpt, but perhaps Example 7.2, taken from near the end of the Credo,[21] will be enough to show how distinct these mass movements are from *Conditor alme siderum* and *Domine non secundum*. In contrast to their smoothed-over homophonic structure, Anchieta here mixes imitative voice pairs, three- and four-voice imitation (not visible in the example, but plentiful elsewhere), and the most deliberate, obvious, declamatory kind of homophony, sometimes with at least an ambiguously rhetorical motive (block chords, everybody together, for 'simul adoratur' for instance, or the orotund lengthening of 'per prophetas'). Note also bars 150 ff., where he inserts a remarkable passage of arching parallel motion in all three voices; this happens in the Gloria too, also to startling effect,[22] and we shall have occasion to notice it elsewhere in Anchieta's works.

The **Kyrie** (handlist 2, R 2) was, as I say, probably written some years after the Gloria and Credo: it did not get into Segovia but appears anonymously in Barcelona 454 and then under Anchieta's name in Tarazona 2/3. It too is troped with one of a series of common Marian tropes, which first glosses the normal Kyrie-Christe-Kyrie structure into Father-Son-Spirit and then emphasizes the relation of each to the

---

19 For the Gloria tune, see *Liber Usualis*, pp. 40–2; on the trope, see for example Higini Anglès, *El còdex musical de las Huelgas* (Barcelona, 1931), vol. I, pp. 119–21.
20 Anglès, MME I, p. 139; Rubio, *Anchieta: Opera Omnia*, introduction p. 36; *Liber Usualis*, pp. 64–73.
21 For this and all such pieces, examples show the Segovia version.
22 Bars 191 ff.

Ex. 7.2 Anchieta, Credo, bb. 132–160

Ex. 7.2 (cont.) Anchieta, Credo, bb. 132–160

per pro - - - phe - tas.

per pro - - phe - tas.

per pro - - phe - tas.

per pro - - phe - tas.

Virgin.[23] Anchieta sets only the troped portions in polyphony; the regular Kyrie and Christe passages were to be done monophonically in a ninefold performance like this:

Kyrie eleison.	chant
Rex, virginum amator, Deus, Mariæ decus, eleison.	polyphony
Kyrie eleison.	chant
Christe eleison.	chant
Christe, Deus de patre, homo natus Maria matre, eleison.	polyphony
Christe eleison.	chant
Kyrie eleison.	chant
O Paraclite obumbrans corpus Mariæ, eleison.	polyphony
Kyrie eleison.	chant

The Kyrie is also based on chant – in this case the Vatican Kyrie IV, for doubles[24] – but this alternatim scheme means that Anchieta has much less space to cover with his polyphony. The result is a more compact, tightly constructed movement than the Gloria or Credo. In Example 7.3 below I have included the opening chant, from the *Liber Usualis*, followed by the first polyphonic section, from Tarazona 2/3, which shows how the chant provides both the opening point of imitation in all voices and, paraphrased, a cantus firmus in the superius throughout. The other sections are similar: the second begins with an alto-bass pair (but only three bars long in contrast to the expansive voice-pair sections of the other movements), and the third with a homophonic opening in the alto, tenor, and bass, the superius joining in at the third bar. None of the voices, beyond the section openings, has more than three semibreves' consecutive rest.

All in all these mass movements are much more forward- or northward-looking, more Josquinian, than what we have seen so far in fifteenth-century Spain. Anchieta is no Josquin, I should immediately add: to my subjective (but I hope sympathetic) ear they seem competent, yet a little stiff and longwinded, like the work of a student who has got the basic idea of what the master is up to, but has not yet gained full control over his materials. Yet there can be no doubt that he is on to something here – something that we can see in some of his other pieces in Segovia.

---

23 See Anglès, *Las Huelgas*, vol. I, pp. 113–16 and vol. III, pp. 1–6 for more on some versions of this Kyrie trope on and off the peninsula.

24 *Liber Usualis*, p. 25.

Ex. 7.3 Anchieta, Marian mass, Kyrie, chant plus bb. 1–25

A Magnificat and Two Motets

In a parallel but less complicated story, Anchieta has left two Magnificats. One, which Rubio calls the *Magnificat [Tertii toni]* (R 10), is in four voices, with some verses a 2 and a 3; it appears only in Tarazona 2/3 and is thus probably a late work. The other, which Rubio calls the *Magnificat [Sexti toni]* and I shall call the **Magnificat a 3** (handlist 48, R 9), is in both Tarazona and Segovia, and must therefore belong to the fifteenth century. It sets the even verses of the text in three voices, MAT clefs,[25] leaving the odd verses to be done in monophony according to the familiar custom.

Example 7.4 shows the second verse, which will serve as representative of the other polyphonic verses. I would place it stylistically somewhere between the Segovia anonymi and Anchieta's mass movements. As in the Kyrie, for example, he paraphrases the chant[26] in the superius and uses it for a fairly simple imitative opening, echoed at the half-verse by a weaker imitation in bass and superius only (bb. 14 ff.),

Ex. 7.4 Anchieta, Magnificat a 3, bb. 1–23

and in bars 8–9 there is another parallel-motion passage such as we saw in the Credo (and again, some milder versions of the same thing in bb. 10–11 and 17–18). But he does nothing nearly so dramatic with voice pairs, declamatory homophony, and so forth: the overall texture is much simpler, with the superius carrying the chant tune mostly in half notes, the tenor working against it in fancier counterpoint, and the bass filling out the harmony, usually copying the rhythm of one voice or the other.

The Marian motet **Virgo et mater** (handlist 66, R 11), preserved in Segovia, Seville 5-5-20, and Tarazona 2/3, is closer in style to the mass movements, though not based on chant.[27] It is in MTTB clefs,[27] and as the opening shows (Example 7.5), it begins with alternating imitative voice pairs, superius-tenor and alto-bass, for 'Virgo et mater', followed by solid declamatory homophony on 'quæ filium Dei'; this gives way to more voice pairs, followed by more homophony, and so on – there is never imitation in more than two voices at a time. Nor can I detect any sort of rhetorical element, however rudimentary, to his use of texture as in the Credo: he seems interested merely in achieving variety between the lines of the motet rather than underlining their meaning.

Ex. 7.5 Anchieta, *Virgo et mater*, bb. 1–13

Domine Jesu Christe (handlist 30, R 3) is preserved not only in Segovia (MTTB clefs) and Tarazona 2/3, but in four other Spanish and three Portuguese sources; evidently it was one of Anchieta's greatest hits, and it is not hard to see why.[28] Nor is it

---

27 In Segovia and Seville; Tarazona has MATB.
28 For further discussion of its transmission see Jane Morlet Hardie, 'The Motets of Francisco de

difficult to understand why Tarazona 5 would mistakenly attribute it to Peñalosa: were I to come upon it anonymously, I might myself be inclined at first glance to place it among Peñalosa's great dramatic Passion motets like *Precor te Domine* or *Deus qui manus tuas*. Here Anchieta is in possession of his usual bag of tricks – short-term four-voice imitation, voice pairs, homophony – but he seems to put them to much more effective use than in the mass movements or *Virgo et mater*. Notice, to begin with, the deliberate restraint of the opening (Example 7.6): solid homophonic blocks of sound, beginning with a breve as we saw so often in the anonymi, but then softened by the superius in the second bar, and then stretching out for a long melisma on the word 'Christe', with just enough motion in the middle voices to ward off monotony, and yet the whole superius fitting within just a fourth.

Ex. 7.6 Anchieta, *Domine Jesu Christe*, bb. 1–10

The next several phrases work in a similar way, perhaps a little more active but essentially in four-voice homophony; then at the text 'et a matre tua mestissime' he uses a short voice pairing to symbolize the solitude of the mother; when he gets to the other mourning women (Example 7.7), he is back in stark declamatory homophony, every word as distinct as it can possibly be. The agony of the passion is subtly underscored by another little passage of parallels (b. 50), and this trails off into drooping four-voice imitation for the tears at 'lacrimis'.

O bone Jesu

Only one piece in Segovia remains to be discussed. I have saved **O bone Jesu** (handlist 53, R 7) for last because its authorship has been long debated,[29] and I have separated it from its companions because the debate concerns whether it belongs in this chapter

Peñalosa and Their Manuscript Sources' (Ph.D. diss., University of Michigan, 1983), vol. II, p. 144, and Rees, *Polyphony in Portugal*, p. 420. Stevenson calls it doubtful in the worklist in *New Grove* 2001, but I see little reason for such doubt.

29   For some representative formulations of this debate see Ludwig Finscher, 'Loyset Compère and his Works', *Musica Disciplina* xii (1958), pp. 105–43, especially p. 124; Norma Klein Baker, 'An Unnumbered Manuscript in the Archives of the Cathedral of Segovia: Its Provenance and History' (Ph.D. diss., University of Maryland, 1978), pp. 49–51; Dionisio Preciado, ed., *Francisco de Peñalosa (ca. 1470–1528): Opera Omnia* (Madrid, 1986–), vol. I, pp. 30, 47; Ros-Fábregas,

Ex. 7.7 Anchieta, *Domine Jesu Christe*, bb. 35–58

'Manuscript Barcelona', vol. I, pp. 263–8; Kenneth Kreitner, 'Franco-Flemish Elements in Tarazona 2 and 3', *Revista de Musicología* xvi (1993), pp. 2567–86, especially pp. 2570–1; Rees, *Polyphony in Portugal*, pp. 424–6; Pedro Calahorra, 'Compositores hispanos en el ms. 2/3 de la Catedral de Tarazona: Copias y variantes', *Fuentes musicales en la península ibérica (ca. 1250–ca. 1550)*, ed. Maricarmen Gómez and Màrius Bernadó (Lleida, 2001), pp. 177–201, especially p. 192; and Tess Knighton, 'Francisco de Peñalosa: New Works Lost and Found', *Encomium Musicæ*, Crawford and Wagstaff, pp. 231–57, especially pp. 250–2.

on Anchieta at all – or anywhere, for that matter, in this book on Spain. Here is the problem in brief:

- In Segovia s.s. (copied, you will recall, as early as 1495–97), *O bone Jesu* is attributed to Anchieta. In favor of this attribution is the antiquity of the source and its apparent proximity to Anchieta; against it is the style of the piece, which is unlike Anchieta's other music in that manuscript.
- In the earliest layer of Barcelona 454 (copied 1500–1510[30]) it is attributed to Peñalosa. This is a little better stylistically, but against it must be weighed the hand of the attribution, which is different from and later than that of the copying,[31] and the conflicting ascription in Tarazona 2/3, the central and otherwise reliable source for Peñalosa.
- In the third book of *Motetti de la Corona,* published in Venice by Ottaviano Petrucci in 1519, it is attributed to Loyset Compère. This too may work stylistically, and any Petrucci ascription tends to command a certain respect, and this one gets at least an oblique support from Barcelona 454, where the piece is copied in a hand otherwise responsible for only northern pieces and right after two known works of Compère;[32] the problem is that the Petrucci print is the only source for *O bone Jesu* outside the Iberian orbit.
- In Tarazona 2/3 (copied in the 1520s or later) it is attributed to Antonio de Ribera. In favor of Ribera, at least for this purpose, is his obscurity – it is the famous name that usually gets applied by mistake – but against him is his other music in 2/3, which is busier and less imaginative than *O bone*, and his biography, which currently begins c1520 and would seem to place him too late to have written something in Segovia.[33]
- In one other Spanish source (Barcelona 5), five Portuguese (Coimbra 12, 32, 48, and 53 and Lisbon 60), and two Guatemalan (Bloomington 8 and Jacaltenango 7) the motet is anonymous.[34] These are not much direct help, except that they further confirm the piece's fame in the Iberian and hispanoamerican world and thereby cast a bit more doubt on the lone Compère attribution in Petrucci.
- As if that weren't enough, the piece is transmitted with several different endings, though the endings don't correspond with the various attributions.[35]

All this might be no more than an interesting curiosity if *O bone Jesu* were not the most famous and popular piece in this whole repertory – largely, as it happens, by virtue of its association with Compère, which won it a place on David Munrow's

[30] Ros-Fábregas, 'Manuscript Barcelona', vol. I, pp. 97–100.
[31] Ibid., vol. I, p. 264.
[32] Ibid.
[33] Stevenson, in *Spanish Music*, p. 189, places him in the papal chapel in 1514; this figure is, however, corrected by in *New Grove* 1980, s.v. 'Ribera, Antonio de', by José M. Llorens, who finds documentation only from c.1520 to 1526. Knighton, in 'Music and Musicians', vol. I, p. 292, adds that Ribera's songs in Palacio are copied in the third and seventh layers, not the original corpus of the manuscript. See also *New Grove* 2001, s.v. 'Ribera, Antonio de', by Tess Knighton.
[34] For more on these sources and this piece in them, see Rees, *Polyphony in Portugal*, pp. 424–6 et passim.
[35] For details, see Ludwig Finscher, ed., *Loyset Compère: Opera Omnia*, Corpus Mensurabilis Musicæ XV (n.p., 1958–), vol. IV, pp. ii–iii and 27–8, and Ros-Fábregas, 'Manuscript Barcelona', vol. I, pp. 263–8.

well-known *Art of the Netherlands* album in 1976.[36] Everybody cares who wrote it, and everybody wants it. So this motet currently appears in the collected-works editions of Compère, Anchieta, and Peñalosa, and would certainly be in Ribera's if he had one.[37] My own inclination is toward Anchieta, if only because the authority of the Segovia manuscript in matters Anchietan is hard to dismiss; but we can return to the question more effectively after a look at the piece itself.

The composer of *O bone Jesu* (in SATR clefs in Segovia) uses all the now-familiar elements: full four-voice counterpoint, usually but not always imitative; contrapuntal voice pairs; and homophony, here of two distinct speeds, the slower of which I might call 'expansive' (moving mostly in breves and semibreves in the original, whole and half notes in most transcriptions) and the faster 'speechlike' (semibreves and minims, or halves and quarters, i.e. roughly the speed of normal speech). What is odd is that instead of alternating these techniques line-by-line for variety, as Anchieta (and everyone else) usually does, *O bone Jesu* starts out contrapuntal and then at bar 30, a little before the halfway point, becomes almost completely homophonic for a very unusual sense of urgency and immediacy:

O bone Jesu:	Semi-imitative counterpoint
illumina oculos meos,	Imitative counterpoint
ne unquam obdormiam in morte;	Voice pair, S-A
ne quando dicat inimicus meus:	Voice pair, T-B
prevalui adversus eum.	Expansive homophony
In manus tuas, Domine,	Expansive homophony
commendo spiritum meum.	Speechlike homophony
Redemisti me Domine,	Speechlike homophony
Deus veritatis.	Semi-imitative counterpoint
O Messias!	Stop-time fermata section
Locutus sum in lingua mea:	Speechlike homophony
notum fac mihi Domine	Speechlike homophony
finem meum.	Non-imitative counterpoint

Two other features of this piece set it apart from its companions: one is the fourth line from the end, 'O Messias!', which is set in solid breves, each crowned with a fermata for a stop-time effect rare among the Spaniards (though it happens in some of Compère's *Motetti missales* and in Ribera's *Ave Maria*[38]), and the other is the opening point of semi-imitation (Example 7.8) with its entries not on the expected perfect intervals (such as the F-F-C-C of *Virgo et mater*) but on G-D-G-C. This does not happen in any of Anchieta's, Ribera's, or Compère's other motets, but interestingly, Peñalosa does it fairly often.[39]

36   Early Music Consort of London, dir. David Munrow, *The Art of the Netherlands*, Seraphim SIC-6104, 1976. When the records were reissued on CD in 1992 (EMI Classics CMS 7 64215 2), the attribution for this piece was changed to include Anchieta and Peñalosa, but not Ribera. Munrow's recording uses the Petrucci ending.

37   Finscher, *Compère: Opera Omnia*, vol. IV, pp. 27–8; Rubio, *Anchieta: Opera Omnia*, pp. 102–6; Preciado, *Peñalosa: Opera Omnia*, vol. I, pp. 267–72; the closest thing currently to a Ribera edition is Pedro Calahorra, ed., *Autores hispanos de los siglos XV–XVI de los MS. 2 y 5 de la catedral de Tarazona*, Polifonía aragonesa IX (Zaragoza, 1995), which contains all the Ribera motets; *O bone Jesu* is found on pp. 61–5.

38   For Compère, see Finscher, *Compère: Opera Omnia*, vol. II, pp. 13, 16, 25, 35; for Ribera, see Calahorra, *Autores hispanos*, pp. 51–4.

39   See *Adoro te*, F–C–B-flat; *Sancta Mater*, D–A–E–A; *Transeunte Domino*, D–G–C.

Ex. 7.8 Anchieta?, *O bone Jesu*, bb. 1–12

Who, then, wrote *O bone Jesu*? As I say, my preference for Anchieta is based on circumstantial evidence, and it may betray a hapless faith in the Segovia-Anchieta connection. On the other hand, the stylistic problems are relatively minor and seem a flimsy reason for excluding him. Of the competitors, Ribera is perhaps the easiest to dispose of: the motet appeared in Segovia about a quarter-century before his first surviving document, and its placement in Tarazona right after an uncontested Ribera motet is probably enough to explain a slip of the pen, a mistaken attribution added to an anonymous piece somewhere along the line. Peñalosa too registers as a mistake: the notes and their attribution in Barcelona 454/A were written by people who apparently didn't even know each other, and Emilio Ros-Fábregas's suggestion that the attributor may have remembered, or thought he remembered, another setting of this same text by Peñalosa[40] is perfectly reasonable. The case for Compère, on the other hand, is disturbingly strong: the appearance of *O bone* in a northern hand in 454/A, and Owen Rees's stemma showing the Petrucci version on one branch of transmission and all others on another, may both point toward an act of importation.[41] But any such account would also need to explain how *O bone Jesu* became so famous below the Pyrenees yet remained so unnoticed above them that it got into no surviving northern or Italian manuscript and saw print only after the composer's death.

So Anchieta it is, at least for now. In any case, it is clear that *O bone Jesu* was a

40   Ros-Fábregas, 'Manuscript Barcelona', vol. I, p. 264.
41   Rees, *Polyphony in Portugal*, p. 426.

popular motet in these circles, and indeed its prominent homophony seems to be the sort of thing that appealed to tastes in Spain, Portugal, and America for some decades to come. Obviously they thought of this piece as their own, and probably it was. And if so, the Petrucci print makes it the one unmistakable case of something in this repertory having an appreciable impact in its own time, and ours, in the wider musical world.

After Segovia

Again: apart from the Kyrie, everything we have seen so far in this chapter is in the Segovia manuscript and therefore, it would seem, from the first decade of Anchieta's known career. (The Kyrie I believe is a little newer, but not much.) This leaves only four pieces of sacred music, and a big gap of time: all four are preserved only in sources from the 1520s and after. One of them I have added to our list of music from the fifteenth century; the others I believe form a separate chronological layer originating after, perhaps well after, the turn of the century.

Libera me Domine (handlist 45, R 6) is a four-voice setting, MATB in Tarazona 2/3, of one of the responsories for the Office for the Dead. It appears in a fair number of Spanish sources, the earliest of which, Tarazona 2/3, was probably copied after the composer's death. I have included it in the handlist because of a suggestion, made first by Tess Knighton and later by Grayson Wagstaff, that this piece and two companions were written for the funeral of Prince Juan in 1497 (i.e. right after Segovia was copied).[42] We can return to these three pieces and their possible circumstances in more detail in chapter 9; this is, however, a good place to look at Anchieta's composition.

Libera me is an alternatim setting of the responsory, featuring short passages (mostly around 15 bars) interlarded among presumably monophonic performance of the chant; it is based on a version of the tune similar to that found in the Vatican sources today,[43] and it uses the chant in a way that we have seen prefigured elsewhere in Anchieta's early works: as Example 7.9, the first polyphonic section, shows, the tune (pitches D-D-C-D-F-E-D-E-F-C-D-D) is used to begin the alto, with the tenor and bass harmonizing it sedately; but then in the fourth bar the superius enters with the same tune, giving some of the effect of imitation, and after that makes it into a slow cantus firmus on top, with just a light paraphrase in the last few bars and all three lower voices homophonically harmonizing. I am reluctant to put too much weight on a stylistic judgement of chronology with a piece like this, which might well be expected to be at least a little conservative, but *mutatis mutandis*, it does seem to fit fairly neatly into the Anchieta style we have seen in Segovia.[44]

Anchieta's three remaining sacred works are all substantial compositions, but

---

[42] Knighton, 'Music and Musicians', vol. I, pp. 177–9 (*Música y músicos*, pp. 140–1); George Grayson Wagstaff, 'Music for the Dead: Polyphonic Settings of the *Officium* and *Missa pro defunctis* by Spanish and Latin American Composers before 1630' (Ph.D. diss., University of Texas, 1995), pp. 195–7.

[43] *Liber Usualis*, pp. 1767–8; but see Wagstaff, 'Music for the Dead', p. 172 et passim for variants and rearrangement of sections.

[44] The note in the altus of b. 15 does not appear in Tarazona; I have added it after Rubio.

Ex. 7.9 Anchieta, *Libera me*, bb. 1–16

there is nothing to connect them to the fifteenth century. The **Salve Regina** (R 12) is found in Barcelona 454/C and Seville 5-5-20 (both probably from the 1520s), Tarazona 2/3, and Barcelona 681 (after c.1545);[45] and the other **Mass** (R 1) and the **Magnificat a 4** (R 10) are in Tarazona 2/3 only. None of these sources, then, is any chronological help, and the texts of the three pieces are part of the everyday liturgy and thus impossible to apply to particular events. I believe they represent Anchieta's sixteenth-century career, after the death of Prince Juan, through the period travelling with Juana, to his retirement from the Aragonese court in the late 1510s.

They are, in other words, not part of our story here except in their sharp technical contrast to the composer's early works. The Magnificat, with its five even verses[46] scored ST, SATB, SSA, AAR, and SS, must be done by a choir large enough for sections to divide and fits into the kind of pattern almost universal in the Magnificats by Peñalosa in Tarazona 2/3.[47] *Salve Regina* shows a hitherto unseen dexterity in handling contrapuntal materials: the 'Vita dulcedo' verse is in the good old slow-cantus-firmus-on-top style, but the 'Ad te suspiramus' verse, for example, has

45 On the dates of these sources, see Ros-Fábregas, 'Manuscript Barcelona', vol. I, pp. 81–8, 224–36, 237–45, and 185–90 respectively.
46 Folio 58, on which one or more voices of verse 12 was presumably written, has been cut out.
47 On the Tarazona Magnificats, see Winfried Kirsch, *Die Quellen der mehrstimmigen Magnificat- und Te Deum-Vertonungen bis zur Mitte des 16. Jahrhunderts* (Tutzing, 1966), nos. 583–84, 904, 960–67, 977, 1045, 1094–95, and 1123; Preciado, *Francisco de Peñalosa: Opera Omnia*, vol. II; and Kenneth Kreitner, 'Peñalosa on Record', *Early Music* xxii (1994), pp. 309–20, especially p. 314.

such advanced features as a migrating cantus firmus and interlocking voice pairs. And the mass is the one piece often cited as a sign of Anchieta's northern-style contrapuntal virtuosity: not only does he use the *L'homme armé tune*, ornamented and transposed to the phrygian mode, as a tenor cantus firmus in his Agnus,[48] the whole piece just breathes an air of vigorous, brilliant counterpoint of a kind very different from his works in Segovia – as can be seen in the Kyrie I (Example 7.10).

Ex. 7.10 Anchieta, *Missa sine nomine*, Kyrie, bb. 1–12

48 See, for example, Kreitner, 'Franco-Flemish Elements', p. 2575.

The Story So Far

Juan de Anchieta's musical career spanned the whole of the critical period between Colombina and Peñalosa. He entered the Castilian court chapel in 1489, his talents were recognized early (he was made chapelmaster to the primogenitor Prince Juan after only six years in the job), and he retired only after Isabella and Ferdinand were dead. He was certainly writing sacred music at the beginning of this period, and there is no reason to believe he was not still writing at the end.

He also led an exceptionally cosmopolitan career for a Spanish musician of this era. By the time Anchieta appeared, the days of imported composers like Urrede were over in Spain; both Ferdinand and Isabella hired exclusively local singers and composers. Of Anchieta's contemporaries, Escobar is not known to have left the peninsula at all, and Peñalosa not till 1517, after the king's death. But Anchieta had two early opportunities for extended study of the state-of-the-art music of northern Europe, first in 1495–97, when Prince Juan was betrothed and then married to Marguerite of Austria, a Burgundian of considerable musical accomplishment and sophistication (and when I believe the Segovia manuscript was copied, with all its northern polyphony), and then from 1504 to 1512, when he travelled with Juana the Mad, spending a great deal of time in Flanders and singing in choirs with such figures as Alexander Agricola and Pierre de la Rue.[49]

So it would only make sense that Anchieta, with his unusual background and influential position, would prove to be a leader of whatever musical revolutions there might be in Spain between the late 1480s and the late 1510s. And so, I believe, he was; or at the very least, the present tour of Anchieta's works – aided by the Segovia manuscript, which allows us to divide his worklist into definitely early (i.e. in) and probably late (out) – makes it possible to trace a quasi-chronological development of his style into four broad phases, each a bit more influenced by northern trends and techniques than the last.

In the late 1480s Anchieta joined a musical world where the norm was a combination of a slow cantus firmus and a smoothed-over homophonic accompaniment, as we saw in so many of the anonymi of Colombina and Segovia; and in *Domine non secundum* he showed that he could produce that style flawlessly. From there, possibly under the influence of the northern pieces he was encountering in Segovia, he adopted a kind of composite style where the writing is still basically homophonic and there is still a cantus firmus, but in which bits of imitation, especially at the beginning, give a little Franco-Flemish cachet to the music without making the demands of serious polyphony on the Spanish ear or pen; *Conditor alme siderum* and the three-voice Magnificat are fair examples, and we saw a few others among the anonymous works of the previous chapter. *Libera me* also fits into this category, though written I believe a little later, in 1497.

In the third phase I would put the Marian mass movements, *Virgo et mater*, *Domine Jesu Christe*, and *O bone Jesu*. Here he takes the mixture of northern and native techniques to the next logical step by alternating more or less rigidly between

[49] Knighton, 'Music and Musicians', vol. I, pp. 251–3 and vol. II, p. 54 (*Música y músicos*, pp. 323–4 and 196); Duggan, 'Queen Joanna'.

full-texture imitation, voice pairs, and stark, declamatory homophonic passages. And finally, the three works, all of them substantial, written too late to get into Segovia show that Anchieta after the turn of the century was fully capable of the most sophisticated northern-style polyphony; the mass in Tarazona is every bit a worthy companion to the virtuosity of Peñalosa.

In short, no one in fifteenth-century Spain wrote in so many musical styles. (His four songs, incidentally, show a comparable variety.) Proving that Anchieta was a revolutionary and not merely a chameleon is quite a different matter, of course, but it may yet be worth raising two points in his favor. The first is that the dramatic motet style so often cited, by me among others, as hallmark and pinnacle of Peñalosa's works[50] is basically only a rhetorical intensification of what I have just called Anchieta's third phase, and that the older composer was writing the same sort of music half a decade before Peñalosa even appeared on the scene.

The other point is a simple statistic. Of the eleven pieces of Spanish church music in the Cancionero de la Colombina, only one appears in any later source; of the seventeen in Segovia s.s. not by Anchieta, also one. But of Anchieta's nine pieces in Segovia, seven were still fashionable enough to be copied into Tarazona 2/3 some thirty years later. Three of his Segovia-era works were included in Coimbra 12 when they were at least fifty years old, and *Libera me* – as we shall see in chapter 9 – remained in use for a very long time indeed. Anchieta seems to have been the first native Spanish composer to have passed the test of time in his own time, and the first whose music was well remembered after his death.

---

[50] See for example Kreitner, 'Peñalosa on Record', 311–12; also Hardie, 'Motets of Peñalosa'; Wolfgang Freis, 'Cristóbal de Morales and the Spanish Motet in the First Half of the Sixteenth Century: An Analytical Study of Selected Motets by Morales and Competitive Settings in SEV-BC 1 and TARAZ-C 2-3' (Ph.D. diss., University of Chicago, 1992), pp. 176–216; and Knighton, 'Peñalosa: New Works'.

8

Barcelona 454

For many years Barcelona 454 was the most baffling of the Spanish manuscripts from this era, the hardest to pin down and characterize cogently, the hardest to use as evidence for any piece's date, provenance, or authenticity.[1] It was known for some strange attributions (Peñalosa's motet *Sancta mater istud agas* is there given to Josquin[2]); for a series of mysterious but unhelpfully late dates, 1525–34, scattered through its pages; and for a fair amount of northern music presented in sometimes unreliable form.[3] It was a reasonably large source – at 190 folios, about the size of Segovia, or twice that of Colombina – but apparently a peripheral one.

Much was explained, however, in 1992 in the doctoral dissertation of Emilio Ros-Fábregas, whose painstaking detective work showed that Barcelona 454 is actually made up of three separate manuscripts that were more or less interrelated to begin with, were partially disassembled and reordered when they were bound together, and had more pieces added to them afterward.[4] It is still a confusing story, to be sure, but at least we seem to know it now, and it gives at least some useful chronological sense of the contents.

Ros-Fábregas divides Barcelona 454 into four sections, which he designates by chronological letters. He sees 454/C as the work of the main scribe of the manuscript and the person responsible for its compilation; he dates it between 1520 and 1525. Section 454/A probably originated outside Spain and received local additions in Catalonia in the first decade of the sixteenth century. Section 454/B has connections to both A and C, and Ros-Fábregas finds it impossible to say whether its date is closer to the one or to the other. And finally, the additions that he lumps together as 454/D

---

[1] Barcelona, Biblioteca de Catalunya, MS M 454 (*Census-Catalogue* BarcBC 454).

[2] M. Antonowycz and W. Elders, eds., *Werken van Josquin des Prés: Supplement* (Amsterdam, 1969), pp. xv–xvi and 41–4.

[3] See for example Richard Taruskin, 'Antoine Busnoys and the *L'Homme armé* Tradition', *Journal of the American Musicological Society* xxxix (1986), pp. 255–93, especially pp. 266–7 n. 24, where he says that 'Certain time signatures [of Busnoys's 'L'homme armé' mass] are more accurately transmitted in Barcelona, Biblioteca Central [*recte* Biblioteca de Catalunya by 1986], MS [*recte* M] 454, than in any Italian source (not surprising, since lines of source transmission between the Low Countries and Spain were often independent and direct), but the version is in other ways defective to the point of uselessness.'

[4] Emilio Ros-Fábregas, 'The Manuscript Barcelona, Biblioteca de Catalunya, M. 454: Study and Edition in the Context of the Iberian and Continental Manuscript Traditions' (Ph.D. diss., City University of New York, 1992); a revised version is in preparation for Edition Reichenberger in Kassel.

are also difficult to date but may be as late as the mid-1530s. Except for the original part of 454/A, he puts it all in Catalonia, probably Barcelona.[5]

Assuming that all of this is right – and little of it is likely to be challenged anytime soon – it is clearly 454/A, whose contents must predate 1510 or so, that is of the most interest to us. I remain cautiously interested in the contents 454/B too. We can take them in order, using Ros-Fábregas's inventory and edition as standard references.

Barcelona 454/A

Ros-Fábregas identifies the section he calls Barcelona 454/A as one main body, folios 73–138, and two separate bifolios later in the manuscript at folios 179, 180, [180 bis], and 181. It includes forty-seven pieces: in his inventory, numbers 23 through 58 (excluding 40, which is a later addition by one of the 454/B scribes) and 96 through 107. It is on a different kind of paper from the rest of the manuscript and it has a separate arabic foliation, showing clearly that it led an independent existence at one point.[6]

It is the work of some eighteen scribes, evidently in two different parts of the world. It began life in the Franco-Flemish area (or conceivably in Spain with northern scribes) as a beautiful book, with ornamental initials, of sacred music by northern composers, mostly Magnificats and Marian motets. Only a few of these are attributed, but from concordances we know they include works of Compère, Brumel, Josquin, and Weerbecke. But at some point after it reached Spain, local scribes added a good many pieces in various genres and styles. What had started out perhaps as a chapel manuscript dedicated to the Virgin, say for the use of a Marian confraternity, ended up as more of a potpourri, though actually most of the Spanish additions, even the songs, are sacred and many are still Marian. Ros-Fábregas believes this section reached its present form, apart from the division and the new foliation, in Barcelona between 1500 and 1510.[7]

So: of the forty-seven pieces in this section, we can remove nineteen that were written by the northern scribes or that can be attributed to northerners even if by Catalan scribes,[8] and sixteen that are fragmentary, monophonic, Castilian-texted, or textless;[9] this leaves twelve compositions putatively by Spaniards, all presumably from the fifteenth or very early sixteenth centuries. We have already seen *O bone Jesu* (handlist 53, Ros-Fábregas inventory no. 56) in Chapter 7, and Torre's *Ne recorderis* (handlist 50, RF 24) is best set aside for consideration in Chapter 9.

5   Ibid., especially vol. I, p. 88 and surrounding (for 454/C); pp. 97–100 (for 454/A); pp. 100–14 (for 454/B); and pp. 115–16 (for 454/D).
6   For a physical description of the manuscript, see ibid., vol. I, pp. 18–28. My folio references will be to the roman foliation that runs through the source as a whole.
7   Ibid., vol. I, pp. 97–100.
8   These include RF numbers 27, 29, 30–33, 37, 38, 49–55 (northern scribes; see ibid., vol. I, p. 21), plus 36 (by Agricola), 57 (by Brumel), and 58 (probably by Brumel: see pp. 258–63). I am also cutting number 35, an anonymous *In illo tempore* by a scribe not otherwise represented in the manuscript, but whose work has a distinctly northern appearance to my eye, as does the style of the piece. It is also damaged and would have to be omitted in any case.
9   These include RF numbers 39 and 107 (fragmentary); 96–97 (monophonic); 43–46, 98, and 100 (Castilian) and 48 and 102–5 (textless).

Kyrie . . . Qui passurus

Kyrie . . . Qui passurus (handlist 43, RF 101) is yet another polyphonic setting of the Kyries tenebrarum, like the examples we saw in Paris 967 and the Segovia manuscript. It is in three voices, MTB clefs, in black chant notation (but a hand Ros-Fábregas identifies as responsible for a number of Spanish pieces in 454/A[10]). Of the settings we have seen, it is structurally closest to the longer one in Segovia (handlist 42, above at Example 6.5): it sets the Kyrie and all three 'Qui' clauses, puts the tune (very close to Segovia's) into the top voice, and harmonizes them – as the notation makes necessary – very rigidly. As Example 8.1 shows, despite being presumably the latest of the Kyries tenebrarum to be written down, this is the most primitive of them all, and rather out of character for the rest of the manuscript.[11]

Ex. 8.1 *Kyrie . . . qui passurus*, sections 1–2

The fabordones

Barcelona 454/A opens with a short setting of **Donec ponam** (handlist 34, RF 23), the second verse of Psalm 109. It is written on the recto side of what was originally the guard sheet of the later-incorporated manuscript, by the same scribe as the first several Spanish pieces inside. On the previous verso (i.e. the other half of the opening but not part of the same original manuscript) is a setting of **Dixit Dominus** (handlist 29, RF 22) the first verse of the same psalm, but in one of the hands of 454/B.[12] They are very similar: in four voices, SATB for *Donec* and SAAB for *Dixit*, rigidly homophonic but for a little flourish at the cadences, with the monotone (mono-chord?) passages of the usual fabordón or falsobordone. Both are in the same mode,

---

[10] Ibid., vol. I, pp. 26–8 and 166.

[11] I am grateful to Dr. Ros-Fábregas for sending me a copy of this piece, which was inadvertently omitted from his dissertation and will soon be published.

[12] Ibid., vol. I, p. 140.

with the reciting tone on an F chord (A in the superius) and a D final.[13] Though falling into separate sections in Ros-Fábregas's scheme, they are clearly meant to go together, and I have no trouble thinking of them as roughly contemporaneous and from the fifteenth century – especially in view of the one fabordón in Colombina, already seen, and the six in Montecassino 871.[14]

Barcelona 454/A has one other such piece, a **textless fabordón** (handlist 67, RF 99) in SSAR clefs (but with very limited ranges), only six bars long. Actually it should probably be called half a fabordón, consisting of one recitation tone plus cadence rather than the usual structure of two half-verses. Presumably no text was given because none was needed for a formula of this kind; even when a fabordón has text given, there is a clear implication, as with psalm tones in chant sources, that it is just a sample. In fact, 454/B has an even more striking case: a group of nine textless fabordones (RF 66–74), in order of mode, with two for mode 1. Possibly these were written (if *written* is even the right word) in the fifteenth century too, though the uncertain but late date of the section, their anonymity, the level of sophistication shown by the mere existence of the clump, and the strength of the tradition into the later sixteenth century all enforce caution.[15]

The glory days of the falsobordone were ahead, and in Italy;[16] these early hispanic specimens attract little musical attention today. But Barcelona 454 at any rate shows that the tradition was strong in Spain at this point – stronger, arguably, than anywhere else in the world. And it is well to remember that, whether in written, memorized, or improvised form, the fabordón may have been the one kind of polyphony most likely to be heard in the urban cathedral service and the style of sacred polyphony most familiar to Spanish churchgoers of every class and station around 1500.

Four anonymi

Three consecutive items of Spanish church music in Barcelona 454/A, numbers 24–26 in the inventory, also appear, in the same order and very similar musical readings, in 454/B as numbers 17–19.[17] This would seem to indicate that at some point the two manuscripts, still circulating separately, were in the same place but were not yet intended to be bound together, so that somebody thought it was worthwhile to copy from the one into the other (probably, but perhaps not necessarily, from A into B[18]). The first of these pieces is Torre's *Ne recorderis*, which we are still saving for later.

---

[13] Compare, for example, the very first Psalm tone in the *Liber Usualis*, p. 128, also on 'Dixit Dominus'.

[14] Isabel Pope and Masakata Kanazawa, eds., *The Music Manuscript Montecassino 871: A Neapolitan Repertory of Sacred and Secular Music of the Late Fifteenth Century* (Oxford, 1978), numbers 7 (by the Spaniard Oriola) and 30–4; see also the commentaries on pp. 32–3, 561–2, and 581–5. See also n. 16 below.

[15] This caution applies even more strongly to three fabordones added still later: RF numbers 87, 93, and 112.

[16] See for example Murray C. Bradshaw, *The Falsobordone: A Study in Renaissance and Baroque Music*, Musicological Studies and Documents XXXIV (n.p., 1978); Bradshaw discusses the Barcelona pieces, among others of the era in Colombina and Montecassino, on pp. 19–39 passim.

[17] Ros-Fábregas, 'Manuscript Barcelona', vol. I, pp. 271–4 and vol. II, pp. 147–53. There are some differences in texting policy between the two versions.

[18] Ibid., vol. I, p. 274 and vol. II, p. 153.

The second is **Alleluia. Dies sanctificatus** (handlist 15, RF 25 [and 18]), a three-voice setting, MTT clefs, of the Alleluia and verse text currently used at mass on Christmas.[19] The tenor uses a tune that appears, with a few variants, in quite a number of Alleluias-and-verses in the *Liber Usualis* today, though never with this text.[20] The chant tune is put into more or less steady breves, and the outer voices are more active but still serve basically to underline the harmonic structure rather than to give a sense of counterpoint. The opening (which is actually a little fancier than the verse portion), Example 8.2, may give a fair idea: it is very much at home with what I have called the archetypal Segovia style – further evidence, perhaps, of the centrality of this style in all parts of fifteenth-century Spain.

Ex. 8.2 *Alleluia. Dies sanctificatus*, bb. 1–12

At the bottom of the same page is a **Benedicamus Domino** (handlist 25, RF 26 [and 19]), in four voices, SSAR clefs. Its superius, all in breves but the second and third notes, uses the same Benedicamus tune, from Gregorian Mass IV,[21] that we have seen in settings from Colombina and Paris 4379 (see above, pp. 45–6 and 55), and the other voices harmonize it simply, with just one unusual feature: the altus is consistently higher than the superius.[22]

Ex. 8.3 *Benedicamus Domino*, bb. 1–9

19 *Liber Usualis*, pp. 409–10.
20 See for example *Liber Usualis*, pp. 320, 394, 490, 805, 848, 1218, 1289, and 1323.
21 *Liber Usualis*, p. 28.
22 Ros-Fábregas's edition ('Manuscript Barcelona', vol. II, pp. 152–3) is taken from 454/B, where

The other two anonymi in this section of the manuscript (RF 41–42) also appear together, though on adjacent openings rather than the same page. They are settings of the Pentecost hymn *Veni creator Spiritus*,[23] in three voices, SAT clefs, and may have been meant to be used together in an alternatim performance as I have already suggested for some other hymn pairs.

The opening of the second (Example 8.4) shows how different they are from the Alleluia and Benedicamus. The bottom line may or may not be intended to function as a cantus firmus (it moves slower here at the beginning, but not always, and does seem to paraphrase the chant tune, but again not always), and the other voices use the tune for a point of imitation that leads into some very vigorous counterpoint. This is like nothing we have seen before, not even the other hymns, which, though perhaps more active than other genres, have still maintained a clear and steady cantus firmus. Moreover, these are the only specimens in the whole manuscript of this hand,[24] which is very legible and distinct and contrasts dark and light strokes in a way more like the northern hands than those that copied known Spanish music. I believe, then, that these two hymn settings either were part of the original northern corpus of 454/A or represent a late Spanish addition, but are in any case not from fifteenth-century Spain.

Ex. 8.4 *Veni creator Spiritus*, bb. 1–9

Alonso de Mondéjar

Four pieces in Barcelona 454/A, all in the same hand, are attributed to Alonso de Mondéjar: *Ave verum/Ave sanctissimum* (RF 28, attributed to Diaz in Tarazona 2/3[25]), a three-voice Magnificat (RF 47), a fourteen-bar textless work (RF 48), and a sacred

this highest-pitched part is labelled 'tenor'; he therefore puts it on the third stave down. In 454/A there are no such markings, so my edition reorders them top to bottom as they are in the source.

23 *Liber Usualis*, p. 885.
24 Ros-Fábregas, 'Manuscript Barcelona', vol. I, p. 27.
25 Ibid., vol. I, pp. 256–8, which also discusses the apparent dual texting in 454/A. The work is anonymous in Coimbra manuscripts 12, 32, and 48; see also Owen Rees, *Polyphony in Portugal c.*

song, *Camino de Santiago* (RF 106). They are joined by eleven songs in the Cancionero de Palacio and one more motet, *Ave rex noster* (AB 203), in the last, undated section of the Segovia manuscript (along with Urrede's *Pange lingua* [S] and a fragment of Torre's *Ne recorderis*).[26]

Mondéjar would thus add a Magnificat and two reasonably substantial motets to our list. The problem is the composer himself: Mondéjar entered the Castilian royal chapel in August of 1502, served there till Isabella's death in 1504, and then moved to the Aragonese court until Ferdinand's death in 1516; we know nothing of his whereabouts before or after.[27] His known dates, in other words, begin four years after Peñalosa's known dates, and the absence of any of his works from the manuscripts before 1500 – all eleven Palacio songs are in a layer copied around 1515[28] – seems to mean that the pieces in Segovia and 454/A are the product of the first years of the sixteenth century, not the fifteenth.

Juan Illario

More or less the opposite case can be made for Juan Illario. To him there is only one known, or rather supposed, contemporary reference: Cristóbal de Escobar cited 'Iohannes Illarius' as an authority in his eight-page *Introduction muy breve de canto llano,* published in Salamanca in the mid-to late 1490s.[29] This is not much to go on, but if Escobar's Illarius, evidently the author of a now-lost treatise is the same person as Illario the composer (whose first name we do not otherwise know), it would show at least that he was in his maturity in the nineties, which in turn suggests that his one piece in Barcelona 454/A could well have been written before 1500.

In Barcelona 454, **O admirabile commercium** (handlist 52, RF 34) is in MATB clefs with only incipits of text; as reconstructed from concordances, the full text begins

1530–c. 1620: Sources from the Monastery of Santa Cruz, Coimbra (New York, 1995), p. 418, and Pedro Calahorra, 'Compositores hispanos en el ms. 2/3 de la Catedral de Tarazona: Copias y variantes', *Fuentes musicales en la península ibérica (ca. 1250–ca. 1550),* ed. Maricarmen Gómez and Màrius Bernadó (Lleida, 2001), pp. 177–201, especially 194–6. On Diaz's identity, see Tessa Wendy Knighton, 'Music and Musicians at the Court of Fernando of Aragon 1474–1516' (Ph.D. diss., Cambridge University, 1983), vol. I, pp. 263–4 (later translated as Tess Knighton, *Música y músicos en la Corte de Fernando el Católico 1474–1516,* trans. Luis Gago [Zaragoza, 2001], p. 328); Knighton identifies the composer as Pedro Diaz de Aux, who served the Aragonese court from 1484 to 1513, though admittedly the name is a common one. See also *DMEH,* s.v. 'Diaz (I)', by Tess Knighton.

26   Robert Stevenson, *Spanish Music in the Age of Columbus* (The Hague, 1960), p. 183; *New Grove* 1980, s.v. 'Mondéjar, Alonso', by Isabel Pope; *New Grove* 2001, s.v. 'Mondéjar, Alonso de', by Tess Knighton. Stevenson also says that Mondéjar is responsible for three Magnificats, where the *New Grove* articles rightly find only one; Pope calls the textless work a motet, and Knighton a villancico.

27   Knighton, 'Music and Musicians', vol. I, p. 285 (*Música y músicos,* p. 338), adds to the documents known to Stevenson and Pope.

28   José Romeu Figueras, *La Música en la Corte de los Reyes Católicos IV: Cancionero Musical de Palacio (siglos XV–XVI),* MME XIV (Barcelona, 1965), pp. 19–20; Mondéjar's compositions are numbers 134, 164, 230, 237, 256, 261, 280, 294, 299, 349, and 373 in Palacio.

29   Johannes Wolf, 'Der Choraltraktat des Christoual de Escobar', in *Gedenkboek aangeboden aan D. D.F. Scheurleer op zijn 70sten verjaardag* (The Hague, 1925), pp. 383–91, especially p. 388; see also Stevenson, *Spanish Music,* pp. 83–5.

(Example 8.5) with that of an antiphon for the feast of the Circumcision[30] but continues with apparently artificial texts also appropriate to the Christmas season.[31] Despite the present-day obscurity of its composer, *O admirabile* was quite a well-known piece, appearing, with substantial variations of text and pitch level, in Tarazona 2/3, four Portuguese sources, and two Guatemalan.[32] And the reasons for its popularity are not hard to spy: the piece has some fairly sophisticated counterpoint, but mostly it seems to be animated by a spirit of fun, with lively triple-meter sections and a snappy – I struggle not to use the word *cute* – triadic opening.

Ex. 8.5 Illario, *O admirabile commercium* (Barcelona reading), bb. 1–9

Only one other piece survives under Illario's name: *Conceptio tua*, a Marian motet preserved only in Tarazona 2/3 and recently edited by Pedro Calahorra.[33] Strictly speaking, perhaps it should be in the handlist, as its composer is documented – assuming the Escobar reference is really to him – only in the fifteenth century. But its

30 *Liber Usualis*, pp. 442–3.
31 Ros-Fábregas, in 'Manuscript Barcelona', vol. II, pp. 216–22, edits the piece with full text; for variants of text in different sources, see also Rees, *Polyphony in Portugal*, pp. 421–4.
32 Ibid.; see also Ros-Fábregas, 'Manuscript Barcelona', vol. I, pp. 144–5 and 278–9, and Calahorra, 'Compositores hispanos', pp. 196–7. In Tarazona, the piece is in SAAR clefs and its pitch is a fourth higher than in Barcelona; the higher pitch seems to be the standard in the later manuscripts. Rees, noting some important rhythmic differences and impossibilities of underlay in the sources, suggests that the piece may have been transmitted instrumentally, which might account for the change of pitch level as well.
33 Pedro Calahorra, ed., *Autores hispanos de los siglos XV–XVI de los MS. 2 y 5 de la catedral de Tarazona*, Polifonía Aragonesa IX (Zaragoza, 1995), pp. 127–32.

humanistic text, thoroughly imitative counterpoint, and late transmission all seem to point toward a sixteenth-century origin. And even if Johannes Illarius is the same as the composer, there is of course no reason why he could not have been about Anchieta's age and remained productive into the 1510s and 1520s – or for that matter been a foreigner with a name Latinized in the treatise and hispanized in the musical sources.[34]

Barcelona 454/B

We have already had a number of occasions to dip into Barcelona 454/B – in fact, we have given our attention to just over half of its twenty-nine compositions.[35] Here is Urrede's *Pange lingua* [T], in possibly its oldest surviving source; here is the plenary mass containing Anchieta's Marian Kyrie and Gloria; here is the *Dixit Dominus* fabordón that goes with the first piece in 454/A; here is the clump of nine fabordones that I regretfully rejected earlier in this chapter; here are the three pieces recopied from 454/A before the two were bound together.

The problem is that it has proven difficult to assign a precise date to 454/B. Ros-Fábregas shows that it was originally an independent manuscript, of Spanish (probably Catalan) origin despite containing works by Ockeghem, Busnoys, and 'Benito', who may be Brumel. It has clear connections to 454/A – as we have seen, several pieces seem to have been copied directly from one to the other – but it also shares its paper type with 454/C, which he dates 1520–25. Ros-Fábregas's hypothesis is that this section was begun around the time Philip the Fair first came to Barcelona in 1503, and that the manuscript as a whole was assembled and completed around 1519, when Charles V visited the city.[36]

This makes 454/B risky for our present chronological purpose: the presence of a piece in this section just doesn't say much about its date. On the other hand, it definitely contains some fairly old repertory – witness Ockeghem, Busnoys, Urrede, the Anchieta movements, the three pieces copied from 454/A, and a song by Lope de Baena, who probably died around 1506[37] – and it may not be unreasonable to browse its anonymi for further possible antiques.

On folios 148v–151v, a single hand has copied a group of four hymns, all in four voices and all anonymous. The first we recognize from concordances as Urrede's

---

[34] See Sydney R. Charles, 'Hillary-Hyllayre: How Many Composers?' *Music and Letters* lv (1974), pp. 61–9; *New Grove* 1980, s.v. 'Hilaire Daleo', by Joshua Rifkin; and *New Grove* 2001, s.v. 'Hylaire', by Jeffrey Dean. Both *New Grove* articles reject their composer(s) as author of these Spanish pieces.

[35] The section, as Ros-Fábregas defines it, is much scattered and interrupted: see his short inventory in 'Manuscript Barcelona', vol. I, pp. 36–8. I omit from consideration the later insertions by scribes K1 and K2.

[36] Ibid., vol. I, pp. 29–38, 110–14, et passim; on the Benito problem, see especially pp. 258–63 and Emilio Ros-Fábregas, 'Phantom Attributions or New Works by Antoine Brumel in an Iberian Manuscript', *Encomium Musicæ: Essays in Memory of Robert Snow*, ed. David Crawford and G. Grayson Wagstaff (Hillsdale, 2002), pp. 259–67.

[37] The song is RF 64, *Amor pues tú nos das plazer*; on Lope de Baena's biography, see *New Grove* 1980, s.v. 'Baena, Lope de', by Isabel Pope; Knighton, 'Music and Musicians', vol. I, p. 255 (*Música y músicos*, p. 325); and *New Grove* 2001, s.v. 'Baena, Lope de', by Isabel Pope and Tess Knighton.

Pange lingua [T] (handlist 57, RF 75), for Corpus Christi; the second is *Ut queant laxis* (RF 76, also appearing in a later layer as RF 5), for the feast of the Nativity of John the Baptist;[38] the third is *Exultet cælum laudibus* (RF 77), probably for the Common of Apostles;[39] and the fourth is *Sacris solemniis* (RF 79; RF 78 is a later interpolation), also for Corpus Christi.[40] These are followed by a fifth hymn, another *Sacris solemniis* setting (RF 80), in a later hand.[41]

These four, later five hymns are significant for several reasons. They seem to be an early testimony to the growth of polyphonic hymn production and hymn conscious-ness in early sixteenth-century Spain: the hymns we have seen in previous sources have been relatively few and have been scattered either through the manuscript (as in Colombina) or among the motets (as in Segovia), but here we may detect an early analogue to the group of twenty hymns, in church-year order, that begins Tarazona 2/3. Bruno Turner has noticed especially the two *Sacris solemniis* settings, the first fancy and the second very plain indeed, a completely homophonic harmonization of the metrical chant, and proposed that they may have placed together for use in an alternatim scheme[42] – a sentiment with which I would agree, adding only that we don't know exactly when the second one was added and thus when the connection was made.

But the intriguing hymn to me is RF 79, the first *Sacris solemniis*, the last of the orig-inal group. Numbers 76 and 77 are both in duple meter and neither has a clearly distinguished cantus firmus; but 79 is in triple meter, with a slow-moving cantus firmus in the tenor and sophisticated non-imitative polyphony in the other voices. Its style is, in other words, much like that of Urrede's *Pange lingua*, which in turn raises the question of whether these two Corpus Christi hymn settings may have travelled together, even whether Urrede might be responsible for both. Without further evidence this must remain a speculation, and I have chosen not to add this hymn to the handlist of fifteenth-century music; but it points up the fundamental difficulty of dealing with these hymn settings in a chronological scheme. Here among just five, clearly meant as a group by somebody, we have a plain chant harmonization, two tenor-cantus-firmus constructions, and two loose paraphrases or free text settings; Urrede's piece probably dates from the 1470s, and the second *Sacris solemniis* may well be fifty years younger.

Finally there is the case of the anonymous **Ave sanctissima Maria**, which appears

[38] *Liber Usualis*, pp. 1504–5; this tune is not used in the Barcelona 454 setting, nor Alva's setting in Tarazona 2/3 (see Rudolf Gerber, ed., *Spanisches Hymnar um 1500*, Das Chorwerk LX [Wolfenbüttel, 1957], pp. 22–4), nor is there an obvious connection between the Spanish pieces till the last phrase.

[39] Ros-Fábregas, 'Manuscript Barcelona', vol. I, p. 77. The text to the hymn as in Barcelona (edited in ibid., vol. II, pp. 331–2) is found in *Antiphonale Monasticum*, pp. 257 (John the Apostle) and 624 (common of Apostles); the corresponding hymns in the *Liber Usualis* (pp. 425–6, 1115–17) have similar but not identical texts. None of the Vatican tunes corresponds to the Barcelona setting.

[40] *Liber Usualis*, pp. 920–2; again, this is not the tune used in Barcelona 454. The Barcelona setting is based on a local Spanish tune, often presented metrically in the sources: see Bruno Turner, 'Spanish Liturgical Hymns: A Matter of Time', *Early Music* xxiii (1995), pp. 473–82, especially p. 476. The Spanish tune is the one used by Peñalosa in Tarazona 2/3: see ibid. and Gerber, *Spanisches Hymnar*, pp. 19–21.

[41] The hand is that of Scribe C, the compiler of the manuscript as a whole; see Ros-Fábregas, 'Manu-script Barcelona', vol. I, p. 38.

[42] Turner, 'Spanish Liturgical Hymns', p. 479.

twice in Barcelona 454 – first (handlist 19, RF 40) in three voices, MTR clefs, within the pages of 454/A but in one of the hands of 454/B; and then (RF 62) in 454/B, in the same hand but in four voices, with an added altus in alto clef.[43] And this altus may stand as a convenient emblem for this manuscript and its era. In the European main-stream around 1500, new alto lines, often marked 'si placet' or the equivalent to indicate their optional nature, were being added to old three-voice works in an apparent effort to update them for new tastes; there are, for example, nine examples, five labelled as such, in Petrucci's *Odhecaton*.[44] Clearly something of the sort is happening here: whether this scribe entered the piece into two separate manuscripts before they were bound together or twice into the same manuscript afterward, the versions obviously had separate, or separable, identities.

And a look at the first nine bars (Example 8.6[45]) will reveal the motivation behind the new voice: the three-voice version is straightforward three-voice smoothed-over homophony, with usually two voices but seldom all three moving together at any given moment, as we have seen so many times in the fifteenth-century manuscripts; the new voice, however, conceals that structure by moving quite a bit faster, weaving above and below the tenor, playing syncopations against the other three. The change may be structurally superficial, but sound of the two is completely different – the difference, I submit, between the fifteenth century and the sixteenth.[46]

The Story So Far

Barcelona 454's complex structure and late overall date mean that it has to be used cautiously in a chronological scheme like this. It doesn't add anything very dramatic to our narrative because it can't: any piece that seriously challenges the view laid out by Colombina and Segovia falls under automatic suspicion of being late, foreign, or both.

But it does have quite a bit of music, and it adds a fair number of pieces to this investigation. Barcelona 454/A has forty-seven compositions altogether: about a third of them (at least) were already there when it was brought down from the north, and among the rest, probably added in Catalonia between 1500 and 1510, I count eight pieces of church music that seem to be from fifteenth-century Spain.[47] Barcelona

---

43 Ros-Fábregas, 'Manuscript Barcelona', vol. I, pp. 147 and 155, with an edition of the four-part version in vol. II, pp. 296–300.

44 Helen Hewitt, with Isabel Pope, eds., *Petrucci: Harmonice Musices Odhecaton A* (Cambridge, 1942), pp. 58–9, 83–6; Hewitt counts five pieces (8, 9, 12, 13, and 20) with *si placet* parts labelled, three (2, 4, and 27) known from concordances, and one (93) recognized from internal evidence. See also, for example, Stephen Self, ed., *The* Si placet *Repertoire of 1480–1530*, Recent Researches in the Music of the Renaissance CVI (Madison, 1996).

45 Edited after Ros-Fábregas, 'Manuscript Barcelona', vol. II, p. 296, which represents only the four-voice, text-incipits-only version (and adds text from another setting elsewhere in the manuscript). The three-voice version has complete text in the tenor and partial text in the superius and some minor differences of rhythm that may imply a different conception of text underlay.

46 Bonnie Blackburn, in 'The Virgin in the Sun: Music and Image for a Prayer Attributed to Sixtus IV', *Journal of the Royal Musical Association* cxxiv (1999), pp. 157–95, remarks (p. 161) that the four-voice version 'is repetitive and depends to a large extent on parallel tenths between the outer voices; the *si placet* voice, as often, thickens the texture but does not improve the piece'.

47 RF numbers 23–26, 34, 56, 99, 101.

Ex. 8.6 *Ave sanctissima Maria,* four-voice version, bb. 1–9

454/B is smaller, twenty-nine pieces, and because some of it may be as late as 1520, I have cautiously identified only five pieces as representing our repertory.[48] The rest of the manuscript is just too late to be much help without other circumstantial evidence.

Among these thirteen compositions (and remember that several of them were introduced in previous chapters and have not been discussed in detail here) we see the usual genres: mass ordinary movements, mass propers, responsories, psalms, hymns, and a few motets on newly written, often Marian texts. We see also the familiar apparent indifference to composers' names; of our thirteen, only two are attributed in Barcelona 454 – *O admirabile commercium* correctly to Illario and *O bone Jesu,* in a later hand and probably wrongly, to Peñalosa. In *Kyrie . . . Qui passurus* and in the fabordones we see the survival of some fairly primitive musical styles, and in the two versions of *Ave sanctissima Maria* we see a corresponding effort to keep abreast of current fashion. And in the northern repertory we can see the fascination Catalan musicians had with the northern mainstream and even its history: Busnoys's *L'homme armé* mass was probably almost sixty years old when it was copied into 454/B.[49]

Indeed, it may be the very normality of the early layers of Barcelona 454 that is their

---

48 RF numbers 9[b], 9[c], 22, 40, and 75; this would of course go up dramatically if we admitted the nine fabordones, RF 66–74.

49 On the date of the Busnoys mass, see Taruskin, 'Antoine Busnoys', especially pp. 257–65 and 288; on its copying in 454/B, see Ros-Fábregas, 'Manuscript Barcelona', vol. I, pp. 109–14, and idem, 'Music and Ceremony during Charles V's 1519 Visit to Barcelona', *Early Music* xxxiii (1995), pp. 374–91.

most important contribution here. As a sometime resident of Catalonia I have become sensitive to the Catalan people's sense of identity, to the mild but palpable offense that can be caused by the careless use of the adjective *Spanish*. Some of this is Franco's work, of course, and should not be allowed to obscure the situation at the end of the middle ages even if it causes my hands to hesitate over the computer keyboard from time to time. Yet it is also true that Catalonia was a separable world even then, with its own linguistic and cultural ties above the Pyrenees. So we might reasonably expect the repertory of a Barcelona manuscript to be quite distinct from that of sources from Seville or Toledo or the Castilian court. But the lesson of Barcelona 454 seems to be the opposite: this source seems, for all its complications, to be part of the same general story, and Barcelona appears in this case to be part of Spain.

9

Tarazona 2/3

It has been hard to know what to do about Tarazona 2/3. It is the largest surviving source of Spanish church music from the time of Ferdinand and Isabella, and for everyone interested in such music it has always been at the center of things. On the other hand, for the present purpose it is disturbingly late; it has never been dated securely, but to the best of my knowledge nobody has ever even hesitantly placed it before 1520, and the prominence of Peñalosa in its contents puts the manuscript also at the center, in effect, of what I have been trying to avoid.

Then again, avoiding it has proven impossible. Already we have seen something over a dozen pieces, from the Urrede *Pange lingua*, written possibly in the 1470s, to a fair number of works by Anchieta and others copied into the Segovia manuscript in the mid-1490s, that found their way into Tarazona 2/3 some decades later. And if 2/3 contains this many provable antiques, it stands to reason that it has others that are harder to spot. They are the subject of this chapter, in which I mean to be stern: tempting as it is to troll the later sources for music that *sounds* like the fifteenth century, it is important to avoid the risk of circularity – of drawing stylistic conclusions from a repertory chosen partly on stylistic grounds – as much as possible. So I shall focus on pieces whose early origins are suggested by external evidence.

Tarazona 2/3

Tarazona 2/3, as I shall call it, began its life as a large volume of some 300 folios which was divided in two (2 and 3, the outer and inner portions) for convenience in the late sixteenth century and remained so until a restoration in 2003; all the existing scholarship thus treats it as two separate sources.[1] It originally had 119, or possibly 118

---

[1] The two halves were called Tarazona, Archivo Capitular de la Catedral, MSS 2 and 3 (*Census-Catalogue*, TarazC 2 and TarazC 3). For some recent descriptions of the manuscript and discussions of its origin, see Jane Morlet Hardie, 'The Motets of Francisco de Peñalosa and their Manuscript Sources' (Ph.D. diss., University of Michigan, 1983), pp. 42–52; Tessa Wendy Knighton, 'Music and Musicians at the Court of Fernando of Aragon, 1474–1516' (Ph.D. diss., Cambridge University, 1983), vol. I, pp. 137–44 (later translated as Tess Knighton, *Música y músicos en la Corte de Fernando el Católico 1474–1516*, trans. Luis Gago [Zaragoza, 2001], pp. 117–21); Emilio Ros-Fábregas, 'The Manuscript Barcelona, Biblioteca de Catalunya, M. 454: Study and Edition in the context of the Iberian and Continental Manuscript Traditions' (Ph.D. diss., City University of New York, 1992), vol. I, pp. 237–44; Wolfgang Freis, 'Cristóbal de Morales and the Spanish Motet in the First Half of the Sixteenth Century: An Analytical Study of

compositions, of which almost all are attributed, and all but a few of the attributions are to certain or probable Iberians.[2]

It is all in one hand, neat and beautiful though not particularly ornamental; evidently it was meant to be used, and the early rebinding shows that used it was. It is carefully planned and executed; the contents are put into meticulous order, and that order is made explicit by a tabla at the beginning, which groups the contents under a system of headings:[3]

Hymnos	20 pieces, in church-year order
Magnificas a tres	3 pieces
Magnificas a quatro	12 pieces
Asperges	4 pieces
Missas a tres	3 pieces
Missas a quatro	14 pieces, ending with the Escobar Requiem
Responsos pro defunctis	2 pieces
Salves	2 pieces
All[elui]as a tres boses	9 pieces, in church-year order
Motetes a tres	9 pieces
Motetes a quatro	35 pieces
Lamentationes a quatro	4 pieces
Deo gracias	1 or 2 pieces

The dominant composer of Tarazona 2/3 by far is Francisco de Peñalosa: Peñalosa is responsible for six of the seventeen masses and part of one other, six of the fifteen Magnificats, three of the four Lamentations, and so on – and the manuscript is for him nearly a sacred Opera Omnia. But it contains significant numbers of works by his most important contemporaries Juan de Anchieta, Pedro de Escobar, and Alonso de Alba, plus a smattering of compositions by evident one-shot wonders, and in general

---

Selected Motets by Morales and Competitive Settings in SEV-BC 1 and TARAZ-C 2-3' (Ph.D. diss., University of Chicago, 1992), pp. 22–5; Kenneth Kreitner, 'Franco-Flemish Elements in Tarazona 2 and 3', *Revista de Musicología* xvi (1993), pp. 2567–86; Pedro Calahorra, 'Compositores hispanos en el ms. 2/3 de la Catedral de Tarazona: Copias y variantes', *Fuentes musicales en la Península Ibérica (ca. 1250–ca. 1550)*, ed. Maricarmen Gómez and Màrius Bernadó (Lleida, 2001), pp. 177–201, and Roberta Freund [Schwartz], 'Tarazona 2/3 y Sevilla 5-5-20: Una consideración de conexiones', in ibid., pp. 203–17.

2   Most published inventories of Tarazona 2/3, including mine, count 119 pieces, but there is an element of potential confusion. Briefly: the last three items in the tabla that opens the manuscript are [a] 'Deo gracias . . . ccc', in the large print used for genre-headings (though the headings do not otherwise include folio numbers); [b] 'Deo gracias all[eliui]a . . . ccc' in the small print used for titles; and [c] the pious tagline 'Laus Deo'. At the end of the manuscript, folio 299v has [x] an anonymous *Deo gratias* setting, with no alleluia, and folio 300 is missing. Hitherto it has been supposed that [a] refers to [x], and [b] to a missing [y] on a now lost folio 300; but it is equally plausible that [a] is a heading with a folio number added by mistake, [b] refers to [x], and there was never a [y].

   A Magnificat by 'Villa' and parts of the two adjoining pieces are now gone from the manuscript, but the missing folios have recently been found at the Biblioteca de Catalunya; see Ros-Fábregas, 'Manuscript Barcelona', vol. I, p. 237 n. 170.

3   The tabla has been published in full in at several places. The most accessible is probably Higinio Anglés, *La música en la Corte de los Reyes Católicos, I: Polifonía religiosa*, MME I (Barcelona, 1941), pp. 122–3; this has a few important errors, however, and a better transcription is in Pedro Calahorra, ed., *Autores hispanos de los siglos XV–XVI de los MS. 2 y 5 de la Catedral de Tarazona*, Polifonía Aragonesa IX (Zaragoza, 1995), pp. 17–21; see also ibid., 'Compositores hispanos', pp. 180–5.

its attributions have carried a good deal of authority with modern scholars.[4] In short, Tarazona 2/3 is our main source, not only of data but of insight on what the Spanish sacred music of this era was like and how it all fit together.

It would be good to know where and especially when the manuscript was assembled; but we don't. Paper studies have so far proven inconclusive; its reliance on liturgical works means there are few if any individual pieces that can be readily dated to use as signposts; its elaborate structure and uniform preparation means that we cannot separate layers of copying; and the lack of biographical information on the manuscript's minor and potentially late composers like Antonio de Ribera, 'Marleth', and 'Rº Morales' makes it impossible to establish even a *terminus post quem*. All the studies cited in note 1 above try to come up with some sort of date, and all admit in the end a degree of frustration.[5] At the moment, possibly the best that can be said is that Tarazona 2/3 contains so much of Peñalosa's sacred music that it must have been collected, at the earliest, toward the end of his career; he died in 1528. My own somewhat intuitive sense is that it was compiled after his death and that it represents a kind of retrospective of an era more or less recently past. I tend, admittedly without any hard evidence, to think of it as being from the mid- to late 1530s, perhaps around the time of the death of Escobar.[6]

Obviously the inclusion of any particular piece in Tarazona 2/3 is not much of a clue to its date. So we must walk cautiously. I have little doubt that there is a fair amount of fifteenth-century music yet to be found within this source, but in this chapter we shall look at only the six compositions for which I think a strong circumstantial case can be made. Three can be tied to events of late 1497, and three more are the work of composers whose known careers did not extend much after 1500.

Funeral Music for Prince Juan

'Thus,' says [Peter] Martyr, who had the melancholy satisfaction of rendering the last sad offices to his royal pupil, 'was laid low the hope of all Spain.' 'Never was there a death,' says another chronicler, 'which occasioned such deep and general lamentation throughout the land.' All the unavailing honors which affection could devise were paid to his memory. His funeral obsequies were celebrated with melancholy splendor, and his remains deposited in the noble Dominican monastery of St. Thomas at Avila, which had been erected by his parents. The court put on a new and deeper mourning than that hitherto used, as if to testify their unwonted grief. All offices, public and private, were closed for forty days; and sable-colored banners were suspended from the walls and portals of the cities. Such extraordinary tokens

---

[4] Several of these conflicts are discussed in ibid.; for my own essay here, see Kenneth Kreitner, '*Ave festiva ferculis* and Josquin's Spanish Reputation', *Journal of the Royal Musical Association* cxxviii (2003), pp. 1–29.

[5] But see especially Ros-Fábregas's dissertation, which takes a fresh look at some old controversies; his study is perhaps the most influential on me.

[6] Ros-Fábregas, in 'Manuscript Barcelona', vol. I, p. 244, even suggests the 1540s or 1550s as a possibility, but tends to favor 1521–28, the years of Peñalosa's final residence in Seville. He has since kindly written me of the possibility that what we now call 2/3 were copied later in the century from an earlier exemplar, possibly connected with Peñalosa.

of public sorrow bear strong testimony to the interest felt in the young prince, independently of his exalted station . . .[7]

No one in the century and a half since has put it into English better than William Prescott: the death of Prince Juan in 1497 was a dreadful thing, and the national mourning for the young prince was of heroic proportions.

Prince Juan has already figured in this narrative as an amateur musician, the employer and pupil of Anchieta, and the possible original owner of the Segovia manuscript. But he was also the keystone of Ferdinand and Isabella's dynastic aspirations: the Catholic Monarchs had one son and four daughters, and the plan was thus for him to inherit the thrones of both Aragón and Castile upon their deaths. Juan was well prepared for, and from all accounts well suited to, such a responsibility, and when he died of plague in October 1497 at nineteen and newly married, his parents and the two nations took it very hard indeed. As Prescott says, a long and intense period of mourning was declared, and memorial obsequies were held all over the peninsula.[8] It was an occasion like none before, and while we don't know for sure that there was polyphonic music at Prince Juan's funeral, it does seem like the right sort of occasion.

And just the right sort of music still exists. Toward the middle of Tarazona 2/3, at the end of the section of 'Missas a quatro', is a Requiem mass by Pedro de Escobar, the oldest such piece in the Spanish orbit; and after that, two 'Responsos pro defunctis': a setting of *Ne recorderis* attributed to Francisco de la Torre and one of *Libera me* by Anchieta. The suggestion that at least some of these were written for the funeral of Prince Juan has been made by Tess Knighton and Grayson Wagstaff,[9] and for a variety of reasons I am inclined to agree. We can return to those reasons after a look at the music.

Escobar's **Missa pro Defunctis** or **Requiem** (handlist 7) is by far the most substantial of these pieces, though apparently not the longest-lived: it survives only in Tarazona 2/3.[10] Escobar sets the introit, Kyrie, gradual, tract, offertory, Sanctus, Agnus Dei, and communion from the Mass for the Dead, all in four voices except the tract, which is in two, then three. The clefs vary from movement to movement but tend to overdramatize some narrow ranges; all but the Kyrie could have been accommodated within MTTB.[11]

In a detailed discussion of the Requiem, Wagstaff has pointed out its most

7   William H. Prescott, *History of the Reign of Ferdinand and Isabella, The Catholic* (New York, 1845), pp. 358–9, documentation omitted.

8   For the services in Barcelona, for example, see Kenneth Kreitner, 'Music and Civic Ceremony in Late-Fifteenth-Century Barcelona' (Ph.D. diss., Duke University, 1990), p. 380.

9   Knighton, 'Music and Musicians', vol. I, pp. 177–8 (*Música y músicos*, pp. 140–1); idem, 'Escobar's Requiem' (recording review), *Early Music* xxvii (1999), pp. 142–4; and George Grayson Wagstaff, 'Music for the Dead: Polyphonic Settings of the *Officium* and *Missa pro defunctis* by Spanish and Latin American Composers before 1630' (Ph.D. diss., University of Texas, 1995), pp. 195–7. Both make other suggestions too, but both come down on Prince Juan as the most probable recipient. See also Tess Knighton, 'Escobar's Requiem' (recording review), *Early Music* xxvii (1999), pp. 142–4.

10 In the current division of the manuscript, the Requiem happens to be divided between mss. 2 and 3. The piece is regrettably still unpublished; I am grateful to Tess Knighton for sending me her edition in manuscript.

11 The superius parts to most of the movements ascend to a G or A above middle C, but the Kyrie for some reason goes regularly up to C and once to E-flat.

significant feature: its placement of the chant (which he can pin to no particular usage) in the superius, normally in steady breves but always clear and obvious even when slightly ornamented; it is an approach familiar from later, more famous Iberian Requiems like those of Morales, Brudieu, Guerrero, Victoria, and Cardoso, and rare off the peninsula. So possibly Escobar was not only a pioneer here, but a trendsetter for hispanic Requiem composers for a century or more to come.[12]

Beyond the chant treatment, it is difficult to characterize this work succinctly. One's first impression, encouraged by the opening to the introit (forty-four breves and five longs within the first fifteen bars), is of a kind of stunned simplicity; but on repeated listenings, the various movements start to take on personalities of their own – the communion brutally homophonic, the offertory the most active and imitative, with frequent excursions by the superius away from the chant – and the mass as a whole to emerge as a subtly constructed and paced work of art. For a specimen of how Escobar blends homophonic and contrapuntal textures, Example 9.1 shows the opening of the Agnus.

Ex. 9.1 Escobar, Requiem, Agnus Dei, bb. 1–20

The discontinuity of range between the Kyrie and the other movements raises at least the possibility that the Requiem was a collaboration, mounted perhaps for efficiency of time after the Prince's sudden death, with the attribution of the piece simplified sometime between its origin and its copying into Tarazona. And in two places – near the end of the tract on the word 'mei' and in the Sanctus at 'gloria tua' – there are

---

12 Wagstaff, 'Music for the Dead', especially pp. 191–229.

even short passages of arching parallel intervals, which I have suggested as a kind of stylistic fingerprint for Anchieta. But there can be little doubt that it works as a varied but unified mass, and one strikingly different from its companions. Escobar's complete mass in Tarazona 2/3 makes an instructive comparison;[13] it is perhaps the most sustained piece of vigorous, muscular writing in the whole repertory, and to anyone familiar with it, the Requiem comes as quite a shock – which of course must have been the whole idea. I hear the Requiem above all as a gesture of restraint, a deliberate turning away from innovation and composerly display, toward a conservative and dignified sound as the dismal occasion demanded. It is immensely effective, as many of Escobar's successors seem to have understood.

Next in the manuscript is **Ne recorderis** (handlist 50), attributed to Francisco de la Torre. It is a setting of a responsory from the Office for the Dead,[14] and Tarazona is not its earliest source: it also appears anonymously in Barcelona 454/A and was copied from there into 454/B,[15] and its superius only, anonymous and in a late hand, is the very last item in Segovia s.s.[16] Wagstaff has identified no less than twenty-nine sources for this piece, all from Spain or Latin America, extending into the late eighteenth century; two others are early enough to be of immediate interest to us here: Toledo 21 (copied c.1525–50), where it is ascribed again to Torre, and Tarazona 5 (c.1515–30), where it is anonymous but is attributed to Sanabria (about whom more shortly) in a library inventory from midcentury.[17]

The piece exists in various versions to accommodate changes of taste and liturgy; the Barcelona 454 version, edited by Emilio Ros-Fábregas,[18] differs at several points from Tarazona's. It is a complex situation,[19] but need not slow us down here: all the manuscripts give just the polyphonic portions of an alternatim performance; both 454 and 2/3 give four blocks of polyphony, of which two must liturgically be repeated; these are interlarded with five monophonic blocks. The polyphonic portions quote the chant more or less literally in the superius, and the three lower voices essentially harmonize it, as the opening block (Example 9.2) shows.[20]

Its structure is unusally economical. Each of the four polyphonic blocks is divided into three little sections, usually by fermatas, and the musical material of these sections is freely reused and recombined. If, for example, we call the three sections of

---

[13] Edited by Anglès in MME I, pp. 125–55.

[14] *Liber Usualis*, pp. 1792–3, which has some variants in the text and a completely different tune; on its liturgical usage in today's Roman and pre-Tridentine Spanish rites, see Wagstaff, 'Music for the Dead', pp. 133–4 et passim.

[15] See Ros-Fábregas, 'Manuscript Barcelona', vol. I, pp. 26, 37, 139, 141, and 271–3.

[16] See, among others, Norma Klein Baker, 'An Unnumbered Manuscript of Polyphony in the Archives of the Cathedral of Segovia: Its Provenance and History' (Ph.D. diss., University of Maryland, 1978), pp. 107 and 208.

[17] Wagstaff, 'Music for the Dead', pp. 138–9 et passim. Dates are as he gives them; I might place Tarazona 5 a little later, but it is admittedly a problematic manuscript. Some late sources also give the piece to Morales, Guerrero, and a certain Pedro Tafulla. On the Sanabria references, see Pedro Calahorra, 'Los fondos musicales en el siglo XVI de la Catedral de Tarazona. I. Inventarios', *Nassarre* viii (1992), pp. 9–56, where it is item number 310; Sanabria's name appears in Calahorra's Inventory 1, which is undated but must precede Inventory 2, dated 1570.

[18] Ros-Fábregas, 'Manuscript Barcelona', vol. II, pp. 147–9.

[19] It is well explained by Wagstaff in 'Music for the Dead', pp. 149–59 et passim.

[20] Ibid., p. 143.

Ex. 9.2   Torre, *Ne recorderis*, bb. 1–13

the first block (bb. 1–3, 4–9, 10–13) *a b c*, then those of the second, 'Dum veneris', become *d e c*, those of 'Dirige' are *f e c*, and those of 'Kyrie' also *f e c* – so that the whole work is built up from six little bits of music.

     Libera me (handlist 45) is next in Tarazona 2/3, attributed to Anchieta.[21] It too is a responsory from the Office for the Dead, and it too had a long and broad career: Wagstaff counts ten sources, all Spanish and all anonymous except 2/3 and Toledo 21 (where it is given to Torre),[22] and F. Rubio Piqueras has reported that as late as the 1920s it was still being sung to profound effect in important funerals at Toledo cathedral, and widely believed there to be the work of Morales.[23] Since we have already looked at this piece in detail in the Anchieta chapter, its style need not be belabored here; suffice it to say that with its alternatim structure, its use of the chant as a cantus firmus in steady breves in the superius, and its generally homophonic approach, it fits in well with *Ne recorderis* and the Requiem, and that its subtle deviations from pure homophony and especially its opening, with a slow imitation prefiguring the cantus firmus in the altus, all fit in with the Anchieta of the mid-1490s.

     So were these three pieces[24] written in 1497 for the funeral of Prince Juan? There is no way to say. No clear record of the music at the funeral has been recovered, and we

---

[21] It is edited by Samuel Rubio in *Juan de Anchieta, Opera Omnia* (Guipuzcoa, 1980), pp. 93–101.

[22] Wagstaff, 'Music for the Dead', pp. 165–6. The same sixteenth-century library inventory that gives *Ne recorderis* to Sanabria gives *Libera me*, which directly precedes it, to Anchieta; see Calahorra, 'Fondos musicales', item number 309.

[23] F. Rubio Piqueras, *Códices polifónicos toledanos* (Toledo, 1925), p. 44, in his discussion of Toledo 21, describes the piece thus: 'terriblemente trágico y de un expresivismo ultraterreno; cuantas veces se escucha, otras tantas nos habla del *más allá* fatídico que se nos acerca. Se ejecuta en los funerales de los Arzobispos y en el día de finados. Muchos atribuyen a Morales la paternidad de esta obra, pero no le corresponde; no hay sino ver el Códice par saber que es de Francisco de la Torre.' It is attributed to Torre both in the tabla and on the page of Toledo 21.

[24] In an earlier incarnation of the handlist – Kenneth Kreitner, 'The Church Music of Fifteenth-Century Spain: A Handlist', *Encomium Musicæ: Essays in Memory of Robert Snow*, ed. David Crawford and G. Grayson Wagstaff (Hillsdale, 2002), pp. 191–207 – I added a fourth: *Paucitas*, another responsory, anonymous, which follows *Ne recorderis* and *Libera me* in Toledo 21 and is in the same general style. On reconsideration, informed by Wagstaff's commentary ('Music for the Dead', pp. 187–8), I see that without a composer's name or a source earlier than Toledo 21, it is hard to justify its inclusion under my current standard. It may well, however, be from the same milieu as the others. See also Robert Stevenson, *Spanish Music in the Age of Columbus* (The Hague, 1960), p. 194.

must always guard against the natural tendency to associate the music we know and the people we know, and to forget how many other possibilities there were that we cannot see at this distance. Yet there can be little doubt, looking at it dispassionately, that each of them was written for an important funeral, and that Juan's funeral was among the most important of the age. And four pieces of evidence, none necessarily conclusive in itself, seem to me to draw the circle still further in.

First, the three pieces, and especially the two responsories, have travelled together. They all three appear together in Tarazona 2/3, and *Ne recorderis* and *Libera me* are placed back-to-back in seven sources. In two others they are present but separated; in other words, of the ten sources of *Libera me*, all but one contain *Ne recorderis* too.[25] For what it is worth, then, quite a few generations of scribes and musicians saw and treated them as a pair.

Second, although their clefs vary, the ranges of their voice parts line up quite neatly: both responsories fit easily within the ranges of the Requiem as a whole, and in fact are compatible with all of its individual movements. As a purely practical matter there is nothing to prevent them from all being the repertory of the same choir – particularly of a large and thereby flexible choir like that of the Castilian court, which in 1497 numbered thirty-three singers.[26]

Third, the three pieces share a general structural approach: all three place the chant in the superius, predominantly in breves, and write the lower parts more or less homophonically. It is risky to try to place this style into a precise chronology; I have already said that I find *Libera me* to be about what we might expect from Anchieta around 1497, but the lack of any other sacred music from Torre and of a chronological picture for Escobar,[27] plus the likelihood that funeral music might naturally take on a more or less conservative cast, makes it hard to go further. Certainly if any of these had been written much after 1500, they would have seemed very conservative indeed in that context.

And fourth, the dates seem to add up, and better for Juan than for anyone else. Anchieta, as we have seen, served at the Castilian courts from 1489 till after Isabella's death; when Prince Juan died, as we saw in Chapter 7, Anchieta was his chapelmaster and certainly would have participated if there was any polyphony at the funeral. Escobar too was in the right place at the right time: his service to Isabella also began in 1489, and would end in 1498.[28] Of all the singers at the Castilian chapel in 1497, they were by far the most eminent composers. Francisco de la Torre is a trickier case: he has been traced at the Aragonese chapel from 1483 to 1494, and then reappears in Seville in 1503; we don't know where he was in 1497, but he was not at the Castilian

---

25 See the source tables in Wagstaff, 'Music for the Dead', pp. 138–9 and 165–6.

26 Knighton, 'Music and Musicians', vol. II, pp. 49–50 (*Música y músicos*, pp. 193–4).

27 The best general discussions of Escobar's sacred style are in Stevenson, *Spanish Music*, pp. 167–74, and Peter Marquis Alexander, 'The Motets of Pedro Escobar' (M.M. thesis, Indiana University, 1976); neither makes any effort at a chronology of his works, probably because his music, like Peñalosa's, survives mostly in manuscripts from near or beyond the end of his life.

28 The most detailed biography of Escobar is in Alexander, 'Motets', pp. 1–19. See also Stevenson, *Spanish Music*, pp. 167–71; *New Grove* 1980, s.v. 'Escobar, Pedro de', by Robert Stevenson (slightly revised by Stevenson for *New Grove* 2001); Knighton, 'Music and Musicians', vol. II, p. 267 (*Música y músicos*, p. 330); *MGG-P*, s.v. 'Escobar, Pedro de', by Tess Knighton; and *DMEH*, s.v. 'Escobar, Pedro de', by Tess Knighton.

court.[29] An intriguing possibility is raised, however, by those inventories of the Tarazona library in which *Ne recorderis* is attributed to Sanabria. Sanabria is a known composer, and we shall return to him in a moment; but Knighton has suggested that 'Sanabria' may be a toponymic, and that the man was also known as Juan Rodríguez de la Torre. If all of this is indeed the same person, then Juan Rodríguez de la Torre de Sanabria would have sung in the Castilian chapel from 1495 to 1504 and thus have been the number three composer there in 1497; it is not hard to imagine the Tarazona 2/3 scribe, working from an exemplar in which *Ne recorderis* was attributed to 'Torre' and not knowing that Torre was Sanabria's name, logically assuming that the reference was to the famous Torre and adding Francisco's first name on his own initiative.[30]

To sum up: if these three pieces were written for the same event, it would have to be an important funeral at or near the Castilian court during the time Anchieta and Escobar were both there, i.e. 1489–98. If Torre is Sanabria, that further narrows things down to 1495–98. Everything points toward the funeral of the crown prince, much beloved and untimely cut down, and an enthusiastic supporter of polyphonic music; nothing, so far as I can see, points away.

Juan Rodríguez [de la Torre] de Sanabria

Whether he is one person or more, Juan Rodríguez [de la Torre] de Sanabria bears a closer look. In spring and summer of 1484 a certain Juan Rodríguez de Sanabria was at the cathedral of Burgos, teaching music to the members of the chapter.[31] In 1487 the post of 'maestro cantor' at the cathedral of Ávila was given to a man called variously, over the course of the document, Juan de Senabria, Juan Rodrigues de Senabria, and Juan Rodríguez.[32] In 1494 Juan de Sanabria became a singer at León cathedral.[33] From 1495 to 1504, Juan Rodríguez de la Torre served in Isabella's chapel, following the queen's body to her funeral in Granada in 1504.[34] Although there is as yet no Rosetta-stone document equating Torre and Sanabria for sure, the flexibility of

---

29   Stevenson, *Spanish Music*, pp. 194–5; *New Grove* 1980, s.v. 'Torre, Francisco de la', by Robert Stevenson; Knighton, 'Music and Musicians', vol. II, p. 299 (*Música y músicos*, p. 345); and *New Grove* 2001, s.v. 'Torre, Francisco de la', by Robert Stevenson, a slight expansion on the 1980 article (but one which assigns *Libera me* to Torre).

30   For biographical information, see Knighton, 'Music and Musicians', vol. I, p. 293 (*Música y músicos*, p. 342), and the next section of this chapter. The suggestion that Sanabria may have written this piece is also made in Tess Knighton, 'Transmisión, difusión y recepción de la polifonía franco-neerlandesa en el reino de Aragón a principios del siglo XVI', *Artigrama* xii (1996–97), pp. 19–38, especially p. 30.

31   José López-Calo, *La música en la Catedral de Burgos* (Burgos, 1996), vol. III, pp. 29–30, docs. 22, 23, 25, 26, and 27. (Document 26 actually refers to him as Juan Fernández de Sanabria, which appears to be an error.) See also Nicolás López Martínez, 'Don Luis de Acuña, el Cabildo de Burgos y la reforma 1456–1495)', *Burgense* ii (1961), pp. 185–317 at p. 288 n. 414; and Jaime Moll, 'El estatuto de maestro cantor de la Catedral de Ávila del año 1487', *Anuario Musical* xxii (1967), pp. 89–95 at p. 90 n. 4.

32   Ibid., especially pp. 91–2.

33   José M.ª Álvarez Pérez, *La musica sacra al servicio de la Catedral de León* (León, 1995), pp. 34–5. Álvarez does not quote the actual document, so his use of the name Juan de Sanabria may not reflect the original spelling.

34   Knighton, 'Music and Musicians', vol. II, p. 293 (*Música y músicos*, p. 343).

Sanabria's name and the dovetailing of dates makes the possibility intriguing. But either scheme places Sanabria's works into the handlist: he disappears from the record either in 1494 or ten years later.

Five works – six if we count *Ne recorderis* – can be associated with Sanabria. The original layer of the Cancionero de Palacio, copied around 1505 by most estimates, has a song, *Donsella por cuyo amor*, attributed to J. Rodriges, which also appears anonymously in the early layer of the Cancionero de la Colombina and thus presumably dates from the early 1480s at the latest; another song in the original layer of Palacio, *Descuidad d'ese cuidado*, is attributed to Juan de Sanabria. And the sixth layer of Palacio, copied a year or so later, contains *Mayoral. . . Dile que Pedro*, attributed to Sanabria.[35] Tarazona 2/3 has two Latin pieces for our consideration.

The first is a hymn, **Ad coenam agni** (handlist 8), SATR clefs, the fourth in the series of hymns that begins the manuscript.[36] The Tarazona version (the only one that survives) preserves the text to the second verse to the hymn for Easter,[37] meaning that the even verses were to be done in polyphony. Example 9.3 shows its most distinctive feature: an imitative beginning in all four voices based on the chant tune. This is actually the only four-voice imitative opening in the entire hymn cycle, and the texture continues with both the tenor and superius loosely based on the chant tune and in imitation with each other. It registers to the eye as a forward-looking piece, but less so to the ear; this is another example of slow imitation, where the imitative subject is in such long note values – here, breves – that it emphasizes dignity rather than excitement.

Sanabria's other contribution to Tarazona 2/3 is a Marian motet, **Lilium sacrum** (handlist 46), STAB clefs; it is the last motet in the manuscript.[38] It is a short piece, less than 70 bars total, but in the small space it packs a variety of musical styles:

Lilium sacrum,	Voice pair, SA
virgo gloriosa,	Voice pair, SA
regina mundi,	Voice pair, SA
domina angelorum	B&T join in, singing 'Lilium sacrum'
et mater peccatorum.	Full ornamented homophony
Ave/Salve salus nostra!	Full imitation, quoting Salve Regina
Clementer petimus	Full non-imitative polyphony

[35] These are numbers 10, 377, and 118 respectively. On the dates of the layers of Palacio, see José Romeu Figueras, *La Música en la Corte de los Reyes Católicos, IV/1–2: Cancionero Musical de Palacio*, MME XIV (Barcelona, 1965), pp. 3–24; Romeu's date for the sixth layer has been updated by Ros-Fábregas in 'Manuscript Barcelona', vol. I, pp. 196–205. See also Stevenson, *Spanish Music*, pp. 193, 243–4, and 295.

[36] It is edited in Rudolf Gerber, ed., *Spanisches Hymnar um 1500*, Das Chorwerk LX (Wolfenbüttel, 1957), pp. 6–7.

[37] This hymn appears in the *Antiphonale Monasticum*, pp. 459 and 467, with a different tune, but Sanabria's tune seems to have been reasonably well known in Spain around this time; tune and text appear together in Barcelona 251, f. 52v, and in the *Intonarium toletanum* of 1515 on f. 7. For this information I am grateful to Màrius Bernadó, who has found the tune with other texts elsewhere in Barcelona 251 and the text with other tunes in the Himnario de Huesca (11th century), f. 26 and in Barcelona, Arxiu de la Corona d'Aragó, Sant Cugat 46 (13th century), f. 174v.

[38] It is edited by Calahorra in *Autores hispanos*, pp. 139–43. Álvarez, in *Música sacra*, p. 35 n. 14, identifies some Lamentations by Sanabria too, but this seems to be a confusion with the section of Lamentations that follows the motet. My discussion of this piece is indebted to an edition of and commentary prepared some years ago by my student Monte Coulter.

Ex. 9.3 Sanabria, *Ad coenam agni*, bb. 1–16

ut preces nostras	Voice pair, SA
Iesu, benignissimo	Voice pair, SA
filio tuo,	Speechlike homophony
domino nostro	Speechlike homophony
et regi nostro,	Speechlike homophony
et patri nostro,	Speechlike homophony
quod, tua gratia mediante,	Speechlike homophony
ante	Speechlike homophony
tribunal	Speechlike homophony
Omnipotentis præsententur	Ditto, dissoving into contrapuntal ending.

This mixed structure is unusual in the proven fifteenth-century repertory and may mean that the piece is later. What it reminds me of, however, is *O bone Jesu*, with its beginning in what appears to be a fairly sophisticated polyphonic style, but in the middle the sudden switch to a rigid dramatic homophony, underlined by very short lines of text (in one case a single preposition) separated by rests. Nor is it difficult to imagine a composer hearing *O bone Jesu* (which we know was a popular piece) and being impressed not only by its power but by its evident simplicity – it does look like the sort of thing one could write without much trouble. If so, if *Lilium sacrum* really is indebted to *O bone Jesu*, it shows how hard the trick actually is.

Juan de Segovia

Tarazona 2/3 also has a three-voice **Magnificat** (handlist 49), even verses, STR clefs, attributed to 'Jo. Segovia'. This is one of those worrisome attributions: Juan was a common first name and Segovia a good-sized city. Knighton has identified him potentially with a singer of that name paid by Isabella in 1493, and the singer with a royal chaplain given a series of benefices between 1487 and 1494;[39] but whether these are all the same man or not, he is clearly a minor composer, and his use of the by now rare three-voice texture for his Magnificat may suggest that he is relatively early. (There are twelve Magnificats a 4 in Tarazona 2/3, versus only three a 3; one of the latter is Anchieta's, which is also in Segovia s.s.)

Example 9.4 gives the opening verse of the Magnificat. It is for the most part a workmanlike piece, similar in sound to, and sharing some licks with, Anchieta's three-voice Magnificat (see Example 7.5 above), though without – to my ear at least – the imagination and skill at handling the materials. The imitative beginning and contrarily-moving eighth notes give an initial impression of contrapuntal activity, but a closer look reveals that at any given moment there are usually two voices moving together; and infelicities like the last beat of bar 16 look more like the sign of a prentice hand than like an error in the manuscript. I have no trouble thinking of this piece as a product of the 1490s, possibly written by Juan de Segovia at the Castilian court under Anchieta's inspiration and/or his eye.[40]

The Story So Far

These six pieces, and the ones we have seen in other chapters, are probably not the only fifteenth-century music in Tarazona 2/3. If we wanted to take a few more steps in this direction, there are a number of things we could do next. For example, if the three-voice Magnificats of Anchieta and Segovia were both written at the Castilian court in the 1490s, could we not add their one companion in 2/3, written in a similar style and compatible clefs, by 'Porto', i.e. Escobar, who was there at the same time?

From there we could branch out in a number of directions, toward more three-voice liturgical music – for example the three such masses in Tarazona 2/3 by Quixada, Alonso de Alba, and Juan Álvarez Almorox, any of whom would be biographically possible[41] – or more works by Escobar, who spent most of the last decade of the century at the court of Isabella and must have written something there besides the Requiem. Or we could start looking at other sources from around the same

---

[39] Knighton, 'Music and Musicians', vol. I, p. 296 (*Música y músicos*, p. 344).

[40] I am indebted here to an edition of the Magnificat prepared some years ago by my student Mark Bradshaw.

[41] On the biography of Almorox, see below, n. 43. On those of Quixada and Alba, see Stevenson, *Spanish Music*, pp. 189 and 164–7, and Knighton, 'Music and Musicians', vol. I, pp. 290 and 249–50 (*Música y músicos*, pp. 341 and 322–3). See also *New Grove* 1980 s.v. 'Alba, Alonso Perez de', by José M. Llorens; *MGG-P*, s.v. 'Alba, Alonso', by Tess W. Knighton; *DMEH*, s.v. 'Alba, Alonso de', by Tess Knighton; and *New Grove* 2001, s.v. 'Alba, Alonso (Pérez) de', by Tess Knighton. Quixada has no article in either edition of the *New Grove*.

Ex. 9.4 Segovia, Magnificat, bb. 1–30

time as Tarazona 2/3, like the later layers of Barcelona 454, or Tarazona 5, or Toledo 21, or Seville 5-5-20, which seems to be closely related to 2/3.[42]

On the other hand, maybe we have already gone too far. My notion of the Escobar, Torre, and Anchieta pieces being written for the funeral of Prince Juan, plausible as it may be, remains something of an untestable hypothesis, and conclusions drawn from biographical data are always risky because the data, especially in Spain at this point, tend to be so fragmentary. Juan de Segovia is a good example: we can really only pin

---

42   See for example Hardie, 'Motets of Peñalosa', pp. 115–17, Ros-Fábregas, 'Manuscript Barcelona', pp. 224–36, and Schwartz, 'Tarazona 2/3 y Sevilla 5-5-20'.

him down (if indeed all those references are to the same person) once, and can document his being alive at all for only eight years. An even more startling cautionary tale is that of Almorox: the traditional principal biographical sources, Stevenson and Knighton, traced him at the Aragonese court from 1482 to 1506, and sporadically to 1510, which sounds like the classic story of a favored singer retiring after long service to the crown – but since their time, José López-Calo has found him serving at the cathedral of Segovia till his death in 1551.[43] This should tell us what we ought to know already but may sometimes forget: that we know much more about the royal courts than about most of the cathedrals in Spain, and that any part of a composer's career spent at a cathedral or a noble court is apt to be that much more of a mystery.[44] So it is probably wisest now to stop searching for more music and take a look at what we have got already.

Of the six pieces we have seen in this chapter, it is the funeral music that intrigues me the most, and especially the Requiem. Escobar's Requiem is by far the largest composition we have encountered – remember that there have been no complete mass ordinaries at all – and for sustained controlled emotion it would be a triumph in any age. It seems strange, then, that of these three items of funeral music, it seems to have been the least popular, that *Ne recorderis*, which is about as modest a piece of polyphony as you could imagine, was the one copied over and over for centuries to come. It may be that *Ne recorderis*, and to a slightly lesser extent *Libera me*, had something of the status of the little Amens in the back of Protestant hymnals today, valued precisely because their position in the service encourages simple tradition over any need to attract attention. What happened to the Requiem was different: it inspired later Iberian composers to write pieces that paid it homage and went beyond.

All this boils down to something that is, on reflection, rather remarkable. Sixteenth-century Spain had a use for the church music of fifteenth-century Spain. The Josquin craze that swept through the peninsula in the 1530s and 1540s[45] must have had something to do with it – perhaps Spanish musicians were newly aware of having Josquins of their own. But whatever the cause, it is a milestone: at the time Tarazona 2/3 was copied, Spain was becoming conscious of having not only a musical practice, but a musical tradition to be proud of.

[43] Stevenson, *Spanish Music*, p. 164; Knighton, 'Music and Musicians', vol. I, p. 290 (*Música y músicos*, p. 322); José López-Calo, *Documentario Musical de la Catedral de Segovia* (Santiago de Compostela, 1990), pp. 34–5, docs. 404–6 et passim. *New Grove* 1980, s.v. 'Almorox, Juan', by Isabel Pope, could not include the Segovia years; the revision of Pope's article *New Grove* 2001, s.v. 'Almorox, Juan Álvarez de', by Tess Knighton, does. See also *MGG-P*, s.v. 'Almorox, Juan Álvarez de', by Tess W. Knighton, and *DMEH*, s.v. 'Almorox, Juan Álvarez de', by Tess Knighton.

[44] On the noble courts of Spain during this period, see Roberta Freund Schwartz, '*En busca de liberalidad*: Music and Musicians in the Courts of the Spanish Nobility, 1470–1640' (Ph.D. diss., University of Illinois, 2001).

[45] My paper '*Ave festiva ferculis*', previously cited, touches on this and was meant as a refinement to Robert Stevenson, 'Josquin in the Music of Spain and Portugal', *Josquin des Prez*, ed. Edward Lowinsky (London, 1976), pp. 217–46. See also Grayson Wagstaff's paper, 'Mary's Own: Josquin's Five-Part Salve Regina and Marian Devotions in Spain', presented at the conference on New Directions in Josquin Scholarship (Princeton, 1999).

10

Sixty-Seven Pieces

The handlist in the Appendix shows sixty-seven pieces of Latin sacred polyphony that I believe were written in Spain between 1400 and 1500. They are probably not all, and they may be too many: there are a few things out there that could be argued onto the list under slightly different rules, and a few now on that might be argued off. It contains one three-movement mass ordinary (the anonymous Kyrie-Sanctus-Agnus group in the Cancionero de la Colombina), one Requiem mass (by Escobar), and three Magnificats (Urrede, Anchieta, and Segovia); the rest is made up of a variety of smaller forms, usually in one movement. This is not a huge repertory to represent an entire large European country and an entire century – it is, if such comparisons mean anything, maybe half the size of Du Fay's surviving sacred output – but for now it will have to do.

Taken for the moment as an undivided whole, it is a repertory very different from those being written and sung in Italy and the north at the same time, as is made clear just by browsing through the table. One thing I notice right away is the number of unica: fully two thirds of the compositions appear in one manuscript only. Evidently, then, we are seeing the remains – the very fractional remains, we have to assume – of a national musical tradition that was not yet centralized. Surviving inventories torment us with descriptions of music books we don't recognize,[1] and the disparate stories proposed for our major manuscripts – Colombina a luxurious courtly cancionero that for some reason turned into an omnium-gatherum, Segovia an orderly collection of everything its compilers could find, Barcelona 454/A a small selection of northern sacred music that was later added to and sewn to other, more varied clumps of musical pages, and Tarazona 2/3 evidently a proper cathedral manuscript – hint at dozens, hundreds of other sources that have been lost, all with stories of their own and music we will never hear.

Of the pieces that do appear in more than one source, almost all appear in Tarazona 2/3, reaffirming the role of that one manuscript in solidifying the tradition, for us at least, in the sixteenth century. There are a few real warhorses, including modest service music like the ferial mass and Torre/Sanabria's *Ne recorderis* and more elaborate pieces, like Anchieta's *Domine Jesu Christe*, that seem to have successfully caught the imagination of the sixteenth century. But no matter how long or how broadly any of this music was used on the peninsula, almost none seems to have percolated out into the mainstream: the only piece on the whole list to be found in a

---

[1] See for example Emilio Ros Fábregas, 'Libros de música en bibliotecas españolas del siglo XVI', *Pliegos de bibliofilia* xv (2001), pp. 37–62; xvi (2001), pp. 33–46, xvii (2002), pp. 17–54.

source outside Spain, Portugal, and the New World is the mysterious *O bone Jesu*, which appears in eleven hispanic manuscripts and one lone Petrucci print.[2]

Another striking feature of this repertory, alluded to a moment ago, is the lack of conventional Kyrie-Gloria-Credo-Sanctus-Agnus mass cycles. Apart from the one little three-movement ferial mass in Colombina, the ordinary of the mass is represented only by isolated movements. Spanish musicians seem to have been aware of the existence of mass cycles elsewhere but not to have cared to produce them themselves; the Segovia manuscript has, or had, seven complete masses by northerners,[3] but only two movements by a Spaniard. Tarazona 2/3, twenty or thirty years later, has sixteen complete KGCSA masses, of which two appear to have been stapled together from movements transmitted separately. It looks, in other words, as though the cyclic mass was a tradition that hit Spain hard, but late.

Similarly, fifteenth-century Spain seems not quite to have caught on to the possibilities of the motet; the handlist is given over almost entirely to texts straight out of the liturgy of mass and office, with just a few, like *Ave sanctissima Maria*, more at home in a book of hours than in the regular service. The most popular text to be set by Spanish musicians? The Kyries tenebrarum, seldom if ever set polyphonically anywhere else. Again, the northern sections of Segovia, with humanistic motets by Obrecht, Isaac, and so forth, make an instructive contemporary contrast, and the contributions of Peñalosa and others to Tarazona 2/3 show that newly-written Latin sacred texts would be put to music in Spain before too long. But whether because of a conservative streak in Spanish religious thought that discouraged the production of new Latin religious texts, or because church music was still too closely tied to chant and improvised polyphony, or because the impulse toward ceremonial, occasional music was diverted in Spain toward the vernacular *romance*, the fifteenth century was different.[4]

The other thing that strikes me while looking over the list is the number of anonymous works. Again, we can contrast this with the northern parts of Segovia and with Tarazona 2/3; in both cases almost everything is attributed. Among the composers whose names appear on the fifteenth-century list, Anchieta is the clear winner with, depending on what you count, ten pieces, and he is followed by a handful (Madrid, Triana, Urrede, and Sanabria) with three or four. So it is not, at least for most of the century, a personality-driven repertory. More important, however, is a stylistic divergence between the anonymi, which tend to be simple and straightforward, and the attributed compositions, which are usually fancier and more complex – a consideration that takes us away from the handlist and into the music itself.

I have not tried to apply a consistent and rigorous critical method to this repertory; instead, while going through the compositions one by one, I have been conscious only of wanting to say what seemed most important and interesting about each and to let

[2] I do not count the presumably Spanish arrangement of Binchois's *Te Deum* in Segovia or the two pieces in Chigi, which appear to have been copied in Spain even though the manuscript did not originate there.

[3] The opening piece, Isaac's *Missa Wol auff gesell von hynnen*, is now fragmentary because of missing folios but presumably was complete originally. Obrecht's *Missa Adieu mes amours* has only Kyrie, Gloria, and Credo in Segovia, though it survives complete elsewhere.

[4] I am indebted here to my correspondence with Tess Knighton; some of these ideas will be developed further in her forthcoming book *Music and Ceremony at the Court of Ferdinand and Isabella*.

the story form itself that way. Stepping back from it now, I see that my main concern has been with rhythm, and with the growth, over the last decades of the century, of an increasingly complex and sophisticated rhythmic organization for sacred music. Six stylistic archetypes have suggested themselves, and they may make useful handholds for talking in general terms about all the kinds of music we have encountered.

a. The **chant harmonization,** in which one line is taken or closely derived from chant and the other(s) move with it in the same or nearly the same rhythm. I include in this archetype the fabordones scattered through several of the manuscripts, but there are various other approaches too. In several cases, like the *Ad honorem* settings in Barcelona 251 and some of the Kyries tenebrarum, the music is unmeasured and presumably moved in the flexible rhythm of chant; in others, like the Lamentations of Paris 967, a mensural rhythm is added, but the voices still tend to move rather rigidly together. All of these pieces seem closely related to what must have been an extensive practice of polyphonic improvisation; often they register, for me at least, as frozen improvisations or maybe just one step into the realm of notation.

b. The **chant accompaniment,** in which the chant is quoted in one voice in steady long note values (normally breves) in the superius or tenor, and the others move faster. This too must be related to improvisational practice, and it covers a wide range of complexities; two things that I notice frequently in the Spanish music, though they are by no means required by the style, are a habit of beginning with long note values in all the voices, giving a momentary impression of the chant harmonization before all the activity begins, and a tendency of the new polyphonic voices to follow each other's rhythm. A *locus classicus* of the archetype is *Alleluia . . . Salve virgo,* from the Segovia manuscript (above, Example 6.9).

c. **Smoothed-over homophony,** which might be thought of as (a) with a hint of (b). Usually there is a cantus firmus, again most often in the superius; and among the new voices, at any given moment at least one is following the rhythm of the chant-bearing voice but there is also usually one defying it to create a sense of motion and independence. It can be a surprisingly subtle and effective style, as shown for example in *Salve sancta parens,* from Colombina (Example 4.5).

d. **Full-fledged contrapuntal writing,** either imitative or non-imitative. This is not nearly so prevalent in Spanish as in northern sources of this period, but neither is it unknown: there are lots of examples of music imported (the mid-century Magnificat in Trent 88 and Colombina, or the northern contents of Segovia), at least one example (Urrede) of a composer imported, and a perhaps gratifying number of composers – well, two, Madrid and Marturià – writing fluently in this style despite being evidently born in Spain and probably older than Anchieta.

e. **Slow imitation,** which may not be truly a separate archetype, but happens often enough to be worthy of comment; perhaps it could be called (d) with a hint of (a) and (b). A good specimen is *O crux ave* from Segovia (example 6.7), which begins with a point of imitation in all four voices, but the substance of the imitation is presented all in breves for an initial impression much closer to a chant harmonization or to so many of the chant accompaniments. It too can work well, as *O crux ave* or, maybe even more effectively, *O bone Jesu* (example 7.8) attest, and I interpret it as the result of Spanish composers seeing and wanting both the structural power that imitation held and the impressive dignity of some of their older polyphonic styles.

f. Finally, **a mixed style** in which homophony and fancy counterpoint exist side-by-side and are played off each other for deliberate effect. It is a style especially celebrated in Peñalosa's motets from well after 1500, but there are at least a few conspicuous examples, about which more in a moment, in Segovia.

I cite complete compositions to illustrate these archetypes, but I do not mean them as rigid categories, pigeonholes for precise sorting. Nor do I wish to make extravagant claims for my system here: the six archetypes, along with various minglings and gray areas among them, can be made to account for most of the church music of fifteenth-century Spain, it is true. But they also amount to a fair description of the whole middle ages and renaissance. To be meaningful, then, the archetypes need to be laid onto some sort of chronological framework to see if the situation can be seen to change over time – to see if there is a story here. I believe there is: I believe that in the last decade of the century, Spanish church polyphony changed from an ideal that favored the, for want of a better word, simpler archetypes like chant harmonization and accompaniment and smoothed-over homophony, to one where northern-style counterpoint was fully accepted and done with confidence.

Musical chronologies are, however, a notoriously slippery business, and ours is no exception. It has had to be built up from manuscript dates and composer biographies; and if there are two things that can be relied on in the fifteenth century, it is that most biographies are misleadingly incomplete and that all manuscript dates will sooner or later turn out to be wrong. I have presented the major sources here, chapter by chapter, in the order in which I believe they were written, but it is sobering to realize how few dates we have that are precise, secure, and uniquivocally meaningful all at once. We have encouraging and useful *termini post quem* for the two main layers of Colombina (1469 and 1492) and most of Segovia s.s. (1495), and beyond those, a tissue of best estimates. But with all these caveats in mind and with, after all, some confidence that things are more prone to adjustments than reversals, we can have a quick tour.

It is quite possible that a few of the Catalan Ars subtilior manuscripts, though I would be reluctant to declare which, were actually written after 1400. But this style seems to have gone soon out of fashion, and after it, for the whole first half of the century, there is no surviving musical source for Spanish church polyphony at all. So the period must remain a mystery for now. But I doubt on the whole that Spanish churches of the early fifteenth century developed a large and sophisticated tradition of written polyphony that has been eradicated without a trace; more likely their polyphony, however much of it there was, was improvised and relatively simple. This has been shown to be the case in Italian churches of roughly the same period, and it seems to be confirmed by the polyphonic works in Barcelona 251, copied for a Barcelona monastery around 1450,[5] and by those in the undated but in some ways similar Paris 967. The six polyphonic compositions in these two sources seem to have strong affinities to an improvisatory practice; I described them above as basically *cantus planus binatim* with one or two additional features – an extra voice, a rhythm added to the chant – which meant that they needed writing down.

---

[5] For fuller explanations of, and the references behind, all this information, see the relevant chapters above; I shall not repeat the details and bibliography here.

The first layer of the Cancionero de la Colombina, copied I believe in the 1470s and early 1480s, has a gathering that was going to be devoted to church music, but was left unfinished with only three entries. All three are by Juan de Triana, and all are in an unusual cleffing (SST or SSR) that may mean they were written for an ensemble of choirboys; they are closest to the chant accompaniment archetype. The second layer of Colombina may have been copied over a long time, but it was probably finished in the early to mid-1490s. Its Latin works – all anonymous – are in a mixture of styles, ranging from tiny bagatelles to a northern Magnificat from the 1450s or so; the pieces that make the strongest impression, like the ferial mass and the motet *Salve sancta parens*, tend toward smoothed-over homophony. And the fourth layer of Paris 4379, which has been associated with Colombina, may have been finished around the same time, but seems to have had higher, or at least more exotic, aspirations: its seven songs are all in French and include works of Du Fay, Busnoys, and Basiron, and its Latin music features ambitious works by Urrede and Madrid in a freely contrapuntal style.

The Segovia manuscript is both the most fruitful for our list and the most persistently controversial. I continue to believe that it was copied in the mid- to late 1490s, somewhere in the orbit of the Castilian courts, possibly for Prince Juan. Segovia is well known for its northern sacred music and for its songs in French, Flemish, and Castilian; but it also contains something over two dozen pieces of Latin music apparently originating in Spain. And this section of Segovia may be the most dramatic vantage point to view the growing chasm between the old and new. The anonymous pieces tend toward the good old chant accompaniments and harmonizations, with a healthy number of smoothed-overs and slow imitations; but the attributed compositions, most numerously the works of Anchieta, are much more self-consciously contrapuntal and northward-looking.

The stylistic contrast between pieces with and without composers' names holds true in the relevant portions of Barcelona 454/A and 454/B, from the years just after 1500, and I consider it to be a sign of something important. The anonymous works seem to come from a world where sacred polyphony was a kind of public property, like chant, belonging to everybody and nobody; the attributed compositions, from one where a mass movement or hymn setting was the work of a particular man – an artistic production, to be associated with his name forever. This cultural shift had taken place in the musical mainstream many decades earlier, and we see it at least starting to happen in Spain in the days of Urrede and Madrid. By the time of the Segovia manuscript and Barcelona 454, the change was well underway, and in our next coherent glimpse of the repertory it seems to be all but complete: Tarazona 2/3 and Seville 5-5-20, which were probably copied in the 1520s or 1530s, are dramatically dominated by attributed works and by works in active counterpoint. Spain had joined the renaissance.

I have so far kept Ferdinand and Isabella in the background for most of this narrative. She was queen of Castile from 1474 to 1504, he king of Aragón from 1479 to 1516, so clearly they presided over the period of musical change that we have been seeing; but their role as agents in that change is harder to disentangle for certain.[6] There can

6   On the Catholic Monarchs and music, see especially Tessa Wendy Knighton, 'Music and Musicians at the Court of Fernando of Aragon, 1474–1516' (Ph.D. diss., Cambridge University, 1983), later translated as Tess Knighton, *Música y músicos en la Corte de Fernando el Católico 1474–1516*,

be little doubt of the Catholic Monarchs' fascination with northern culture in general, or of their reliance on the Burgundian court in particular as a model for the kind of ceremonial tone they wanted to establish at their own courts. And sacred music would seem to be an obvious candidate to take part in this process: it was one arena where northern superiority was unquestioned, and its artworks were both portable (unlike, say, architecture) and accessible across language barriers, and it fit logically into just the kinds of ceremonies where it could be best shown off.

If this is what you want to do, and you have the money, there are two easy ways: you can send talent scouts to the north to hire singer/composers for your chapel choir, or you can commission manuscripts of the most prestigious foreign music and have your choir sing it. Both methods were famously followed by Ferdinand and Isabella's contemporaries in Italy, and both had also been used by their Spanish predecessors – hence all the French music in the Aragonese court manuscripts around 1400, and hence the presence of musicians like Urrede and Enrique de Paris on the peninsula at the time their own reigns began. But both of the Catholic Monarchs went the other way: they hired almost exclusively Iberian singers for their choirs, and they made no discernable effort to bring in northern polyphony for them to sing. What Franco-Flemish music survives in Spanish sources seems to be more or less haphazard and much of it, like the one Magnificat in Colombina or the original corpus of Barcelona 454/A, had little or nothing to do with the royal chapels. The one big exception, of course, is the Segovia manuscript, but this seems more a happy byproduct of the increasing contact between the Castilian court and the north in the mid-1490s than the result of a systematic royal collection effort.

It is tempting to see all this as a matter of personal musical taste – to envision the Catholic Monarchs liking the local music and patronizing what they wanted to hear – or at least as a conscious gesture of musical nationalism like, say, commissioning one's coronation march from William Walton. But things are always more complicated than that: the policies governing the court chapels of Aragón and Castile were inevitably bound up in Ferdinand and Isabella's plans for religious reform, which were themselves motivated by a complicated mixture of spiritual zeal and political cunning. They filled their households, chapels included, with Spaniards as part of the web of power with which they were drawing in the old kingdoms and loyalties, and the musicians who came in inevitably brought their local traditions with them. Yet I don't think it is quite wrong to imagine that Spanish composers of the late fifteenth and early sixteenth centuries saw themselves as charged to create a national music, just as their royal employers were creating a nation. And it is a delicate job. The goal, I think, admittedly at quite a few years' remove, must have been to write sacred music that acknowledged northern ideals but was not swamped by them, music that could stand unashamed with the masterpieces of contemporary European music but would at the same time retain something distinctly, audibly Spanish. What they did, we can start to see at the end of the fifteenth century, but it becomes clearer after a look at what it would develop into in the 1510s and 1520s.

trans. Luis Gago (Zaragoza, 2001); idem, 'Northern Influence on Cultural Developments in the Iberian Peninsula during the Fifteenth Century', *Renaissance Studies* i (1987), pp. 221–37; and the forthcoming *Music and Ceremony*. See also many of the works of Higinio Anglés in the bibliography, especially *La música en la corte de los Reyes Católicos*, MME I, V, X, and (with Josep Romeu Figueras) XIV (Barcelona, 1941–65).

A fair amount has been written about the musical styles, particularly those of the motets, in Tarazona 2/3, and this is probably not the place to belabor or extend the secondary literature.[7] We have seen some of the fifteenth-century pieces that are still preserved there, and there are others, like the cycle of nine three-voice Alleluias by Alba, Escobar, and Hernández, all in solid chant-accompaniment style, that may be additional survivals or perhaps *hommages* to earlier times.[8] But what jumps out of Tarazona 2/3, especially to the eye and ear accustomed to the sacred music of Segovia, Colombina, and so forth, is the number of compositions showing a much higher degree of contrapuntal sophistication. This we have also seen firsthand, at least briefly, in my little discussion of Anchieta's late works, and the observations made there can be extended outward. To overgeneralize greatly: the masses of Tarazona 2/3, and particularly the six four-voice masses of Peñalosa and the one apiece of Anchieta and Escobar, are written in a fully mature imitative polyphonic style, with a sometimes dazzling rhythmic strength and an impressive command of textures and techniques; the hymn cycle is also predominantly in a very vigorous counterpoint; the Magnificats and Lamentations likewise, though perhaps a little repressed by their reciting-tone past; and so on through the *Salve Regina* settings of Escobar and Alba, and many of the liturgical motets of Peñalosa. Not all the liturgical music, I should add, is like this, but enough: it is as though Iberian composers in the teens and twenties needed to show, just in case anybody was watching, that they could do it, that they were certified members of the international society of polyphonists.

In the devotional motets, however, they seem to have a deeper and for us more interesting purpose. The most famous examples are Peñalosa's great Passion motets like *Precor te Domine*, and in them Peñalosa uses all the polyphonic tricks of his masses, plus one more – strips, sometimes long strips, of declamatory homophony are sewn deftly into the fabric at just the most dramatic portions of the text, with keen attention to the rhythm of the words and the pace of the often grisly images being depicted, for at their best, a truly hair-raising effect.[9] Peñalosa may be the most celebrated practitioner of this style, but it must be noted that he had no patent on it; it is

---

[7]   For a representative sample of writings in English: Robert Stevenson, *Spanish Music in the Age of Columbus* (The Hague, 1960); Peter Marquis Alexander, 'The Motets of Pedro Escobar'(M.M. thesis, Indiana University, 1976); Jane Morlet Hardie, 'The Motets of Francisco de Peñalosa and their Manuscript Sources' (Ph.D. diss., University of Michigan, 1983); Wolfgang Freis, 'Cristóbal de Morales and the Spanish Motet in the First Half of the Sixteenth Century: An Analytical Study of Selected Motets by Morales and Competitive Settings in SEV-BC 1 and TARAZ-C 2-3' (Ph.D. diss., University of Chicago, 1992); Kenneth Kreitner, 'Franco-Flemish Elements in Tarazona 2 and 3', *Revista de Musicología* xvi (1993), pp. 2567–86; idem, 'Peñalosa on Record', *Early Music* xxii (1994), pp. 309–18; and Tess Knighton,'Francisco de Peñalosa: New Works Lost and Found', *Encomium Musicæ: Essays in Memory of Robert Snow*, ed. David Crawford and G. Grayson Wagstaff (Hillsdale, 2002), pp. 231–57.

[8]   See for example Alexander, 'Motets of Escobar', especially pp. 52–5 and 234–41; I am indebted here also to a term paper and edition by my student David McNair. The nine Alleluias, arranged in the manuscript in church-year order, are quite a bit alike, yet it is currently difficult to reconcile the biographies of the composers into a scheme where they were written as a group rather than merely assembled (like the hymn group) by the compiler of Tarazona 2/3.

[9]   See for example Tess Knighton, 'Devotional piety and musical developments at the court of Ferdinand and Isabella', <http://www.sun.rhul.ac.uk/Music/ILM/ID/Vol_0/Art/twk.html>, 2 August 2002.

part of what animates Escobar's most popular and influential composition, *Clamabat autem*,[10] and as we have seen, Anchieta, in *Domine Jesu Christe*, another Passion motet, had already used it early enough to be copied into Segovia.

There is nothing quite like this music anywhere else in the renaissance, and whether it is a response to conscious encouragement by Ferdinand and Isabella to create a kind of sacred music that was distinctly Spanish, or if it just developed in the natural interchange of court and cathedral musicians in the early sixteenth century, the result is the same, and immensely moving. But here we overstep the temporal limits of the book. All I will suggest is that what makes these motets work so well is a greater than usual tolerance for homophony and a keen understanding of what simplicity can do that fancy counterpoint can't – and that, raised in the musical world we have been examining here, composers like Peñalosa knew homophony, and simplicity, the way sailors know water.

---

[10] For a recent analysis of this remarkable piece, see Freis, 'Cristóbal de Morales', pp. 284–8.

Appendix

Handlist of Fifteenth-Century Spanish Church Music

A. Mass Ordinary Movements and Cycles

No.	Title	Composer	Source(s)*	Page
1	[Missa de feria] ([Kyrie]; Sanctus; Agnus)	anonymous	Colombina, nos. 45–47 Toledo 21 7 others†	48
2	Kyrie . . . Rex virginum	Anchieta	Barcelona 454 Tarazona 2/3, no. 55	111
	Kyrie . . . Qui passurus Kyrie . . . Qui expansis		*see* table B *see* table B	
3	Gloria	Madrid	Paris 4379/D, no. 11	58
4	Gloria . . . Spiritus et alme	Anchieta	Segovia, no. 10 Barcelona 454 Tarazona 2/3, no. 55	111
5	Credo	anonymous	Barcelona 251, no. 3	30
6	Credo	Anchieta	Segovia, no. 9 Tarazona 2/3, no. 55 Coimbra 12	111
7	Missa pro defunctis (Requiem; Kyrie; Requiem; Sicut cervus; Domine Jesu; Sanctus; Agnus; Absolve)	Escobar	Tarazona 2/3, no. 56	143

B. Propers, Office, Motets, etc. (arranged alphabetically)

No.	Title	Composer	Source(s)*	Page
8	Ad coenam agni	Sanabria	Tarazona 2/3, no. 4	149
9	Ad honorem . . . Ave regina	anonymous	Barcelona 251, no. 1	30
10	Ad honorem . . . Salve regina	anonymous	Barcelona 251, no. 2	30
11	Aleph. Quomodo obscuratum	anonymous	Segovia, no. 74	92
12	Aleph. Quomodo obtexit	anonymous	Paris 967, no. 2	33
13	Aleph. Viæ Sion lugent	anonymous	Segovia, no. 75	92
14	Alleluia	anonymous	Segovia, no. 72	95

*† See pp. 165–6 below.

No.	Title	Composer	Source(s)*	Page
15	Alleluia. Dies sanctificatus	anonymous	Barcelona 454, no. 18 Barcelona 454, no. 25	131
16	Alleluia. Salve virgo	anonymous	Segovia, no. 73	94
17	Asperges me	Madrid	Chigi, no. 40	58
18	Ave sanctissima Maria	anonymous	Segovia, no. 102	96
19	Ave sanctissima Maria	anonymous	Barcelona 454, no. 40 {Barcelona 454, no. 62}	137
20	Ave sanctissimum / Ave verum	Mondéjar? Diaz?	Barcelona 454, no. 40 Tarazona 2.3, no. 102 4 others†	132
21	Ave verum corpus	anonymous	Segovia, no. 76	87
22	Benedicamus Domino [i]	Triana	Colombina, no. 80	45
23	Benedicamus Domino [ii]	Triana	Colombina, no. 81	45
24	Benedicamus Domino	anonymous	Paris 4379/D, no. 12	55
25	Benedicamus Domino	anonymous	Barcelona 454, no. 19 Barcelona 454, no. 26	131
26	Conditor alme siderum	Anchieta	Segovia, no. 100	106
27	Conditor alme siderum	Marturià	Segovia, no. 101	83
28	Dic nobis Maria	anonymous	Colombina, no. 79	52
29	Dixit Dominus	anonymous	Barcelona 454, no. 22	129
30	Domine Jesu Christe	Anchieta	Segovia, no. 26 Seville 5-5-20 Tarazona 2/3, no. 106 6 others†	116
31	Domine non secundum	Madrid	Paris 4379/D, no. 10	56
32	Domine non secundum	Anchieta	Segovia, no. 99, 28	106
33	Dona jube benedicere	anonymous	Paris 967, no. 1	33
34	Donec ponam	anonymous	Barcelona 454, no. 23	129
35	Hosanna salvifica	anonymous	Segovia, no. 71	95
36	Imperatrix reginarum	anonymous	Segovia, no. 70	96
37	In exitu Israel de Egipto	anonymous	Colombina, no. 68	51
38	Juste judex Jesu Christe	Triana	Colombina, no. 82	45
39	Juste judex Jesu Christe	anonymous	Segovia, no. 35	87
40	Kyrie . . . Qui expansis	anonymous	Segovia, no. 29	91
41	Kyrie . . . Qui passurus	anonymous	Paris 967, no. 3	34
42	Kyrie . . . Qui passurus	anonymous	Segovia, no. 32	88
43	Kyrie . . . Qui passurus	anonymous	Barcelona 454, no. 101	129
44	Laudate eum	anonymous	Colombina, no. 29	53
45	Libera me	Anchieta	Tarazona 2/3, no. 58 9 others†	122
46	Lilium sacrum	Sanabria	Tarazona 2/3, no. 113	149
47	Magnificat	Urrede	Paris 4379/D, no. 14 Coimbra 12 (Lisbon 60)	70
48	Magnificat (a 3)	Anchieta	Segovia, no. 68 Tarazona 2/3, no. 22	115
49	Magnificat	Segovia	Tarazona 2/3, no. 23	151

No.	Title	Composer	Source(s)*	Page
50	Ne recorderis	Torre [=Sanabria?]	Barcelona 454, no. 17 Barcelona 454, no. 24 Tarazona 2/3, no. 57 (Segovia, no. 204) 25 others†	145
51	Nunc dimittis	Urrede	Paris 4379/D, no. 13	68
52	O admirabile commercium	Illario	Barcelona 454, no. 34 Tarazona 2/3, no. 101 6 others†	133
53	O bone Jesu	Anchieta? Peñalosa? Ribera? Compère?	Segovia, no. 33 Barcelona 454, no. 56 Tarazona 2/3, no. 100 9 others†	117
54	O crux ave	anonymous	Segovia, no. 31	91
55	O gloriosa domina	anonymous	Colombina, no. 55	52
56	Omnipotentem semper	anonymous	Colombina, no. 39	53
	Osanna salvifica		*see* Hosanna	
57	Pange lingua [T]	Urrede	Barcelona 454, no. 75 Tarazona 2/3, no. 9 17 others†	73
58	Pange lingua [S]	Urrede	Segovia, no. 202	73
59	Qui fecit celum et terram	anonymous	Colombina, no. 77	52
60	Salve sancta facies	anonymous	Segovia, no. 69	96
61	Salve sancta parens	anonymous	Colombina, no. 63	49
62	Sancta Maria ora pro nobis	anonymous	Segovia, no. 98	96
63	Te Deum	Binchois/anon.	Segovia, no. 34	85
64	Veni creator spiritus	Alba	Segovia, no. 30 Tarazona 2/3, no. 7	82
65	Vidi aquam	anonymous [=Madrid?]	Chigi, no. 41	58
66	Virgo et mater	Anchieta	Segovia, no. 27 Seville 5-5-20 Tarazona 2/3, no. 104	116
67	[Textless fabordón]	anonymous	Barcelona 454, no. 99	130

* Parentheses indicate incompleteness; curly brackets indicate extra voice. Inventory numbers for the major manuscripts are taken from the following:

Barcelona 454	Ros-Fábregas dissertation
Chigi codex	Kellman, *JAMS* 1958
Colombina	Querol, MME XXXIII
Paris 4379/D	Fallows, *Rivista Italiana di Musicologia* 1993
Segovia s.s.	Anglés, MME I; also Baker dissertation
Tarazona 2/3	Kreitner, *Revista de Musicología* 1993

Concordances assembled from literature above plus Knighton, Wagstaff, and Kirk dissertations, Rees, *Polyphony in Portugal*, etc.

† Additional sources, for pieces with more than five:

Missa de Feria: Escorial 4 (attr. Voluda); Escorial 4 (Sanctus, Benedictus, Agnus); Escorial 5 (Sanctus, Benedictus); Montserrat 750; New York 278 (Sanctus, Benedictus); Toledo 24 (Kyrie, Sanctus, Benedictus); Toledo s.s. (Benedictus, Agnus).

Ave sanctissimum (Mondéjar/Díaz): Coimbra 12, 32, 48; Lisbon 60.

Domine Jesu Christe (Anchieta): Coimbra 12, 32; Lisbon 60; Valladolid 5, s.s.; Tarazona 5.

Libera me (Anchieta): Escorial 10; Granada 6; Montserrat 753; New York 380-861; Tarazona 5; Toledo 1, 21, 22; Valladolid 5.

Ne recorderis (Torre/Sanabria): Ávila 1, 2, 9; Bloomington 4, 7; Chicago 4; Coimbra 34; Escorial 7, 10; Guadalupe 3; Granada 6; Madrid 6832; Mexico City 3; Montserrat 753, 1085; New York 380-861; Oporto 12; Puebla 3; Segovia 3; Silos 21; Tarazona 5; Toledo 1, 21; Valencia 9; Valladolid 5.

O admirabile commercium (Ylario): Bloomington 4, 8; Coimbra 12, 32, 48, 53.

O bone Jesu (Anchieta etc.): Barcelona 5; Bloomington 8; Coimbra 12, 32, 48, 53; Jacaltenango 7; Lisbon 60; 1519[2].

Pange lingua [T] (Urrede): Bloomington 8, 9; Burgos s.s.; Granada 3, LE, CR(5); Guadalupe (1); Lerma 1; Plasencia 4; Puebla 19; Segovia 2; Toledo 25; Tudela (2), (3); Valencia 173, 176, 179; also intabulations, arrangements, etc.

Bibliography

Aguirre Rincón, Soterraña. *Ginés de Boluda (ca. 1545–des. 1604): Biografía y obra musical.* Valladolid, 1995.

Alexander, Peter Marquis. 'The Motets of Pedro Escobar.' M.M. thesis, Indiana University, 1976.

Altés i Aguilo, Francesc Xavier, ed. *Llibre Vermell de Montserrat: Edició facsímil parcial del manuscrit núm. 1 de la Biblioteca de L'Abadia de Montserrat.* Llibres del Mil.lenari II. Barcelona, 1989.

Álvarez Pérez, José M.ª. *La música sacra al servicio de la Catedral de León.* León, 1995.

Anglès, Higini. *El còdex musical de las Huelgas.* Biblioteca de Catalunya: Publicacions del Departament de Música VI. Barcelona, 1931.

Anglès, Higinio. 'Die spanische Liedkunst im 15. und Amfang des 16. Jahrhunderts.' *Theodor Kroyer: Festschrift zum sechzigsten Geburtstage am 9. September 1933*, ed. Hermann Zenck, Helmut Schultz, and Walter Gerstenberg, pp. 62–8. Regensburg, 1933.

Anglès, Higini. *La música a Catalunya fins al segle XIII.* Biblioteca de Catalunya: Publicacions del Departament de Música X. Barcelona, 1935.

Anglés, Higinio. 'Un manuscrit inconnu avec polyphonie du XVe siècle conservé à la cathédrale de Ségovie (Espagne).' *Acta Musicologica* viii (1936), pp. 3–17.

Anglés, Higinio, ed. *La música en la Corte de los Reyes Católicos, I: Polifonía religiosa.* Monumentos de la Música Española I. Barcelona, 1941; 2nd edn. 1960.

Anglés, Higinio, ed. *La música en la Corte de Carlos V.* Monumentos de la Música Española II. Barcelona, 1944; 2nd edn. 1965.

Anglés, Higinio. 'El "Pange Lingua" de Johannes Urreda, maestro de capilla del Rey Fernando el Católico.' *Anuario Musical* vii (1952), pp. 193–200.

Anglés, Higinio, ed. *Antonio de Cabezón (1510–1566): Obras de música para tecla, arpa y vihuela . . .* Monumentos de la Música Española XXVII–XXVIII. Barcelona, 1966.

Anglés, Higinio, and Josep Romeu Figueras, eds. *La música en la corte de los Reyes Católicos: Cancionero Musical de Palacio (siglos XV–XVI).* Monumentos de la Música Española V, X, XIV. Barcelona, 1947–65.

Antiphonale Monasticum pro diurnis horas, edn. no. 818. Paris, 1934.

Atlas, Allan W. *Music at the Aragonese Court of Naples.* Cambridge, 1985.

Atlas, Allan W. 'Aggio visto lo mappanundo: A New Reconstruction.' *Studies in Musical Sources and Style: Essays in Honor of Jan LaRue*, ed. Eugene K. Wolf and Edward H. Roesner, pp. 109–20. Madison, 1990.

Atlas, Allan W. *Renaissance Music: Music in Western Europe, 1400–1600.* New York, 1998.

Auden, W.H. *Selected Poems*, ed. Edward Mendelson. New York, 1979.

Baker, Norma Klein. 'An Unnumbered Manuscript of Polyphony in the Archives of the Cathedral of Segovia: Its Provenance and History.' Ph.D. dissertation, University of Maryland, 1978.

Banks, Jon. 'Performing the Instrumental Music in the Segovia Codex', *Early Music* xxvii (1999), pp. 295–309.

Bellingham, Bruce, and Edward G. Evans, Jr. *Sixteenth-Century Bicinia: A Complete Edition of*

Munich, Bayerische Staatsbibliothek, Ms. Ms. 260. Recent Researches in Renaissance Music XVI–XVII. Madison, 1974.

Bermudo, Juan. *El libro llamado declaracion de instrumentos musicales.* Osuna, 1555; rept. Kassel, 1957.

Bernadó i Tarragona, Màrius. 'El repertori himnòdic del *Cantorale Sancti Ieronimi* (Barcelona: Bibliotetca de Catalunya, M 251).' Licenciado thesis, Universitat Autònoma de Barcelona, 1992.

Bernadó, Màrius. 'The Hymns of the *Intonarium Toletanum* (1515): Some Peculiarities.' *Cantus Planus* i (1993), pp. 367–96.

Bernard, Madeleine. *Répertoire de manuscrits médiévaux contenant des notations musicales, v. III: Bibliothèques Parisiennes Arsenal, Nationale (musique), Universitaire, École des beaux-arts et fonds privés.* Paris, 1974.

Blackburn, Bonnie J. 'For Whom Do the Singers Sing?' *Early Music* xxv (1997), pp. 593–609.

Blackburn, Bonnie. 'The Virgin in the Sun: Music and Image for a Prayer Attributed to Sixtus IV.' *Journal of the Royal Musical Association* cxxiv (1999), pp. 157–95.

Blake, Jon Vincent. '*Libro de la cámara real del Príncipe don Juan e officios de su casa e servicio ordinario* de Gonzalo Fernández de Oviedo y Valdés – según el manuscrito autógrafo Escorial e.iv.8: Estudio, transcripción y notas.' Ph.D. dissertation, University of North Carolina at Chapel Hill, 1975.

Borgerding, Todd Michael. 'The Motet and Spanish Religiosity ca. 1550–1610.' Ph.D. dissertation, University of Michigan, 1997.

Borgerding, Todd. '*Ay arte de contrapunto*: Improvised Vocal Polyphony and Ritual in Early Modern Spain.' Unpublished paper.

Bradshaw, Murray C. *The Falsobordone: A Study in Renaissance and Baroque Music.* Musicological Studies and Documents XXXIV. N.p., 1978.

Brown, Howard Mayer. *Music in the Renaissance.* Englewood Cliffs, 1976; 2nd edn., with Louise K. Stein. Upper Saddle River, 1999.

Brown, Howard Mayer. 'On Veronica and Josquin.' *New Perspectives in Music: Essays in Honor of Eileen Southern,* ed. Josephine Wright and Samuel A. Floyd, Jr., pp. 49–61. Detroit Monographs in Musicology/ Studies in Music XI. Warren, Michigan, 1992.

Cabero Pueyo, Bernat. 'El fragmento con polifonía litúrgica del siglo XV, E-Ahl 1474/17: Estudio comparativo sobre el Kyrie *Summe clementissime*.' *Anuario Musical* xlvii (1992), pp. 39–80.

Calahorra, Pedro. 'Los fondos musicales en el siglo XVI de la Catedral de Tarazona. I. Inventarios.' *Nassarre* viii (1992), pp. 9–56.

Calahorra, Pedro, ed. *Autores hispanos de los siglos XV–XVI de los MS. 2 y 5 de la catedral de Tarazona.* Polifonía Aragonesa IX. Zaragoza, 1995.

Calahorra, Pedro. 'Compositores hispanos en el ms. 2/3 de la Catedral de Tarazona: Copias y variantes', *Fuentes musicales en la Península Ibérica (ca. 1250–ca. 1550),* ed. Maricarmen Gómez and Màrius Bernadó, pp. 177–201. Lleida, 2001.

Carbonell, Pedro Miquel. *Opúsculos inéditos del cronista catalan Pedro Miguel Carbonell,* ed. Manuel de Bofarull y de Sartório. Colección de documentos inéditos del Archivo General de la Corona de Aragón XVII. Barcelona, 1864.

Casares Rodicio, Emilio, ed. *Diccionario de la música Española e Hispanoamericana.* Madrid, 1999– .

Cattin, Giulio, and Francesco Facchin, with Maria del Carmen Gómez, eds. *French Sacred Music.* Polyphonic Music of the Fourteenth Century XXIII. Monaco, 1989.

Census-Catalogue of Manuscript Sources of Polyphonic Music, 1400–1550. Renaissance Manuscript Studies I. Neuhausen-Stuttgart, 1979–88.

Charles, Sydney R. 'Hillary-Hyllayre: How Many Composers?' *Music and Letters* lv (1974), pp. 61–9.

Codex Tridentinus 88. Rome, 1970.

Coster, Adolphe. 'Juan de Anchieta et la famille de Loyola.' *Revue Hispanique* lxxix (1930), pp. 1–322.

Cumming, Julie E. *The Motet in the Age of Du Fay.* Cambridge, 1999.

Denley, Daniel. 'The Mystery of Anchieta's *Missa de nostra dona.*' Senior paper, University of Memphis, 1998.

Donovan, Richard. *The Liturgical Drama in Medieval Spain.* Toronto, 1958.

Dreves, Guido Maria, ed. *Cantiones et muteti: Lieder und Motetten des Mittelalters.* Analecta Hymnica Medii Aevi XX. Leipzig, 1895.

Duggan, Mary Kay. 'Queen Joanna and the Musicians.' *Musica Disciplina* xxx (1976), pp. 73–95.

Durán i Sanpere, Agustí. *Barcelona i la seva història.* Barcelona, 1972–75.

D'Accone, Frank A. *The Civic Muse: Music and Musicians in Siena during the Middle Ages and the Renaissance.* Chicago, 1997.

Early Music Consort of London, dir. David Munrow. *The Art of the Netherlands.* Seraphim SIC6104, 1976. CD reissue, EMI Classics CMS 7 64215 2, 1992.

Fallows, David. 'Specific Information on the Ensembles for Composed Polyphony, 1400–1474.' *Studies in the Performance of Late Mediaeval Music,* ed. Stanley Boorman, pp. 109–59. Cambridge, 1983.

Fallows, David. 'A Glimpse of the Lost Years: Spanish Polyphonic Song, 1450–70.' *New Perspectives in Music: Essays in Honor of Eileen Southern,* ed. Josephine Wright and Samuel A. Floyd, Jr., pp. 19–36. Detroit Monographs in Musicology/ Studies in Music XI. Warren, Michigan, 1992.

Fallows, David. 'I fogli parigini del Cancionero Musical e del manoscritto teorico della Biblioteca Colombina.' *Rivista Italiana di Musicologia* xvii (1992), pp. 25–40.

Fallows, David. 'The End of the Ars Subtilior.' *Basler Jahrbuch für historische Musikpraxis* xx (1996), pp. 21–40.

Fallows, David. *A Catalogue of Polyphonic Song, 1450–1480.* Oxford, 1999.

Fernández de Oviedo, Gonzalo. *Libro de la camara real del prínçipe don Juan e offiçios de su casa e seruiçio ordinario,* ed. J.M. Escudero de la Peña. Madrid, 1870.

Ferreira, Manuel Pedro. 'Braga, Toledo and Sahagún: The Testimony of a Sixteenth-Century Liturgical Manuscript.' *Fuentes musicales en la península ibérica (ca.1250–ca.1550),* ed. Maricarmen Gómez and Màrius Bernadó, pp. 11–33. Lleida, 2001.

Finscher, Ludwig. 'Loyset Compère and his Works.' *Musica Disciplina* xii (1958), pp. 105–43.

Finscher, Ludwig, ed. *Loyset Compère: Opera Omnia.* Corpus Mensurabilis Musicae XV. N.p., 1958–72.

Finscher, Ludwig, ed. *Die Musik in Geschichte und Gegenwart,* 2nd edn. Kassel, 1994– .

Freis, Wolfgang. 'Cristóbal de Morales and the Spanish Motet in the First Half of the Sixteenth Century: An Analytical Study of Selected Motets by Morales and Competitive Settings in SEV-BC 1 and TARAZ-C 2-3.' Ph.D. dissertation, University of Chicago, 1992.

Freund, Roberta. *See* Schwartz, Roberta Freund.

Gallo, F. Alberto. ' "Cantus planus binatim": Polifonia primitiva in fonte tardive.' *Quadrivium* vii (1966), pp. 79–89.

García Fraile, Damaso. 'La cátedra de música de la Universidad de Salamanca durante diecisiete años del siglo XV (1464–1481).' *Anuario Musical* xlvi (1991), pp. 57–101.

Gastoué, A. 'Manuscrits et fragments de musique liturgique, à la bibliothèque du Conservatoire, à Paris.' *Revue de Musicologie* xiii (1932), pp. 1–9.

Gerber, Rebecca Lynn. 'The Manuscript Trent, Castello del Buonconsiglio, 88: A Study of Fifteenth-Century Manuscript Transmission and Repertory.' Ph.D. dissertation, University of California, Santa Barbara, 1984.

Gerber, Rebecca L. *Johannes Cornago: Complete Works*. Recent Researches in the Music of the Middle Ages and Renaissance XV. Madison, 1984.

Gerber, Rudolf. 'Spanische Hymnensätze um 1500.' *Archiv für Musikwissenschaft* x (1953), pp. 165–84.

Gerber, Rudolf, ed. *Spanisches Hymnar um 1500*. Das Chorwerk LX. Wolfenbüttel, 1957.

Gómez Muntané, M.ª del Carmen. *La música en la casa real catalano-aragonesa durante los años 1336–1432*. Barcelona, 1977.

Gómez, María del Carmen. 'Neue Quellen mit mehrstimmiger geistlicher Musik des 14. Jahrhunderts in Spanien.' *Acta Musicologica* l (1978), pp. 208–16.

Gómez, María del Carmen. 'Más códices con polifonía del siglo XIV en España.' *Acta Musicologica* liii (1981), pp. 85–90.

Gómez, M.ª Carmen. 'A propósito de un Credo polifónico del "Cantorale S. Jeronimi" (E-Bd 251).' *Revista de Musicología* iv (1981), pp. 309–315.

Gómez Muntané, M.ª Carmen. 'El manuscrito M 971 de la Biblioteca de Catalunya (Misa de Barcelona).' *Butlletí de la Biblioteca de Catalunya* x (1982–84), pp. 159–290.

Gómez, M.ª Carmen. 'Musique et musiciens dans les chapelles de la maison royale d'Aragon (1336–1413).' *Musica Disciplina* xxxviii (1984), pp. 67–86.

Gómez, María del Carmen. 'Quelques remarques sur le répertoire sacré de l'Ars nova provenant de l'ancien royaume d'Aragon.' *Acta Musicologica* lvii (1985), pp. 166–79.

Gómez, M. Carmen. 'Un nuevo manuscrito con polifonía antiqua en el Archivo Diocesano de Solsona.' *Recerca Musicologica* v (1985), pp. 5–11.

Gómez, María del Carmen.'Sobre el papel de España en la música europea del siglo XIV y primer tercio del siglo XV.' *España en la música de occidente*, ed. Emilio Casares Rodicio, Ismael Fernández de la Cuesta, and José López-Calo,vol. 1, pp. 45–7. Madrid, 1987.

Gómez Muntané, M.ª Carmen. *El Llibre Vermell de Montserrat: Cantos y danzas s. XIV*. Barcelona, 1990.

Gómez, Mª Carmen. 'Autour du répertoire du XIVe siècle du manuscrit M 1361 de la Bibliothèque Nationale de Madrid.' *L'Ars Nova Italiana del Trecento* vi (1992), pp. 193–207.

Gómez Muntané, M.ª Carmen. *Polifonía de la Corona de Aragón: Siglos XIV y XV*. Polifonía Aragonesa VIII. Zaragoza, 1993.

Gómez Muntané, Maricarmen. 'Enricus Foxer, alias Enrique de Paris (†1487/8).' *Nassarre* ix (1993): 139–46.

Gómez i Muntané, M.ª Carme. *La música medieval*, 3rd edn. Barcelona, 1998.

Gómez, Maricarmen. 'Una fuente desatendida con repertorio sacro mensural de fines del medioevo: el contoral del convento de la Concepción de Palma de Mallorca [E-Pm].' *Nassarre* xiv (1998), pp. 333–72.

Gómez, Maricarmen. 'Acerca las vías de difusión de la polifonía antigua en Castilla y León: del Códice Calixtino al Códice de las Huelgas.' *El Códice Calixtino y la música de su tiempo*, ed. José López-Calo and Carlos Villanueva, pp. 163–80. La Coruña, 2001.

Gómez Muntané, Maricarmen. *La música medieval en España*. Kassel, 2001.

Gómez, Maricarmen. 'La polifonía vocal española del Renacimiento hacia el Barroco: el caso de los villancicos de Navidad.' *Nassarre* xvii (2001), pp. 77–114.

Graduale Sacrosanctæ Romanæ Ecclesiæ. Solesmes and Tournai, 1974.

Gran enciclopèdia catalana, 2nd edn. Barcelona, 1986–98.

Gregori i Cifré, Josep Maria. 'La música del renaixement a la catedral de Barcelona, 1450–1580. Doctoral thesis, Universitat Autònoma de Barcelona, 1986.

Haberkamp, Gertraut. *Die weltliche Vokalmusik in Spanien um 1500*. Tutzing, 1968.

Hardie, Jane Morlet. 'The Motets of Francisco de Peñalosa and their Manuscript Sources.' Ph.D. dissertation, University of Michigan, 1983.

Hardie, Jane Morlet. 'Kyries tenebrarum in Sixteenth-Century Spain.' *Nassarre* iv (1988), pp. 161–94.

Hardie, Jane Morlet. 'Lamentations in Spanish Sources before 1568: Notes towards a Geography.' *Revista de Musicología* xvi (1993), pp. 912–42.

Hardie, Jane Morlet. 'Lamentations Chant in Spanish Sources: A Preliminary Report.' *Chant and its Peripheries: Essays in Honour of Terence Bailey,* ed. Bryan Gillingham and Paul Merkley, Musicological Studies LXII, pp. 370–89. Ottawa, 1998.

Hardie, Jane Morlet. 'Proto-Mensural Notation in Pre-Pius V Spanish Liturgical Sources.' *Studia Musicologica Academiae Scientiarum Hungaricae* xxxix (1998), pp. 195–200.

Hardie, Jane Morlet. 'Circles of Relationship: Chant and Polyphony in the Lamentations of Francisco de Peñalosa.' *Alamire Foundation Yearbook* iv (2000, published 2002), pp. 465–74.

Hardie, Jane Morlet. 'Lamentations Chants in Iberian Sources before 1568.' *Fuentes musicales en la Península Ibérica (ca. 1250–ca. 1550),* ed. Màrius Bernadó and Maricarmen Gómez, pp. 271–87. Lleida, 2001.

Harrison, Frank Ll., with Elizabeth Rutson and A.G. Rigg, eds. *Motets of French Provenance.* Polyphonic Music of the Fourteenth Century V. Monaco, 1968.

Hewitt, Helen, ed. *Petrucci: Harmonice Musices Odhecaton A.* Cambridge, Massachusetts, 1942.

Hoppin, Richard. *Medieval Music.* New York, 1978.

Hughes, Robert. *Barcelona.* New York, 1992.

Intonarium Toletanum. Toledo, 1515.

Josephson, Nors F. ed. *Early Sixteenth-Century Sacred Music from the Papal Chapel.* Corpus Mensurabilis Musicae XCV. N.p., 1982.

Kämper, Dietrich. 'Das Lehr- und Instrumentalduo um 1500 in Italien.' *Die Musikforschung* xviii (1965), pp. 242–63.

Kaye, Philip, ed. *The Sacred Music of Gilles Binchois.* Oxford, 1992.

Kellman, Herbert. 'The Origins of the Chigi Codex: The Date, Provenance, and Original Ownership of Rome, Biblioteca Vaticana, Chigiana, C.VIII.234.' *Journal of the American Musicological Society* xi (1958), pp. 6–19.

Kellman, Herbert, ed. *Vatican City, Biblioteca Apostolica Vaticana, MS Chigi C VIII 234.* Renaissance Music in Facsimile XXII. New York, 1987.

Kirk, Douglas Karl. 'Churching the Shawms in Renaissance Spain: Lerma, Archivo de San Pedro, Ms. Mus. 1.' Ph.D. dissertation, McGill University, 1993.

Kirsch, Winfried. *Die Quellen der mehrstimmigen Magnificat- und Te Deum-Vertonungen bis zur Mitte des 16. Jahrhunderts.* Tutzing, 1966.

Knighton, Tessa Wendy. 'Music and Musicians at the Court of Fernando of Aragon, 1474–1516.' Ph.D. dissertation, Cambridge University, 1983.

Knighton, Tess. 'Northern Influence on Cultural Developments in the Iberian Peninsula during the Fifteenth Century.' *Renaissance Studies* i (1987), pp. 221–37.

Knighton, Tess. 'A Newly Discovered Keyboard Source (Gonzalo de Baena's *Arte nouamente inuentada pera aprender a tanger,* Lisbon, 1540): A Preliminary Report.' *Plainsong and Medieval Music* v (1996), pp. 81–112.

Knighton, Tess. 'Transmisión, difusión y recepción de la polifonía franco-neerlandesa en el reino de Aragón a principios del siglo XVI.' *Artigrama* xii (1996–97), pp. 19–38.

Knighton, Tess. 'Escobar's Requiem,' recording review. *Early Music* xxvii (1999), pp. 142–4.

Knighton, Tess. *Música y músicos en la corte de Fernando el Católico, 1474–1516,* trans. Luis Gago. Zaragoza, 2001.

Knighton, Tess. 'Devotional Piety and Musical Developments at the Court of Ferdinand and Isabella.' <http://www.sun.rhul.ac.uk/Music/ILM/ID/Vol_0/Art1/twk.html>, 2 August 2002.

Knighton, Tess. 'Francisco de Peñalosa: New Works Lost and Found.' *Encomium Musicæ: Essays in Memory of Robert Snow,* ed. David Crawford and G. Grayson Wagstaff, pp. 231–57. Hillsdale, 2002.

Knighton, Tess. *Music and Ceremony at the Court of Ferdinand and Isabella.* London, in preparation.

Kreitner, Kenneth Richard. 'Music and Civic Ceremony in Late-Fifteenth-Century Barcelona.' Ph.D. dissertation, Duke University, 1990.

Kreitner, Kenneth. 'Minstrels in Spanish Churches, 1400–1600.' *Early Music* xx (1992), pp. 532–46.

Kreitner, Kenneth. 'Franco-Flemish Elements in Tarazona 2 and 3.' *Revista de Musicología* xvi (1993), pp. 2567–86.

Kreitner, Kenneth. 'Peñalosa on Record.' *Early Music* xxii (1994), pp. 309–18.

Kreitner, Kenneth. 'Music in the Corpus Christi Procession of Fifteenth-Century Barcelona.' *Early Music History* xiv (1995), pp. 153–204.

Kreitner, Kenneth. 'The Church Music of Fifteenth-Century Spain.' Paper read at the annual meeting of the American Musicological Society, New York, 1995.

Kreitner, Kenneth. 'The Musical Warhorses of Juan de Urrede.' Paper read at the conference Legacies: 500 Years of Printed Music, Denton, 2001.

Kreitner, Kenneth. 'The Dates (?) of the Cancionero de la Colombina.' *Fuentes musicales en la península ibérica (ca. 1250–ca. 1500),* ed. Maricarmen Gómez and Màrius Bernadó, pp. 121–40. Lleida, 2001.

Kreitner, Kenneth. 'The Church Music of Fifteenth-Century Spain: A Handlist.' *Encomium Musicæ: Essays in Memory of Robert Snow,* ed. David Crawford and G. Grayson Wagstaff, pp. 191–207. Hillsdale, 2002.

Kreitner, Kenneth. '*Ave festiva ferculis* and Josquin's Spanish Reputation.' *Journal of the Royal Musical Association* cxxviii (2003), pp. 1–29.

Lawes, Robert Clement, Jr. 'The Seville Cancionero: Transcription and Commentary.' Ph.D. dissertation, North Texas State College, 1960.

León Tello, Francisco José. *Estudios de história de la teoría musical.* Madrid, 1962.

Liber Usualis, The, edn. no. 801. Tournai, 1938.

López Calo, José. *La música en la catedral de Granada en el siglo XVI.* Granada, 1963.

López-Calo, José. *La música medieval en Galicia.* La Coruña, 1982.

López-Calo, José. *Documentario Musical de la Catedral de Segovia.* Santiago de Compostela, 1990.

López-Calo, José. *La música en la Catedral de Burgos.* Burgos, 1996.

López Martínez, Nicolás. 'Don Luis de Acuña, el Cabildo de Burgos y la reforma 1456–1495.' *Burgense* ii (1961), pp. 185–317.

Lowinsky, Edward E., ed. *The Medici Codex of 1518.* Chicago, 1968.

Massenkeil, Günther. 'Zur Lamentationskomposition des 15. Jahrhunderts.' *Archiv für Musikwissenschaft* xviii (1961), pp. 103–14.

Massenkeil, Günther, ed. *Mehrstimmige Lamentationen aus der ersten Hälfte des 16. Jahrhunderts.* Musikalische Denkmäler VI. Mainz, 1965.

Meconi, Honey. 'Art-Song Reworkings: An Overview.' *Journal of the Royal Musical Association* cxix (1994), pp. 1–42.

Meconi, Honey. 'Poliziano, *Primavera,* and Perugia 431: New Light on *Fortuna desperata.*' *Antoine Busnoys: Method, Meaning, and Context in Late Medieval Music,* ed. Paula Higgins, pp. 463–503. Oxford, 1999.

Miller, Patrick. 'A Chronology of the Works of Juan de Anchieta.' Paper read at the annual meeting of the American Musicological Society, South-Central Chapter, Atlanta, April 1995.

Moll, Jaime. 'El estatuto de maestro cantor de la Catedral de Ávila del año 1487.' *Anuario Musical* xxii (1967), pp. 89–95.

Nelson, Bernadette. 'Binchois Revisited: The Segovia Te Deum and Falsobordone Practice.' Unpublished paper.

Nelson, Kathleen E. *Medieval Liturgical Music of Zamora.* Musicological Studies LXVII. Ottawa, 1996.

Nelson, Kathleen E. '*Conlaudemus omnes pie* and *Deo nos agentes*: Polyphony in a Fourteenth-Century source of the Church of Zamora.' *Fuentes musicales en la península ibérica (ca. 1250–ca. 1550)*, ed. Maricarmen Gómez and Màrius Bernadó, pp. 109–19. Lleida, 2001.

Nelson, Kathleen E. 'Two Twelfth-Century Fragments in Zamora: Representatives of a Period in Transition.' *Encomium Musicæ: Essays in Memory of Robert Snow*, ed. David Crawford and G. Grayson Wagstaff, pp. 161–74. Hillsdale, 2002.

Noone, Michael. *Music and Musicians in the Escorial Liturgy under the Hapsburgs, 1563–1700.* Rochester, 1998.

Nosow, Robert. 'Early Fifteenth-Century Spanish Polyphony from an Altarpiece in Kansas City.' Paper read at the congress of the International Musicological Society, Leuven, 2002.

Perales de la Cal, Ramon, F. Albertos, and Hilario Sanz, eds., *Cancionero de la Catedral de Segovia.* Segovia, 1977.

Perkins, Leeman L. *Music in the Age of the Renaissance.* New York, 1999.

Picker, Martin. *The Chanson Albums of Marguerite of Austria.* Berkeley, 1965.

Plamenac, Dragan. 'A Reconstruction of the French Chansonnier in the Biblioteca Colombina, Seville.' *The Musical Quarterly* xxxvii (1951), pp. 501–42.

Plamenac, Dragan, ed. *Facsimile Reproduction of the Manuscripts Sevilla 5-1-43 & Paris N.A. Fr. 4379 (Pt. 1).* Publications of Mediaeval Musical Manuscripts VIII. Brooklyn, 1962.

Planchart, Alejandro. 'Music in the Christian Courts of Spain', *Musical Repercussions of 1492*, ed. Carol E. Robertson, pp. 149–66. Washington, 1992.

Pope, Isabel, and Masakata Kanazawa, eds. *The Music Manuscript Montecassino 871: A Neapolitan Repertory of Sacred and Secular Music of the Late Fifteenth Century.* Oxford, 1978.

Preciado, Dionisio. *Francisco de Peñalosa (ca. 1470–1528): Opera Omnia.* Madrid, 1986– .

Preciado, Dionisio, ed. *Juan de Anchieta (c. 1462–1523): Cuatro Pasiones polifónicas.* Madrid, 1995.

Preciado, Dionisio. 'Juan de Anchieta (c. 1462–1523) y los Salmos del Códice Musical de la Parroquia de Santiago de Valladolid.' *Encomium Musicæ: Essays in Memory of Robert Snow*, ed. David Crawford and G. Grayson Wagstaff, pp. 209–29. Hillsdale, 2002.

Prescott, William H. *History of the Reign of Ferdinand and Isabella, The Catholic.* New York, 1845.

Querol Gavaldá, Miguel, ed. *Cancionero Musical de la Colombina.* Monumentos de la Música Española XXXIII. Barcelona, 1971.

Randel, Don Michael, ed. *The New Harvard Dictionary of Music.* Cambridge, Massachusetts, 1986.

Reaney, Gilbert. *Manuscripts of Polyphonic Music (c. 1320–1400).* RISM B.IV.2. Munich, 1969.

Rees, Owen Lewis. 'Sixteenth- and Early Seventeenth-Century Polyphony from the Monastery of Santa Cruz, Coimbra, Portugal.' Ph.D. dissertation, Cambridge University, 1991.

Rees, Owen. *Polyphony in Portugal, c. 1530–c. 1620: Sources from the Monastery of Santa Cruz, Coimbra.* New York, 1995.

Reese, Gustave. *Music in the Renaissance.* New York, 1954.

Reynaud, François. *La polyphonie tolédane et son milieu: Des premiers témoignages aux environs de 1600.* Brepols, 1996.

Rifkin, Joshua. 'Busnoys and Italy: The Evidence of Two Songs.' *Antoine Busnoys: Method, Meaning, and Context in Late Medieval Music*, ed. Paula Higgins, pp. 505–71. Oxford, 1999.

Rincon, Juan. *Processionarij Toletani prima pars.* Toledo, 1562.

Robertson, Anne Walters. 'Which Vitry? The Witness of the Trinity Motet from the Roman de Fauvel.' *Hearing the Motet: Essays on the Motet of the Middle Ages and Renaissance*, ed. Dolores Pesce, pp. 52–81. Oxford, 1997.

Ros-Fábregas, Emilio. 'The Manuscript Barcelona, Biblioteca de Catalunya, M. 454: Study and

Edition in the Context of the Iberian and Continental Manuscript Traditions.' Ph.D. dissertation, City University of New York, 1992.

Ros-Fábregas, Emilio. 'Music and Ceremony during Charles V's 1519 Visit to Barcelona.' *Early Music* xxxiii (1995), pp. 374–91.

Ros Fábregas, Emilio. 'Libros de música en bibliotecas españolas del siglo XVI.' *Pliegos de bibliofília* xv (2001), pp. 37–62; xvi (2001), pp. 33–46; xvii (2002), pp. 17–54.

Ros-Fábregas, Emilio. 'Phantom Attributions or New Works by Antoine Brumel in an Iberian Manuscript.' *Encomium Musicæ: Essays in Memory of Robert Snow*, ed. David Crawford and G. Grayson Wagstaff, pp. 259–67. Hillsdale, 2002.

Rosa y López, Simón de la. *Los seises de la catedral de Sevilla: Ensayo de investigación histórica.* Seville, 1904.

Roth, Adalbert. *Studien zum frühen repertoire der päpstlichen Kapelle unter dem Pontificat Sixtus' IV. (1471–1484): Die Chorbücher 14 und 51 des Fondo Capella Sistina der Biblioteca Apostolica Vaticana.* Vatican City, 1991.

Rubio, P. Samuel, 'Las glosas de Antonio de Cabezón y de otros autores sobre el "Pange lingua" de Juan de Urreda.' *Anuario Musical* xxi (1966), pp. 45–59.

Rubio, Samuel, ed. *Juan de Anchieta: Opera Omnia.* Guipuzcoa, 1980.

Rubio Piqueras, F. *Música y músicos toledanos: Contribución de su estudio.* Toledo, 1923.

Rubio Piqueras, F. *Códices polifónicos toledanos.* Toledo, 1925.

Sadie, Stanley, ed. *The New Grove Dictionary of Music and Musicians.* London, 1980; 2nd edn., with John Tyrell, ed., London, 2001.

Schrade, Leo, ed., *The* Roman de Fauvel*; The Works of Philippe de Vitry; French Cycles of the* Ordinarium Missæ. Polyphonic Music of the Fourteenth Century I. Monaco, 1956, rept. 1974.

Schwartz, Roberta Freund. '*En busca de liberalidad*: Music and Musicians in the Courts of the Spanish Nobility, 1470–1640.' Ph.D. dissertation, University of Illinois, 2001.

[Schwartz], Roberta Freund. 'Tarazona 2/3 y Sevilla 5-5-20: Una consideración de conexiones.' *Fuentes musicales en la Península Ibérica (ca. 1250–ca. 1550),* ed. Maricarmen Gómez and Màrius Bernadó, pp. 203–17. Lleida, 2001.

Self, Stephen, ed. *The* Si placet *Repertoire of 1480–1530.* Recent Researches in the Music of the Renaissance CVI. Madison, 1996.

Sherr, Richard. '*Illibata Dei virgo nutrix* and Josquin's Roman Style.' *Journal of the American Musicological Society* xli (1988), pp. 434–64.

Sierra Pérez. José. *Fr. Martín de Villanueva: obras completas.* Escorial, 1997.

Smijers, A., M. Antonowycz, and W. Elders, eds. *Werken van Josquin des Près.* Amsterdam, 1921–69.

Snow, Robert J., ed. *A New-World Collection of Polyphony for Holy Week and the Salve Service: Guatemala City, Cathedral Archive, Music MS 4.* Monuments of Renaissance Music IX. Chicago, 1996.

Spitzer, John. ' "Oh! Susanna": Oral Transmission and Tune Transformation." *Journal of the American Musicological Society* xlvii (1994), pp. 90–136.

Stäblein, Bruno. *Monumenta monodica medii aevi I: Hymnen (I): Die mittelalterlichen Hymnenmelodien des Abendlandes.* Kassel, 1956.

Stäblein-Harder, H. *Fourteenth-Century Mass Music in France.* Corpus Mensurabilis Musicæ XXIX. N.p., 1962.

Stäblein-Harder, H. *Fourteenth-Century Mass Music in France.* Musicological Studies and Documents VII. N.p., 1962.

Stevenson, Robert. *Spanish Music in the Age of Columbus.* The Hague, 1960.

Stevenson, Robert. *Juan Bermudo.* The Hague, 1960.

Stevenson, Robert. 'Josquin in the Music of Spain and Portugal.' *Josquin des Prez*, ed. Edward E. Lowinsky, pp. 217–46. London, 1976.

Stevenson, Robert. 'Spanish Musical Impact beyond the Pyrenees (1250–1500).' *España en la música de occidente*, ed. Emilio Casares Rodicio, Ismael Fernández de la Cuesta, and José López-Calo, vol. I, pp. 115–64. Madrid, 1987.

Strohm, Reinhard. *Music in Late Medieval Bruges*. Oxford, 1985.

Strohm, Reinhard. 'The Close of the Middle Ages.' *Antiquity and the Middle Ages*, ed. James McKinnon, pp. 269–312. Englewood Cliffs, 1990.

Strohm, Reinhard. *The Rise of European Music, 1380–1500*. Cambridge, 1993.

Taruskin, Richard. 'Antoine Busnoys and the *L'homme armé* tradition.' *Journal of the American Musicological Society* xxxix (1986), pp. 255–93.

Turner, Bruno, 'Spanish Liturgical Hymns: A Matter of Time.' *Early Music* xxiii (1995), pp. 473–82.

Turner, Bruno. *Five Spanish Liturgical Hymns*. Marvig, 1996.

Variæ Preces, edn. no. 808. Solesmes, 1901.

Wagstaff, George Grayson. 'Music for the Dead: Polyphonic Settings of the *Officium* and *Missa pro defunctis* by Spanish and Latin American Composers before 1630.' Ph.D. dissertation, University of Texas, 1995.

Wagstaff, Grayson. 'Mary's Own: Josquin's Five-Part Salve Regina and Marian Devotions in Spain.' Paper read at conference, New Directions in Josquin Scholarship, Princeton, 1999.

Ward, Tom. *The Polyphonic Office Hymn from 1400–1520: A Descriptive Inventory*. Renaissance Manuscript Studies III. Neuhausen-Stuttgart, 1979.

Wolf, Johannes. 'Der Choraltraktat des Christoual de Escobar.' *Gedenkboek aangeboden aan D. D.F. Scheurleer op zijn 70sten verjaardag*, pp. 383–91. The Hague, 1925.

Wright, Craig. *Music and Ceremony at Notre Dame of Paris, 500–1500*. Cambridge, 1989.

Index